# *Faith in the Letter of James*

# *Faith in the Letter of James*

## Disestablishment and the Church of England with Special Reference to English Ethnicity

David Isiorho *and* Linda Isiorho

*Foreword by Patricia Bidmead*

WIPF & STOCK • Eugene, Oregon

FAITH IN THE LETTER OF JAMES
Disestablishment and the Church of England with Special Reference to English Ethnicity



Wipf & Stock
An Imprint of Wipf and Stock Publishers
199 W. 8th Ave., Suite 3
Eugene, OR 97401

www.wipfandstock.com

PAPERBACK ISBN: 979-8-3852-5460-6
HARDCOVER ISBN: 979-8-3852-5461-3
EBOOK ISBN: 979-8-3852-5462-0

VERSION NUMBER 03/26/26

*What does the Lord require of you but to do justice, and to love kindness, and to walk humbly with your God?*

*—Micah 6:8*

David and Linda Isiorho, in faith, are trying to serve God in Christ Jesus. They have always encouraged each other, sharing the same theology and politics, to do what Jesus did—challenge the institution and support the faith of the faithful. They dedicate this book to each other and the love that is between them and all this held in the greater love of God.

# Contents

# Foreword

David and Linda isiorho, in their commentary on the letter of James, draw their readers' attention to the impossibility of giving support to the British monarchy on the one hand and promoting the Christian faith, as understood by the letter of James, on the other. The epistle is about a preference for God or mammon, and a choice has to be made. To my mind, an established church structure giving preferential treatment to the wealthy and privileged is not a genuine church. The monarch claims the divine right of leadership in the Church of England by reason of heredity. The assumption is that the monarch as the supreme head of this institution is likely to embrace morality. The institution is propped up by nepotism and maintained through the manipulation of state education and excessive media control. Disagreements and infighting in the royal family have raised issues of racism, as we saw in Prince Harry's departure, believing his wife had been discriminated against. Corruption was also an issue, as Andrew Mountbatten-Windsor was associated with pedophiles, thus presenting a new context and opportunity to argue for the abolition of the monarchy in its last days as an archaic institution and to question its relationship to the Church of England.

In the early church, the Roman emperors claimed to be divine, and the assertion that Jesus was Lord was highly offensive to them. In the fourth century, the Roman Empire incorporated Christianity into the state and declared all kings were anointed by God. A reading of 1 Sam reveals that it was clearly said in asking for an earthly sovereign, the Israelites had rejected God. So the history of Christianity, like that of Judaism, is one of conflict between the earthly kings and the prophets. Monarchy is linked to secular power and militarism, and in the New Testament, little can be found to support it. The idea that a monarch can be the supreme head of a church in the Anglican Communion is in conflict with the letter of James and a betrayal of the Christian gospel. Clearly, keeping the monarchy in the twenty-first century sends out the message that Christians should grovel and submit to the royals as though they are divine and deserving of veneration. Faith in the letter of James shows that true followers of the faith cannot bow their knee to any earthly monarch. They can only genuflect before God.

David and Linda Isiorho show through their accessible scholarship that the Church of England should be disestablished. That as an institution, it should oppose all forms of state control, whether that be from the Crown or from the prime minister of the day, acting on behalf of the Crown. I commend the authors of faith in the letter of James for their biblical understanding and challenging observations.

Pat Bidmead
Poet and Activist

Declaration of Interest:
Anglican clergy without preferment

# Introduction

## Safeguarding the Church of England: Incompetent, Spineless, and Probably Both

At the end of 2024, a major news item appeared worldwide, in the newspapers and on television, concerning safeguarding failures in the hierarchy of the Church of England. We ask our readers in their prayers to remember those who were victims of the abuse perpetrated in the Church of England and especially, at that time, the victims of John Smyth. In our prayers, we must acknowledge that the allegations were covered up and mishandled by then-Archbishop of Canterbury, the Most Rev. Justin Welby, and by the institution of the Church of England. The official line was that we should also pray for Welby, but many people were unhappy about this, since he was not the victim of abuse but rather a senior officeholder who failed to do his duty. And what a terrible legacy he has left the Church of England following a speech in the House of Lords, which offended many of those who had been abused. Surely, it must serve as a summons to the whole church to recommit to the priority of making our church a safer place for children and vulnerable adults. Sadly, the church hierarchy is populated by many senior officeholders who have proven to be incompetent managers, whose faith and social background seem hugely different from that of the congregation of the Letter of James.

So, we start this book on a sad note, giving focus to an archbishop's resignation and calling for competence and professionalism on the part of senior leadership. We sent an email of support to the Right Rev. Dr. Helen-Ann Hartley, the bishop of Newcastle, following her call for Archbishop Welby to stand down. We appreciated her courage in using her position to speak truth to power during that challenging time. We felt that the Spirit of God was here and had shined into this darkened church institution. We should be people of the light, and we should be able to stand scrutiny and take accountability. In Welby's case, there is also the classism of old Etonians and the like, forming their close testudos. Bishop Hartley also called upon the archbishop of York to stand down, but he remained in post despite serious safeguarding concerns about appointments he had made while bishop of Chelmsford. His grace would not go, and he had the support of the rest of the hierarchy who did not want to be left without an archbishop. We are all servants of righteousness and have every right to ask for reassurance from the institution of the Church that the next archbishops of Canterbury and York would exercise their ministries with the professionalism and competence required for those roles.

In the first half of 2025, the Church of England General Synod started to review its safeguarding structures. There was much discussion about what independent scrutiny might look like and less about who would deliver such a policy. So, what does it mean to adopt an independent safeguarding policy? What does it really look like? Our concern then and now is that the Church of England will create a safeguarding model replicating the existing system and collaborating with the same personnel, some of whom have been found wanting, particularly at a senior level. Safeguarding should be about protecting people from harm, not maintaining the institution's image at the expense of the most vulnerable.

This book is about the Church of England and its establishment status in English society and the Anglican Communion. So, clearly, we have to pray for the humility of the Church of England and its willingness to repent, learn, and change. That is a big ask, given its history, which is colonial. It follows from this that in recent years, the Church of England as an institution has come under global scrutiny and, at the time of publication for this book, remains in crisis. This scandal will remain the context for church history and theological writing for many years to come. This is the legacy of Justin Welby and the context for *Faith in the Letter of James.*

We contacted a small number of senior officeholders and potential members of the future hierarchy, most of whom did not return our emails. The spineless lack of response just tells the faithful that the Westminster Church and its associates does not want a discussion that could lead to any significant change to its privileged and establishment status. Those who are aspiring to this hierarchy—to get their top jobs—may well have to ask themselves, before God, when and where did they leave the faith of the church as understood by the Letter of James? This may sound judgmental but so is the Scripture that is the subject of our commentary. We did hear from an archbishop who is leading a disestablished church, but they refused to get involved in this discussion because they had previously served in the Church of England. Need we say any more?

As authors of *Faith in the Letter of James: Disestablishment and the Church of England*, we are not doing a hard sell to get people to agree with us about the disestablishment of the Church of England, but rather, we want to start a serious debate within the Church and beyond. This is not an adversarial polemic, and for this reason, we welcome criticism of our approach. There are five chapters of theological commentary and reflection. People may well draw different conclusions from their reading of the Letter of James. This may sound very liberal on our part, but hopefully, we are genuine in what we say. Some of our endorsements come from people who don't advocate disestablishment but want this book to be read widely. So far, as authors, we don't claim to have a monopoly on how the Christian faith is to be practiced, even though it may seem like that when we are challenging the establishment. We only know what God has given us to say as *doers of the word*, which is the subject of our first chapter, and we want to share that with our readers. So, following the Letter of James, we understand the Christian faith and its ministry should not be a career structure for the privileged and wealthy.[1] Our prayer, as it was with James, our Lord's brother, that what we proclaim on earth will be understood as a prophetic act of witness even in heaven. Praise be to God.

## Questions About Church and State

Throughout this commentary, we ask questions about Anglicanism and the Church of England. What is the church relationship to the British state and where has it got to as an institutional expression of the Christian faith? This book is not a conventional commentary, so it will not be crammed with loads of Greek words or a preoccupation with authorship and the direction of diasporic travel for the gospel message. There are books like that on the market, and if that is what floats a potential reader's

1. See Isiorho, *Faith in Church Newspapers*, 116.

boat, then this reflection is not for them. We will consider, however, the Greek words of *chronos* and *kairos* in the endnote of our first chapter—"Doers of the Word." This is a contextual and theological commentary, so we shall be concerned with what the Letter of James means to us today reading the New Testament in the language and structure of the Anglicized edition of the NRSV. In other words, we want to apply the theology of James to our own context and ask, in the light of its teaching, if the Church of England should be disestablished. One of our authors, David, is dyslexic and diaphasic, who has no Greek language skills and feels alienated from that form of discourse. He is neurodivergent and has things to say outside of the box. Linda, on the other hand, knows all about Greek words and has a translation of the New Testament readily available on her desk.[2] They agreed that a lot of this scholarly work has already been done by William Barclay[3] and others, so they did not need to repeat it. This is a theological commentary, so there was no need to evaluate every verse of Scripture but rather get a sense of the wider context of this catholic epistle. We, the authors of the commentary, believe the letter to have come from the pen of James, the bother of Jesus, who was a leader of the Jerusalem Church. Our thinking here is that its Jewishness and strict moralism is a sign of authenticity. A pseudonymous writing would have given more weight to authorship. We do not think this letter is a reworked homily or a later independent work with Christian additions. This letter is not a haphazard collection of ethical teaching but rather an apocalyptic instruction in a time of moral uncertainty. As to historical context, it was written either during the last decade before the fall of the Jerusalem temple or after following economic recovery. And just to think completely outside of the box, maybe this church community is located outside Palestine. For us, the authors of this commentary, the contextual importance is not geographical or time specific. We don't know where all this took place, but what is important is to explore through these texts the traditional understanding of evangelism and discipleship. James is about testing the faith in situations of economic deprivation that enables God's mission of church in God's world. Faith, generosity, and inclusivity are the values that mark out the Christian readers of the Letter of James.

2. Douglas, *New Greek-English Interlinear New Testament.*

3. Barclay, *Letters of James and Peter.*

## Englishness

The purpose of this introduction is to define the Church of England, not exclusive by its doctrines but also by its ethnic identity, and to appreciate this as a signifier of Englishness.[4] We will attempt to do this by exploring trajectories that continue to tie Englishness and the English people to an ambiguous relationship to the Church of England. An important trajectory concerns aesthetics as an indicator of Englishness in the Anglican Church. The way that the English represent England to themselves has routinely involved the Church. The Church is a recurrent provider of caricatures and characters in English literature and the arts. Our first reference point is the concept of Protestantism. We will attempt to place Christianity within the context of Englishness in order to determine the contemporary relationship between Protestantism and Catholicism. This is a trajectory about religion as a boundary marker, distinguishing the true English Protestant from a Catholic foreigner. Coronations and royal weddings are set-piece occasions on which the Church of England provides state rituals that express a boundary-marking principle. In this Introduction, we will be concerned with the concept of authority as it operates within the Anglican tradition of the Church of England.

So, just to recap, this commentary is a contextual theology—a way of talking about God through the lens of the specific situation of the church, which James addresses. This context considers the political and economic factors that frame social and cultural experiences. So, our God-talk is relevant if it is rooted in the lived experience of people in particular contexts. As contextual theologians, we engage with the Bible to promote social justice through an understanding of the human experience of inequality and marginalization. So, the important characteristics of our discipline are experience, culture, and social justice, and they are an important starting point for theological reflection. In other words, this is how we talk about God as the driver of our being and who is there for the people in this world, the marginalized. All this shapes our Christian faith as something real, related to this world and the life beyond. This reasoning takes place not in a vacuum but rather in a context that advocates a faith perspective that favors the oppressed. Our contextual theology is a signpost to liberation and is heavenly influenced by the work of Gustavo Gutierrez. We will review the work of this amazing theologian in the

4. See Isiorho, *Black Clergy Discontent*, 215; Isiorho, *Mission, Anguish, and Defiance*, 119; Isiorho, *Faith in Unions*, 100; Isiorho, *Faith in Church Newspapers*, 125.

conclusion to this book. In this context, the Christian faith is a source for epiphany and resurrection.

## About This Book

So does *Faith in the Letter of James* have any rivals? To our knowledge, there are none. Colin Buchanan published *Cut the Connection: Disestablishment and the Church of England* in 1994.[5] Following Buchanan, *Faith in the Letter of James* advocates the abolition of the establishment system, which gives the prime minister of the day the final say in the appointment of diocesan bishops, which are, in effect, Crown appointments. Buchanan's argument, which we support, is that although the Church of England has gained its place in English society as a result of its establishment status, it should now sever its connection with the state. This is an important but limited starting point. So, how is *Faith in the Letter of James* different from *Cut the Connection*? The latter is a political discourse about how the Church of England should be independent of government structures. The former is a theological argument for disestablishment based on the teaching of the New Testament Letter of James. *Cut the Connection* does not seriously engage with Scripture or English ethnicity. *Faith in the Letter of James* is an original book and one of crucial importance for church history and ecclesiology, but also to urban and contextual theology. It would make a good textbook for theological students undertaking pastoral education and also for students of sociology and sociology of religion, history, and social change.

There have been books that are substantially in favor of Church of England establishment. We draw our readers attention to the work of Mark Chapman, Judith Maltby, and William Whyte.[6] We review contributions made by Martyn Percy and Elaine Graham later in this introduction. We also note the work of Bob Morris.[7] We found this later collection of writings not worthy of serious review for a book on disestablishment. It adopts a broad definition of establishment to include Scotland and talks about what it calls "facile arguments" for disestablishment in the Church of England. There are papers on disestablishment, but these focus on Ireland, Wales, and church state relations in Scandinavia. The only

5. Buchanan, *Cut the Connection.*

6. Chapman et al., *Established Church.*

7. Morris, *Church and State.*

relevant point from our position is that it warns of a constitutional crisis if the next UK monarch was not willing to swear allegiance to the Church of England. If this were to happen, there would be a call for disestablishment so that the heir could come to the throne. We say, bring it on.

## Tradition, Doctrine, and Authority

Anglicanism, as a denominational tradition within the Christian religion, is premised upon a relationship between church tradition, the Bible, and reason. It is distinguished from other reformed traditions by its liturgy and formularies that are to be found in *The Book of Common Prayer*. Anglican witness to the Christian faith is also founded upon church laws or canons. However, for Stephen Neil, Anglicanism is not a theological system with its own doctrines.

> There are no special Anglican theological doctrines, there is no particular Anglican theology. The Church of England is the Catholic Church in England. It teaches all the doctrines of the Catholic Faith, as these are to be found in Holy Scripture, as they are summarized in the Apostles, the Nicene, and the Athanasian Creeds, and as they are set forth in the decisions of the first four General Councils of the undivided Church.[8]

Stephen Sykes takes exception to the idea that the Church of England has no doctrines of its own and merely expresses the doctrines of the universal church.[9] In order to persist with this line of argument, Sykes has to adopt an understanding of church doctrine that is broad enough to include any elucidation of foundation documents and specific enough to be synonymous with Anglican liturgy. The special Anglican doctrine argument claims that Anglicanism has its own doctrine of the church expressed in theological categories that are contained in *The Book of Common Prayer.*

After the Reformation, it was to the Bible that Christians went for validation of their faith, but the Bible as the foundation document still required interpretation if it was to be read intelligibly. For Anglicanism, there is an important distinction between scriptural doctrines that are believed to be necessary for salvation on the one hand and other types of traditional doctrine that are not so considered. However, Anglicanism as

8. Neil, *Anglicanism*, 416.

9. Sykes, *Unashamed Anglicanism*.

a guardian of Scripture does accept the possibility that it may teach things contrary to the Bible and that the church can be in error, which brings us back to Anglicanism as a tradition within Christendom, encompassing the doctrines of the universal church. For Sykes, the very choosing and affirming of such doctrines amounts to the establishment of new doctrines. The new doctrine for old argument is premised upon an understanding of Anglicanism as a conscious "pick n mix" of theological doctrines, taking the Church of England beyond mere Christianity.

Thus, when the English Church left the See of Rome, it had to decide which traditions were correct and which were misleading or irrelevant, or even distortions of the Christian faith. This relationship between Scripture and tradition is made clear in Article VI.

> Holy Scripture containeth all things necessary to salvation. In the name of the Holy Scripture, we do understand those standard books of the Old and New Testament, of whose authority was never any doubt in the Church. All the books of the New Testament, as they are commonly received, we do receive, and account them canonical.[10]

And in Article XX, we find,

> The Church hath power to decree rites or ceremonies, and authority in controversies of faith: and yet it is not lawful for the Church to ordain anything that is contrary to God's word written, neither may it so expound one place of scripture that it is repugnant to another. Wherefore, although the Church be a witness and a keeper of Holy Writ, yet as it ought not to decree any thing against the same, so beside the same ought it not to enforce any thing to be believed for necessity of salvation.[11]

The Anglican notion of essential and non-essential doctrines, as a theological and doctrinal criterion upon which Anglicanism can be distinguished from other denominations within Christendom, is difficult to operationalize without an historical appreciation of the concept of reason. The combination of Scripture and church tradition, guided by a notion of reason, requires some elucidation. A post-Enlightenment approach would see reason opposed to faith in the same way that science is seen in opposition to superstition. Reason is not synonymous with the intellect and rationalism, rather it has a theological meaning implying an

10. *Book of Common Prayer*, 564.

11. *Book of Common Prayer*, 568.

externally implanted truth-seeking principle that would govern the intellectual faculties. Thus, this reason is an informed theological conscience that allows Christians to make sense of their history.

This Christian system of doctrine is a particular interpretation of the Bible that takes reason beyond the common sense of the new doctrines for old argument. As far as we, the authors of this commentary, are concerned, a theological perspective or consciousness on its own does not amount to the construction of a new theological or doctrinal system. Clearly, the Anglican reformers did not believe they were inventing a new doctrine of the church. Rather, they sought to be true to the existing doctrines of the Christian church as understood in a faithful understanding of the Holy Scriptures. So, Anglicanism as a tradition of Christian witness has its origins in the authority issues of the universal church.

The modern Anglican experience of authority is reflected not only in certain important documents, such as prayer books, ordinals, and articles of faith, but also in important events in the life of the churches of which it is composed. This in turn is reflected in the documents of the Lambeth Conference. The 1948 Lambeth Conference Report on the Anglican Communion offers us a picture of dispersed, as opposed to centralized, authority based upon a number of elements that are fused and unified in the offering of public worship.[12] These include Scripture, tradition, creeds, the ministry of word and sacraments, the witness of saints, and the *consensus fidelium*. According to the above report, the inherited authority of the Anglican Communion is derived from a single divine source—the authority of the eternal Father, the incarnate Son, and the life-giving Spirit.

A biblical and historical understanding of the ministry of Jesus has led many Christians to question the contemporary understanding and exercise of authority. Jesus did not come to lord it over others but rather to serve. Furthermore, the very power of God is the power of weakness as expressed in the humility of the cross (1 Cor 1:18–31, Phil 2:5–10). The Bible also tells that the followers of Jesus must expect to suffer (2 Thess 1:5; Romans 8:17; 2 Cor 1:5; Phil 3:10; 1 Peter). This suffering can only be transformed by the power of the gospel for those who believe in Jesus and who can thereby participate in the ultimate triumph of God. We are personally empowered by God through our belief in Jesus as Lord and Savior. Thus, everlasting life is given to us by Christ, who is the only mediator between ourselves and God.

12. Anglican Communion, *Lambeth Conference*.

This understanding of the power of the gospel leads us to the authority of the ministry through which it is proclaimed. This authority is concerned with the declaration of truth as understood by those who exercise it. Thus, St. Paul claimed that God's power worked in and through him (2 Cor 13:3–4) and that he had been given divine authority (2 Cor 13:10). In this letter to the church at Corinth, Paul understands himself as having authority, as Christ's steward and servant, to confront the disorder and disunity of this community (2 Cor 11:34).

The authority of the ministry of the gospel leads us to consider the power of the church that is distributed in one way or another in church organizations. The Church of England's claim to authority can be traced back to Parliament in the sixteenth century, but as we have already stated, if we follow Williams, it has no doctrines of its own, save those of the universal church. In the "Thirty-Nine Articles of Religion," we find two types of authority related to living subject to the word of God:

- Firstly, authority to decree rites and ceremonies in particular national churches;
- Secondly, authority in controversies concerning faith.[13]

In the ordinal, we find a hierarchical pattern of authority: a chain of command that includes archbishop, bishop, priest, and deacon, which is accompanied by the prescription of specified duties pertaining to each office. Priests and bishops are required to promise that they will study Scripture and dispute erroneous opinion. Bishops are expected to govern the Church, to interpret Scriptures in disputes, and to exercise authority in a gentle and constructive manner. This does not suggest any mechanism for accountability of that office.

• • •

According to Alwyn Williams, Anglicanism owes its foundation to the Reformation of the sixteenth century and that an important characteristic of this in the English context has been its conservatism and its tentative caution.[14] The English Reformation left unchanged the parochial and diocesan structure of former times. One difference was the use of English rather than Latin in the liturgy, but the creed remained that of the universal church and the pattern of worship underwent only minor

13. *Book of Common Prayer*, article 20, p. 568.

14. Williams, *Anglican Tradition*.

revision. Thus, the English parish functioned much as it had done for many centuries before. Parish life in the nineteenth century was rural with clergy freehold and the autonomy that went with it. The life of this parochial structure centered upon the local church, which was often isolated from the rest of the world. The typical vicar was not a theologian, but he cared for the needs of the sick and visited his flock. This was the age of the hunting parson and the dutiful church-going English. According to Williams, the Church of the nineteenth century was an austere institution that expressed a drab and conservative piety.

This was the context in which ecclesiastical parties within the Church began to emerge, but divisions were not characterized by the ceremonial or by leanings to Roman Catholicism. "High Church" meant Tory and strict following of *The Book of Common Prayer*; "Low Church" meant support for the Whig party in Parliament. The first Evangelicals in the Church of England, comments Williams, "were inspired to preach the Gospel with a new intensity and converting power."[15] As an ascending group with an intellectual base at Cambridge, they soon gained influential friends. This Evangelical grouping played an important part in the social concerns of their day, including the abolition of slavery and the development of the Sunday school movement. Since this was a time of great missionary expansion abroad, it is not difficult to agree with Williams's conclusions that the Evangelicals of the nineteenth century were the home guard of the Church of England.

The Evangelical ascendancy had probably reached its peak by the 1830s. The Church's role in the life of the nation, despite the achievements of the early Evangelicals, was perceived by many as conservative and uncertain. On to this stage, a second great party was to emerge. This was the Oxford movement, deriving its name from an intellectual base at Oxford University. From now on, "High Church" was no longer associated with or defined as support for Tory members of Parliament. This brand of "High Church" did include strict adherence to *The Book of Common Prayer* and high stands of morality. This group believed the Church to be a divine society and, as such, it could not be an extension or appendix to the British state. This did not mean that those who subscribed to this stand of orthodoxy were anti-state or were ignorant of the historical link between the Church of England and the institutions of government. Williams comments thus:

15. Williams, *Anglican Tradition*, 66.

> The leaders of the Oxford Movement in their tracts and sermons and correspondence and agitations were proclaiming what, for most Englishmen, was a new doctrine of the independence of a spiritual society whose trust-deeds were written in no Act of Parliament nor in any tacit compromise with the state.[16]

The Oxford movement was essentially evangelical in the traditional sense of that word. It was concerned with rousing the faithful to action and reminding the lapsed of their Christian heritage. It advocated a strict moralism and restored public worship to a central place in the life of the nation. Williams says that despite its radicalism, the Oxford movement was conservative, and he likens this to the concept of Englishness as a kind of dignified reserve. Williams comments as follows:

> Strong and stirring as the impact of the movement was, it was yet also like many another English "revolution" intensely conservative in spirit. It recalled churchmen to ancient principles and practices forgotten or commonly neglected in the drowsy Hanoverian days. The teaching of the Fathers, the lives of the saints, the doctrine and discipline of the Prayer Book . . . all were used to invigorate the life of a Church which had, as a whole, long been unused to these reminders of the austerity and dignity of its lineage.[17]

Thanks to the Oxford movement, the rising industrial populations now had something of heaven brought down to earth—something real and coherent expressed in art and music. Williams tells us,

> A stern reserve and a strict moralism were marked features of the Movement's early days. . . . But as it spread into town and country throughout England it came increasingly to use and to propagate the color, the pageantry, the ceremonial, the music, the tradition of ecclesiastical art and architecture congenial to men concerned to revive the sense of an ancient and magnificent heritage among those to whom a more austere and intellectual approach would have had little force or meaning.[18]

The mid-nineteenth century were years when the Church of England not only became more conscious of itself but aware of the social and economic conditions of the broad mass of the British people. It was this that gave birth to the Christian socialist movement of Charles Kingsley and

16. Williams, *Anglican Tradition*, 89.
17. Williams, *Anglican Tradition*, 90.
18. Williams, *Anglican Tradition*, 91.

William Morris. The dominant ecclesiastical party in the Church of England was Anglo-Catholic, who demanded a greater independence from the state. Meanwhile, liberal and Evangelical parties remained staunchly loyal to the state and were, on the whole, politically conservative.

## Britishness

According to David McDowall, the British define themselves as a nation through the concepts of tolerance, decency, moderation, consensus, and compromise with an emphasis upon modesty and understatement. In this respect, comments McDowall, the British are no different from any other society.[19] Britishness is also associated with embarrassment about intellectual and artistic achievement. McDowall does make a distinction between Anglo-Saxon and Celtic communities, but he nevertheless seems to use the term British as a generic to include English, Welsh, Scottish, and even Irish experience, while at the same time only making those distinctions in those sections of his work that accuse the English of defining the UK as English. Thus, on the whole, distinctions are not made between these cultural groupings, and the term *Britishness* is used even when the term *Englishness* would seem more in line with the characteristic and attributes described. McDowall notes the nostalgic preoccupation of the British with the countryside as a kind of mental retreat from the reality of where most people live in the UK.[20] However, McDowall contrasts this lament for the good life in the countryside with what he calls urban subculture. Here, Teds, mods, rockers, bikers, skinheads, punks, and Rastafarians have been marginalized and alienated from British culture.[21]

19. McDowall, *Britain in Close-Up*, 102.

20. McDowall, *Britain in Close-Up*, 105–6. "As a nation, the British have made a mental retreat from the urban environment. They have a deep nostalgia for an idealized world of neat hedgerows, cottages and great country houses, surrounded by parkland, that clever eighteenth-century style of gardening that looked natural. The nostalgia stems partly from a sense of loss which has lingered since the Industrial revolution two centuries ago, and from a romantic love of nature which has been such a powerful theme in English literature. . . . Britain is a country where over 80 per cent of the population live in towns of 50,000 inhabitants or more. Yet most reject the urban industrial culture, viewing life in the city as an unnatural economic necessity."

21. McDowall, *Britain in Close-Up*, 110. "Among those who reject the English cottage culture in favour of a popular urban culture, some remained deeply dissatisfied with their place in society. Teds, Mods, Rockers, Bikers, skinheads, punks and Rastafarians, the sub-culture of the politically or economically weaker segments of society, all have their roots in the poorer parts of towns."

John Oakland defines what it is to be English within the context of contemporary British culture with the clear recognition that social and cultural values are subject to change as the result of historical processes. He notes the tension and unresolved conflicts between the four nationality groups: England, Wales, Ireland,[22] and Scotland, which make up the UK. He sees English identity as the most potent of the four, as defined by norms to which the others both react in hostility and, at the same time, to some extent, maintain their own identity as a result of this relationship.[23] Oakland concludes that these attributes are, in fact, stereotypes and that their value is limited in describing the dynamic that governs the identity politics of the four nations that make up the UK. We can conclude that what these nations do have in common is the experience of empire as a world power and their subsequent suspicion of foreigners who were formerly held in economic and political subjection.

There are historical reasons for English dominance within the UK, namely the unification under the English Crown. Thus, power resides geographically in London and the home countries. Oakland describes a fractured society with as many divisions within these nations as between them. For Oakland, the whole debate about Britishness has come about partly as a result of these divisions but also because of claims that non-white immigration has been detrimental to national identity, which is about the preservation of whiteness as an English norm.[24] A case study by John Eade in the 1990s demonstrates the racialized response of a section of the native English toward the Islamic presence in Tower Hamlets.[25] Their opposition to the use of a Georgian Huguenot building as a mosque

22. We assume he is referring to Northan and not Southern Ireland, though it is not specified.

23. Oakland, *British Civilization*, 62. "The English might like to see themselves as calm, reasonable, patient and commonsensical people, who should be distinguished from the excitable, romantic and impulsive Celts. The Celts, on the other hand, may consider the English to be arrogant, patronizing and cold, and themselves as having all the virtues. The English, and sometimes the British as a whole, are often thought of as restrained, reserved, unemotional, private and independent individuals, with a respect for the amateur and the eccentric. Underlying all, there is supposed to be a dry sense of humor which specializes in understatement, irony, self-deprecation and an enjoyment in using the language in very flexible ways. Such qualities may be offset by certain aggressiveness, stubbornness and lack of co-operation. The British appear to have a relaxed attitude towards work and economic production, and have often been characterized as tolerant and somewhat lazy, with a happy-go-lucky attitude to life."

24. See Isiorho, *Faith in Unions*, 34–61.

25. Eade, "Changing Landscapes."

is cloaked in the garb of conservation and national heritage. This building had been used formerly as a Methodist chapel but had been seriously neglected despite its great architectural worth. The Spitalfields Historic Building Trust wanted to stop the lawful owners of the Brick Lane Great Mosque from making internal alterations to the fabric of this building. The conservationists objected to the construction of a new floor, since this would involve the destruction of galleries and pews of the former chapel. For Eade, conservationist politics become racialized politics in the hands of a social grouping who are characterized by gentrification. The decline of empire on the one hand and the rise of Thatcherism on the other led many people to embrace neoconservative ideologies, which gave them a false sense Britain's importance on the world stage.[26] For Goran Therbourn, the collective identity is also by definition a public identity, which provides a secular expression for Christianity.[27] Therbourn saw this Christian identity as social celebration and rites of passage rather than the active pursuit of theological understanding. So, nationality, nationalism, and ethnicity are concepts within European identity formation that seek to replace the present with an idealized perception of the past.[28]

## A Challenge to the British State by George Bell

The next section of this introduction will consider the relationship between church and state during the Second War World. We will do this by examining the work and teaching of Bishop George Bell of Chichester and ask if there are implications for the debate about disestablishment of the Church of England. Through a sociological exposition of the teaching of George Bell, we will seek to develop a theological understanding of the relationship between church and state for our own time.

George Bell was appointed dean of Canterbury in 1924 and was bishop of Chichester from 1929 until his retirement in 1957. Bell stood openly against the Hitler regime from the beginning and supported his friend Dietrich Bonhoeffer and the Confessing Church in their struggle against the Nazi government in Germany. Bell came into conflict with the British state when he refused to accept the doctrine that the war must be waged ruthlessly, not merely against the Nazi and the armed forces but

26. Husband, "Political Context of Muslim Communities."

27. Therbourn, *European Modernity and Beyond.*

28. See Wright, *On Living.*

against the whole German people. Bell believed himself to be acting in accordance with the mind of Christ in making this challenge to the British state. There can be little doubt that he had taken a principled position based upon firmly held convictions. For Donald MacKinnon, Bell is "an authentic apostle."[29] Adrian Hastings describes Bell as "a man of immense compassion and obstinate consistency in clinging to cause."[30] Considering he was an Anglican Bishop with much ecclesiastical experience, Bell was certainly aware of the likely reaction to his pronouncements concerning the obliteration bombing and the internment of aliens to which he was strongly opposed. For Bell, the enemy was not the German people but the tyrants of the Third Reich. So, did he pay the price of his convictions? Did Bell's speeches during the war destroy his chances of succeeding to the seat of Canterbury? Was preferment denied to him by Winston Churchill on account of the challenge he made to the British state during the Second World War? Kenneth Slack talks about "an implacable refusal; to forgive the man who has betrayed the establishment from within. That was Bell's offence, and it was to the end unpardonable."[31] However, Slack does not seem to think Bell was overlooked as such but rather that he did not have the support of the Church or the nation to take on the archbishop role.[32] According to Andrew Chandler, there was "a restless, irresolvable debate in Church circles, a debate that even now does not go away."[33] Given the secrecy around the appointment procedures then and now, we shall never know with any certainty.

When war broke out in 1939, the German Evangelical Church was already divided into two camps—those who, like Bonhoeffer and the Confessing Church, were opposed to Hitler, and those who supported Hitler, the so-called German Christians. The latter group wanted a church subservient to the state, while the aim of the former was to safeguard its independence. This state of affairs created a major dilemma for the ecumenical movement of the day, since the committees and conferences of that movement were to be chosen by the churches they represented. The German Christians could not be totally excluded from ecumenical activities. However, this did not prevent George Bell from using his position as chairperson of the Life and Work Movement to denounce

29. MacKinnon, *Stripping of the Altars*, 83.

30. Hastings, *History of English Christianity*, 341

31. Slack, *George Bell*, 123–24.

32. Slack, *George Bell*, 112–16.

33. Chandler, *George Bell*, 173.

the disciplinary measures that had been taken by that church against ministers of the gospel on account of their loyalty to the fundamental principles of Christian faith.

Following the invasion of Austria, the official Reich Church decreed, as a birthday present for Hitler, that all pastors should have to take an oath of loyalty to the Fuhrer. During the summer of 1938, resistance began to wane and even the Confessing pastors began to take the oath. During this crisis, the Confessing Church produced a confession of the church's guilt and a prayer that the danger of war might be averted. This was immediately denounced by the SS as a treasonable action. When war finally broke out, the Council of Brethren, which had set up the Confessing Church, distributed leaflets to Christian theologians claiming that, since war was not a matter of individual responsibility, it was possible to be a soldier with a good conscience.

Hitler's coming to power in 1933 saw the expulsion from Germany large numbers of people, especially those with Jewish ancestry. A group of refugees who had been designated by the Nazis as non-Aryan Christians was brought to the attention of George Bell, who tried to awaken the church and the British public to their plight. According to Bell, the church had "a special duty to plead the cause of the suffering, whether Jew or Gentile."[34] At the outbreak of war in 1939, the British government interned all aliens of enemy origin who had lived and worked in Britain before the commencement of hostilities.[35] With the support of the archbishops of Canterbury and York, Bell approached the home secretary with a view to bringing about the release of six German pastors, the majority of whom were opposed to Hitler. This Bell achieved through the appeals procedure.

However, with the invasion of Holland, Belgium, and France by German forces, the British government took its internment policy a stage further and arrested not just those who had lived and worked in Britain before the war but all male aliens of German origin. Many of the people caught in this net were those who had fled to Britain to escape Nazi persecution. For Bell, it was an outrage that those refugees whom he had helped to escape from tyranny in Germany would now find themselves behind the barbed wire of English internment camps.[36]

34. Bell, *Church and Humanity*, 117.

35. See Bell, *Church and Humanity*, 1–21.

36. See Lafitte, *Internment of Aliens*, cited in Chandler, *George Bell*, 78; Gillman and Gillman, *Papers of Francois Lafitte*; Cesarani and Kushner, *Internment of Aliens*.

On February 9, 1944, Bell condemned the obliteration bombing of Germany and declared the church should speak out against the methods of barbarism and tyranny, which threatened civilian populations outside the military zone.[37] A letter in the *Church Times* was as follows—"If Europe is civilized at all, what can excuse the bombing of towns by night and the harassing of non-combatants who work by day and cannot sleep when night comes?"[38] He denounced the bombing of Dresden. In a speech to the House of Lords, he comments thus:

> It is no longer definite military and industrial objectives which are the aim of the bombers but the whole town area by area is plotted carefully out. Thus an area is singled out and plastered on one night, that area is singled out and plastered on another night a third a fourth; a fifth area is similarly singled out and plastered night after night till to use the language of the Chief of Bomber Command with regard to Berlin, "The heart of Nazi Germany ceases to beat." How can there be discrimination in such matters when civilians, monuments, military objectives, and industrial objectives all together form the target? How can the bombers aim at anything more than a great space when they see nothing and the bombing is blind?[39]

There are different approaches to Christian discipleship, which have been influential in the relationship of the church and state. There is the school of thought that says Christian discipleship requires the Christian rule of love to be the guiding principle in all relations of life without a single exception. If Christians cannot persuade society to adopt the Christian way, then they should withdraw from society and live as a separate body. Another approach declares that the standards that govern Christian disciples in their intimate personal life are not applicable in the wider sphere of common life. Finally, there is the viewpoint that affirms there is available a moral standard for the common life that is not the full commandment of the Christian gospel but has some relation to it and should approximate more nearly towards it. Bell suggests that it is this latter position that most Christians accept and commends it on the grounds that it demands the establishment of justice.[40]

37. See Chandler, "Church of England," 930–31.

38. *Church Times*, April 17, 1941, 5, cited in Chandler, *George Bell*, 113.

39. Bell, *Church and Humanity*, 134–35.

40. See Bell, *Christianity and World Order.*

Bell regarded the doctrine of the "just war" as an appropriate guide to the commitment of Christians to the support of the state during the Second World War. So, for Bell, the church had a responsibility to define righteousness as part of its prophetic role in the world.[41] The following conditions have been recognized in the church as necessary for a "just war." It must be waged by a legitimate authority. It must be in a just cause proportionate to the suffering and death that comes about by its waging. It must be undertaken with the right intention, which ultimately is a just and lasting peace. The war should be a last resort, when all peaceful remedies are exhausted. There should be reasonable expectation of success. The mode of conducting the war should be morally legitimate. The innocent must not be killed by indiscriminate slaughter. It must not result in disproportionate suffering to the enemy population, to the home population, or to the international community. According to the just war tradition, a particular war is justified only if all the above criteria are met.[42] Both the cause for which one goes to war and the methods by which one fights must be just.

The war against Germany can be understood as legitimate, since all other means to the morally just solution to the conflict were exhausted before resorting to arms. When Britain declared war on Germany, she had a just cause—the German invasion of Poland. In this context, war is described as just if employed to defend a stable order or morally preferable cause against threats of destruction or the use of injustice. Thus, the goals for which Britain fought were just and the opponent was unjust. The war was explicitly declared by a legitimate authority and its formal declaration of war preceded armed conflict. Thus, Germany had every opportunity to abandon its unjust activities and prevent war. Furthermore, the war was conducted by military means that promised a reasonable attainment of moral and political objectives being sought.

Bell's argument was that the ends do not justify the means. He did not believe that modern warfare, with its indiscriminate bombing of civilian populations, could in any way be described as the war of the just.[43] The just war theory entailed selective immunity for certain parts of the enemy population, particularly for non-combatants. Non-combatants are all those not directly involved in the manufacture, direction, or use of

41. Bell, *Church and Humanity*, 22–31.

42. Bell, *Church and Humanity*, 22–31; Chandler, *George Bell*, 75.

43. See Bell, *Church and Humanity*, 129–41.

weapons. In a just war, no military action may be aimed directly at non-combatants. That is not to say that civilians may never be injured. If an army justly destroyed a military target and nearby non-combatants are killed, that is an unintended side effect, which is permissible within limits. However, the principle of proportionality applies here, which specifies that there must be a reasonable expectation that good results of the war exceed the bad. This principle applies both to the whole enterprise of the war and to specific tactics in the course of battle.

Rowan Williams uses the example of George Bell to justify an implicit but unconvincing argument for church establishment. In a brief contribution to *The Church and Humanity*,[44] the challenge to the British state is initially sanitized as something to do with art and culture, as if these important attributes could be reduced to relics to be found in a museum or church archive. This is the world of Englishness, with its long dry sentences referenced by ibid. and op cit.[45] Bell is seen as someone creating routes into the establishment and giving a voice to the powerless in a system that presumably had a listening ear. Furthermore, Bell is portrayed as presiding over an establishment that did not require systemic change, even though the government of the day had gone astray with its policy on obliteration bombing and the internment of aliens. For Williams, this is about the church acting as a guardian for the "morally coherent society," otherwise known as the "nation," which is dependent upon the church for guidance.[46]

According to Williams, an established church needs to be "coherently aware" of its larger global context, as this is where the Church of England operates.[47] Presumably, this is about the Church of England presiding over the rest of the Anglican Communion in the absence of an elected presiding bishop.[48] For the writers of this commentary, these comments on establishment from Williams sound dangerously like the promotion of colonialism. We will deal with the concepts of colonialism and neocolonialism in the context of the church structures later in our manuscript when we consider the work of Franz Fanon and Gustavo Gutierrez.

44. See Chandler, *Church and Humanity.*

45. Chandler, *Church and Humanity*, 209.

46. Williams, "Church of the Nation," 214.

47. Williams, "Church of the Nation," 217.

48. The role of the archbishop of Canterbury is *primus inter pares*—first among equals. In reality, the archbishop of Canterbury is the colonial head of the Anglican Communion.

For Bell, the state has no ultimate omnipotent authority of its own. From the time of the incarnation, the church has stood over and against the state as a witness to the sovereignty of God. The state derives its authority from God and is subordinate to God. For this reason, the functions of church and state are not synonymous. Williams is reluctant to see church and state as potential rivals, even though "the state is the guarantor of order, justice, and civil liberty,"[49] while the church "is charged with the gospel of God's redeeming love."[50] However, for Bell, power is an important characteristic of the state, which enables it to maintain order. So, according to Bell, "The State has a function, and the Church has a function. They are distinct."[51] In order to advocate church establishment, Williams plays down this distinction by suggesting a harmony of structures, which Bell would not own.

Bell knew, on the outbreak of war, that all the resources of the state would be called upon. He also knew that his task as a bishop was to make it clear that the church was not such a resource. The church was not an appendage of the nation. The church primarily represents the Christian gospel, which brings forgiveness and salvation. Bell believed that the church in any country fails to be the church if it forgets that its members in one country have a fellowship with its members in every other country. By opposing government policy during the Second World War, Bell helped the church to remain the church despite its attempts to become the mouthpiece of the state. Bell had demonstrated in his pronouncements that the dehumanized brutality of Nazism had entered the thinking of those who would oppose it—the state that had opposed the Nazis by obliteration bombing and indiscriminate internment.

## Implicit Establishment by Literature and Depictions of Clergy

We move now to the trajectory that looks at Englishness as it is seen through the pages of the English novel. Here, church and society are linked through a *Deep England* portrayal of the English cleric.[52] Thus, from Chaucer to Fielding and beyond, through Jane Austen to George

49. Bell, "Church's Function in War-Time," para. 2.

50. Bell, "Church's Function in War-Time," para. 2.

51. Bell, "Church's Function in War-Time," para. 2.

52. See Wright, *On Living*.

Eliot[53] and to Susan Howatch, something to do with the condition and portrayal of the church and of the clergy has been a strong indicator of how the English depict their notion of themselves and of their practice of religion. Two common themes have been the comic potential of persons of the cloth and the sense of a departure from the glories and the certainties of old. Yet, the simple English word *nostalgia* is the only one available to cover this; at least, that does have the connotation of recollection and reinvention, with all the additional overtones of dubiety that retrospection brings.

*The Canterbury Tales* is an early tour de force for the English tradition of travel and shrewd observation as twin balances in which whatever is under scrutiny is weighed and invariably found wanting. The church figures in this collection are notable for either their stupidity or their venialness.

The picaresque exploitation of this comic potential continues in Fielding, especially with Parson Adams in *Joseph Andrews*.[54] The early opening comments in the continuing debate of rural simplicity and virtue versus the depravity of city life are inherent in the texture and pattern of Fielding's work and are continued in the church's deliberations of today—still unresolved apart from the cloaking miasma of sentiment. Of the character, Adams, Fielding remarks in his preface to *Joseph Andrews*,

> It is designed a character of perfect simplicity; and as the goodness of his heart will recommend him to the gentlemen of the cloth; for whom, while they are worthy of their sacred order, no man could possibly have greater respect. They will therefore excuse me, notwithstanding the low adventures in which he is engaged, that I have made him a clergyman; since no other office could have given him so many opportunities of displaying his worthy inclinations.[55]

The opening description within the novel of the inimitable Parson Adams is thus:

> Mr Abraham Adams was an excellent scholar. . . . He was, besides, a man of good sense, good parts, and good nature; but was at the same time as entirely ignorant of the ways of this world as an infant just entered into it could possibly be.[56]

53. Her given name was Mary Ann Evans; her pen name was George Eliot.

54. Fielding, *Joseph Andrews*.

55. Fielding, *Joseph Andrews*, 54.

56. Fielding, *Joseph Andrews*, 65.

*Joseph Andrews* concerns the adventures of a young and naive poor man who travels between the two worlds of London sophistication and vice to the bucolic simplicity of the rural life. Joseph is a comely man who is subject to the constant attentions of amorous females. His companion and mentor is Abraham Adams, a complex and yet engaging, open character who is depicted as a moderate scholar—shrewd, uxorious, and productive, yet vigorous and ready to fight for what he believes is right. It is the combination of his parts that is funny. You do not expect a Church of England clergyman to display a brawny fist, nor to end up tied to a bed post, besmirched in a pigsty, or accidentally in bed with Lady Booby. These mishaps are comic, yet Adams manages to keep our affection and our respect. His overriding characteristic is his candor. You could not swear to the consequences if you trusted your life to him, but you could be certain that he would, at the very least, suffer with you. Adams understands that the main tenets of the Christian faith are to be taken at their face value. Faith, truth, compassion, forgiveness are concrete in their reality for him. The book is the story of Joseph's pilgrimage but also of Adams's and of how his values do stand the test of time and trial. That is why, despite the near buffoonery of his predicaments, Adams retains something of the air of a genuine hero, except for his great flaw: his all too evident humanity.

The satirical edge behind all of this is that it is somewhat unexpected that Adams should be a parson. The clergy are perhaps expected to be members of the more formal aspects of society, and those were precisely the parts that Fielding castigates for their self-serving heartlessness and infidelity. Whilst it would be too simplistic to say that Fielding contrasts the wickedness of town life with the rural virtues, there is, as a frame for the action and the discourse of the novel, the sense that the countryside, with a properly ordered social structure of squire, parson, and villagers, is the way in which mortal happiness can best be pursued.

The date of publication of *Joseph Andrews* was 1742; some thirty years later, Jane Austen was born and would grow up to be recognized as one of the most quintessential English writers, whose tiny pictures, intricately painted on the famous metaphorical inch of ivory, have been only recently exploited by the English-hungry Hollywood moguls avariciously searching for the pot of gold that is Englishness quaintly expressed to a western world that has lost its sense of self and is seeking an alibi. In her first written novel, *Northanger Abbey*, a clergyman is the romantic hero who acts as a counterfoil to the more gothic excesses of the naive heroine.

Henry Tilney is depicted as a man of good sense and of good family who knew how to conduct himself and yet retain a sense of fun. Catherine Morland is the daughter of a well-to-do clergyman, so the atmosphere of vicarages and of English country life is extraordinarily strong throughout the novel. Indeed, it is consciously drawn upon to refute the inferior species of the gothic novel, with its Italianate overtones, which is depicted as a specious and exotic invader into the national consciousness.

The clergyman, Henry Tilney, is very much a precursor of the more roundly developed George Knightley in *Emma*, Jane Austen's later and, arguably, finest work. Mr. Knightley's "high superiority of character" is a symptom of his Englishness, of the decency and moderation, self-restraint, and general good breeding that have become synonymous with the best of the English way of life. Ronald Blythe, in his introduction to the Penguin edition of *Emma* in 1966, describes Knightley thus:

> Mr Knightley is the timeless Englishman, the real thing, modest, unaffected, somewhat inadequate of speech (loquacity is not a masculine virtue in England), just, intelligent but not intellectual, loving rather than lover-like, and *landed*.[57]

This serves as a fair description of Henry as of Mr. Knightley. The clergy, as scions and types of the Church of England, were to be members of the landed gentry, usually younger sons, naturally, who were not to be too enthusiastic about anything. They made a virtue out of the tepidity that was so roundly condemned in Laodicea. How they would encounter Pentecost in any Lucan sense is a prospect that can only make the mind boggle.

Returning to Henry and his horror when he at last understands exactly what suspicions Catherine has been entertaining about the circumstances of his mother's death, and sadly, this sounds like a contemporary royal story.

> Dear Miss Morland, consider the dreadful nature of the suspicions you have entertained. What have you been judging from? Remember the country and the age in which we live. Remember that we are English, that we are Christians. Consult your own understanding, your own sense of the probable, your own observation of what is passing around you. Does our education prepare us for such atrocities? Do our laws connive at them? Could they be perpetrated without being known, in a country

57. Jane Austin, *Northanger Abbey*, 16.

> like this, where social and literary intercourse is on such a footing, where every man is surrounded by a neighbourhood of voluntary spies, and where roads and newspapers lay everything open?[58]

The nature of Henry Tilney's vocation is never discussed, presumably because such matters need no elaboration. Admittedly, it is through Catherine's eyes that his churchy connections are viewed, but she is the daughter of a vicarage herself, so when she is seen as thinking, "Now, there was nothing so charming to her imagination as the unpretending comfort of a well-connected parsonage,"[59] we have to hear this as important. Nowhere is the gospel mentioned. The icons of restraint, good taste, and general decency are liberally scattered, but the Lord of the universe humbled into human form on the most merciful of rescue missions, well, that would not be English to allude to that, now, would it?

Any list of other famous Janeite parsons must include Mr. Collins from *Pride and Prejudice*.[60] This self-serving toady of a parson typifies all the worst of the Church of England in its long love affair with the rich and landed. Mr. Collins is besotted with his patron, Lady Catherine de Bourgh, who is plainly revealed by the merciless pen of the author to be a shallow person obsessed with appearance, to the detriment of genuine worth. She is exactly the sort of person who should be challenged by any servant of the gospel, yet the sycophancy exhibited by Mr. Collins shows what glamour the English tradition of snobbery holds. If being a clergyman is something to do with being the younger son, then built into that is the anxiety that all almost-outsiders feel to be more in than the inmost circle. Status, not mission, becomes the mainspring of life in a fascinating triumph for the lord of misrule. Rationality and morality are alike discarded. Perhaps part of the blessing of the church's present position is that more of the clergy and members are able to stand in radical critique of society in a way not possible to people such as Mr. Collins. One of the particular struggles of the Church of England must be its relationship with the establishment and the values that it typifies. You cannot serve two lords, but the Church of England does its darnedest.

By 1872, almost sixty years after the publication of *Pride and Prejudice*, another woman writer, who has been associated with depictions of

58. Austen, *Northanger Abbey*, 165.
59. Austen, *Northanger Abbey*, 198–99.
60. Austen, *Pride and Prejudice*.

English life, published her great novel *Middlemarch*. George Eliot has always been admired for her powers of observation and her ability to portray interesting characters with credibility as well as accuracy. With her background in philosophical studies and her own social position, she was well placed to chronicle her times by examining the recent past. *Middlemarch* looks back over several decades of great change in the English way of life and a shift in the locus of power from the landed gentry to the manufacturing and retailing classes. The railway, the newspapers, the rise and influence of nonconformity were all issues that moved her. There is a nostalgia in the narrator's voice that is profound and very English. She refers to Fielding, who was an author she admired, as having "the happiness to be dead a hundred and twenty years ago."[61] She continues at the beginning of chapter 15,

> But Fielding lived when the days were longer (for time, like money, is measured by our needs) when summer afternoons were spacious, and the clock ticked slowly in the winter evenings. We belated historians must not linger after his example.[62]

• • •

*Middlemarch* is concerned with the lives of three young women, Dorothea Brooke, Rosamond Vincy, and Mary Garth, and the processes by which they choose their life partners. Dorothea is upper class, from county stock, landed, with money and position. She inhabits a very consciously English world that Jane Austen could have depicted. Rosamond is a merchant's daughter; she lives in the town from money made by her father and is very aware of straining after gentility. Her desire is to imitate her betters, that curious English trait of negating one's own struggle and worth to pretend to be members of a quite different social class. We see the agony of that struggle in Rosamond, who moves us to pity despite her shallow pretensions. Mary Garth is from the stock that once might have been called yeoman.[63] Her grandmother could have been Harriet Smith, Emma Woodhouse's protégé.[64] She is respectable but impoverished,

61. Eliot, *Middlemarch*, 141.

62. Eliot, *Middlemarch*, 141.

63. It could mean a person who is a freehold landholder on a landed estate occupying a lower middle-class position between the gentry and the laborers.

64. The character of Harriet Smith can be found in Jane Austen's novel *Emma*, where she is a boarding student at Mrs. Goddard's school. This impressionable young woman

clinging to a strong set of moral values, inhabiting a world somewhere between town and country.

There are five types of clergymen seen in *Middlemarch*. First, there is Casaubon, the disastrous first choice of Dorothea. He is of landed, moneyed origin. He is a scholarly but remote figure, dry as dust, pursuing a goal of such remoteness as to be completely irrelevant. He looks backward to the Classical era and appears to have some disdain for the modern world. He is cultured in that very English sense of the word. When he goes on his sedate version of the grand tour, he spends hours toiling away in libraries, seriously neglecting his wife on their honeymoon. A figure who is a member of the chorus, so to speak, is Cadwallader, the rector. His wife plays a minor comic role in the action, and his situation is common enough not to warrant deep detail, which makes it interesting for our purposes. He is of good birth but impoverished, the younger son syndrome. He very much inhabits the present moment and cheerfully goes about his own interests, going fishing and so forth, leaving the duties of anxiety to his wife. It is impossible to imagine either of these clerics having the Jabbok relationship with God that is so biblical.[65] They may have wrestled on shores between day and night until they limped, but this is not shown in the novel. Their world does not include indicators of spirituality or of devotion and piety.

The next clergyman worthy of note is Farebrother, whose parish, unlike those of his two colleagues, is in the town itself. It is not a rich living, and he has a struggle to provide for himself and for his mother, his aunt, and his sister. Mrs. Farebrother is of the old school. She declares to Lydgate, in chapter 17,

> When I was young, Mr Lydgate, there was never any question about right and wrong. We knew our catechism, and that was enough; we learned our creed and our duty. Every respectable church person had the same opinions. But now if you speak out of the Prayer-book itself, you are liable to be contradicted.[66]

Her father was a clergyman, so Camden Farebrother inherits that tradition of impoverished gentility, so poor that his aunt "steals" sugar and other titbits from his table in order to be able to give to the really poor

---

becomes Emma Woodhouse's protégé and close friend. Harriet is given bad advice as to her matchmaking endeavors, which has negative consequences for this character.

65. Gen 32:22–31.

66. Austin, *Middlemarch*, 169–70.

families that she visits. Sadly, for Farebrother, it seemed he "felt himself not altogether in the right vocation."[67] This strain led him into several difficulties, especially financial. He is a figure that eventually attains nobility but who is also seriously impaired. He is engaged in a struggle, and his faithfulness is seen particularly in his loyalty to his dependent female relatives. Farebrother is modern, an urban and domestic hero whose trials and tribulations are easily accessible to the modern reader. In his denial of himself, by not pursuing Mary Garth nor by distressing her with a show of ardor when she was at her most vulnerable, he reveals himself to be a genuinely good person but on a small scale. George Eliot's world, although too crowded for one inch of ivory, nevertheless has the same sense of scale as Jane Austen's while having a wider frame of reference.

The other two types of clergy shown in *Middlemarch* are the curates, who are never personally delineated but are depicted as extremely poor and prolific with children that are available for upper-class women to play with; Celia Brooke enjoys this pastime. The curates serve the upper classes; they are the vicarious functionaries of the rectors and, by consequence, inhabit a shadowy, in-between world. The remaining type of clergyman is the nonconformist pastor, allied with Bulstrode, who stands as the most cowardly, vicious, and hypocritical of men in this novel. They are also connected with the working classes, whereas all the other types of religious persons are allied to the upper classes. They are firmly on the periphery of so-called polite society.

The Englishness of this book as a whole lies in the obsession with birth and fortune that runs through it. People are either happy that they are lucky in their birth, or they strive to achieve that goal of being like their betters. A significant part of the rigid social structure is signified by the clergymen and their activities. The book as a whole shows the shift from landed to landlessness, from wealth by birth to individual acquisition, from easily inherited culture to laboriously acquired knowledge through study and self-deprivation. *Middlemarch* shows a society under change and, therefore, under attack. Its moral foundations are not certain, hence Mrs. Farebrother's *cri de coeur* quoted above. It is a world in flux, where an earlier, probably mythical world of constancy contained, amongst other things, the church in its center. So far, our clergy have been significant because they were recognizable as emblems. The church had a role and the types of clergy portrayed could be located within that

67. Austin, *Middlemarch*, 172.

world. The men were well within the range of average, either being totally predictable or by being caricatures coming within the range of burlesque, suggesting that they were not typical but amusing by contrast.

To read Susan Howatch is to encounter an author who has chosen to focus on the church, but now the church is so marginalized in society that she has to make her central figures people who are extraordinary. The ordinariness of earlier clerical depictions will not do. In order to make the church interesting for the average reader, she has to break through that aura of indifference and ignorance by making her characters amazing. Yet, the echoes of Mrs. Farebrother's nostalgia for the certainties of yore necessitate this fascination with the church, which ought to embody eternal values and constancy. We want the church to be solid and to be dependable, and we are angry that it is not; therefore, we have to have it staffed by maniacs and deviants.

Susan Howatch was born in 1940 in Surrey but has spent significant amounts of time living overseas, first in America, then in Ireland.[68] This gives her the sharp eye of a return observer. She has written a hugely successful series of six substantial novels based on the interwoven lives of several "successful" churchmen and covering the period of the Second World War up to the sixties. The titles are interesting: *Glittering Images*, *Glamorous Powers*, *Ultimate Prizes*, *Scandalous Risks*, *Mystical Paths*, and *Absolute Truths*. The idea for the series occurred to her when she was living in Salisbury in a flat overlooking the cathedral, which broods like a stranded leviathan over that ancient city and is the embodiment of old English usage.[69] She has thoroughly researched her work, basing many of her ideas and characters on historical figures, incorporating some in their own identity, such as her depiction of George Bell. Most of the novels, with the exception of *Scandalous Risks*, have clergymen as their narrators. Without exception, her heroes rise to be senior churchmen and are remarkable for their extraordinary personalities. The norm is eccentricity, and the style is self-consciously English. Howatch notes the decline in living standard of the clergy from the days before the war, when bishops lived in palaces, wore gaiters, and kept a good cellar, to the modern era of boxes for vicarages and smaller houses for bishops. Her characters brood a great deal and suffer huge agonies. They commit numerous faults and

68. This information is found on the inside cover page in the series of her novels.

69. This is also found on the inside cover page in the series.

sins, but each display a certain charismatic energy and fascination for the reader—Alex Haley meets George Eliot.

The Englishness of the Church of England pervades these contemporary English novels. You really can imagine Susan Howatch sitting, gazing at Salisbury Cathedral as she writes: the gracious houses, the easy way with money and private schools, the assumption that one knows how to behave and one follows certain codes, such as using the pronoun "one." Churchmen have regular contact with the landed classes, although that causes some social crises for the parvenu. Her world is a dizzying mixture of the stuffy and the traumatic, a fairly accurate portrait of the present church in its state of upheaval. Like the embodiment of the nation, the Church of England in Howatch's world is being shaken out of the old, imperial ways into a new path, which is clouded by uncertainty. Howatch chronicles a church that is riven by self-doubt and by change. She clearly outlines some of the historical processes involved. She sees the struggle for power between the Anglo-Catholic and the Evangelical wings of the Church of England. She notes the tension between the prophetic and the institutional. Her truly dangerous characters are linked to George Bell, who was, despite the legacy of the Oxford movement, the only English bishop vehemently opposed to the British government policy of terror-bombing German cities and the indiscriminate internment of aliens during the Second World War.

Howatch's less radical characters are scandalous, indulging in moral laxities, often resulting in illegitimate children. At least Howatch does permit the clergy to have sex lives, as opposed to the stereotypical expectation of some form of neuter life of popular imagination. This all too human aspect of her clerical figures is one way in which Howatch details the turbulent life of the Church of England in the middle years of this century. The rise of radical theology, the questioning of tradition, and the loss of confidence together with the decline in attendance. Her clergy move between extremes, from the psychic mystic to the cynical manager. She, too, conveys this sense of nostalgia that hankers after the old certainties and, as such, can be linked to Wright's concept of deep England, portraying a world that never existed except in the selective memory of the privileged.[70] The world of English literature acts as a signpost to a deep Anglicanism, which is preoccupied with its past and with itself.

70. See Wright, *On Living*; Isiorho, *Faith in Unions*, 57–60.

## Methodism—A Distant but Anglican Sibling

So, is Methodism a repository of working class Englishness? Well, who can tell; but certainly, the purpose of this next section of the introduction, like its predecessor, is to define a denominational faith not by its doctrines but by its social identity. We consider the social context of two novels by George Eliot, *Middlemarch* and *Adam Bede*, which ties the development Methodism to the Industrial Revolution and demonstrates a repository of working class Englishness. George Eliot has always been admired for her powers of observation and her ability to portray interesting characters with credibility as well as accuracy. With her background in philosophical studies and her own social position, she was in an ideal position to cast a critical and interested eye over the nation's recent history.

George Eliot writes in layers of history, often going back to the age before her own, when huge changes were beginning, giving her the benefit of hindsight. It can be argued that her work falls within the broad genre known as "condition of England" novels, focusing on the impact of social fracture through the growing divide between town and country, factory and farming, which was opening up ever more widely. Eliot is more than that as she is such a consummate portrayer of the real world, the "old women scraping carrots with their work-worn hands"[71] are as much part of the stream of history as those whose names survive the ravages of time. "Therefore let Art always remind us of them; therefore let us always have men ready to give the loving pains of a life to the faithful representing of commonplace things—men who see beauty in these commonplace things, and delight in showing how kindly the light of heaven falls on them."[72]

So, Eliot was a writer of fiction, but she was also fascinated by the impact of wide changes upon the lives of ordinary people. She saw herself as a chronicler, using a strong sense of realism to make her work not merely possessed of verisimilitude but actually dealing with the truth through the lens of fiction. Eliot writes sympathetically about Methodism, perhaps being influenced by the memory of her aunt by marriage, Elizabeth Tomlinson Evans, who was a Methodist preacher. It is from a conversation with her aunt that Eliot began to formulate the idea of the infanticide in *Adam Bede*. In a conversation one day, her aunt recalled

71. Eliot, *Adam Bede*, 162.

72. Eliot, *Adam Bede*, 162.

a Mary Voce, whom she had supported right up to the scaffold as the unfortunate woman was sentenced to death for her crime.[73]

• • •

Methodism as a form of Protestantism is different from its distant sibling, Anglicanism, having its origins in the cell structure of self-sustained religious societies, whose context was the laboring and mining communities of the Industrial Revolution. Methodism is as much a religion of dissenting groups as it was that of the poor, but, although the two are clearly related, they are not necessarily the same. For Edward Thompson, Methodism may have been armed with the trappings of dissent, nevertheless, it was a religion for those exploited by capitalism in the growing industrial towns. This church would eventually surrender its nonconformity to the establishment but in its own particular way.[74] Thompson suggests three reasons as to why Methodism was able to hold on to its working-class adherents, despite a lack of any real benefit to working class interests. Firstly, there was an indoctrination program delivered by a system of evangelical Sunday schools, teaching that children came into the world in a state of sin, and therefore, their wills would have to be broken to overcome their original nature.[75]

The story of John and Betty Wise, which was told to children to correct sinful ways, is useful to illustrate the point of indoctrination and the psychological torture visited upon children. John's father impresses upon him the sanctity of the Sabbath, but his sister fails to take on this important teaching by going for a walk on Sunday. Both children were roundly admonished and given a Bible-thumping lesson, first from Genesis, which advocates stoning for people who collect sticks on the Sabbath, and then from 2 Kgs 2:23—the story of the forty-two children who are killed for mocking the bald-headed prophet, Elisha. Watts' hymn explains the situation thus:

> When children in their wanton play,
> Served old Elisha so;
> And bid the prophet go his way,
> "Go up, thou bald-head, go!"

73. Eliot, *Adam Bede*, xv.

74. Thompson, *Making of the English*, 385–86.

75. Thompson, *Making of the English*, 412.

God quickly stop their wicked breath,
And sent two raging bears,
That tore them limb from limb to death,
With blood, and groans, and tears.[76]

The Elisha story is used here to threaten children into submission. There is no attempt at liberal Bible criticism to ask what is going on in this text. It is a straightforward attempt to present a revengeful God who wants children to be obedient and compliant with adult wishes. We cannot leave the Elisha story in the hands of child abusers without some kind of explanation. For one thing, there are some very interesting contradictions. Elisha succeeded Elijah as prophet in Israel and was renowned for many good deeds, possibly even resurrecting a poor woman's son. Are we to believe that the God, whose word we think of as love incarnate, actually would send bears to consume forty-two children—not scare them or maim a few, but kill forty-two—that's a lot of carnage. What was the heinous crime these youths had committed? They called Elisha "baldy." They taunted him with "go up," possibly a reference to the way Elijah, his predecessor, had been taken up to heaven. Presumably, Elisha took great offense at this brief encounter. Some scholars have suggested that the bald head was a reference to leprosy, as lepers had to shave their heads as a sign of their being set aside as unclean. Yet, Elisha heals people, notably Naaman, of leprosy. We think he simply threw a fit. Or it could have been coincidence that the children got attacked. Maybe their shrill cries disturbed the bears, who took umbrage; but then, why didn't Elisha, with his powers, protect these children? Maybe Elisha wanted this to be written as he was fed up of being taunted about his baldness. Maybe the message is "do not mess with bald men because they will get you." Maybe there is no message, and the passage is a quirk of history; its use in Sunday schools certainly is a quirk, one that we baulk at today.

To return to Thompson, Methodism encompassed a work ethic that gave to working people a substitute community to replace the more traditional community structures that they had left behind in the rural areas. Unlike its distant sibling, the Church of England, the urban landscape was not an established place for the landed gentry but rather a new space where, perhaps, the working class might take some ownership, setting the pace themselves. The uprooted and abandoned newcomers from closely-knit mining, fishing, and weaving communities flocked to Methodism.

76. Wise, *History of John Wise*.

Moreover, for migrant workers going from town to town, Methodism could be a home from home, very much as the early church for the first Christians.[77] Methodism used a strong emotional appeal to recruit its followers. Open, hysteria and paroxysms were not the rule of Methodism, but reminders of hellfire sometimes were associated with significant growth of support, particularly among the working class in the North of England.[78]

David Hempton claims that Thompson asked the right questions, namely, why did Methodism as a religious movement come into existence and why did it expand in various geological locations? However, he accuses Thompson of bias on the grounds of his atheism, which is assumed to follow from a Marxist approach to history. Hampton's argument is that too much emphasis has been placed upon the individual motives of faith adherence and the medium through which it was transmitted. Thus, if Thompson believes religion to be irrational and illusionary, then it follows that the only conclusions he can reach are those that explain the phenomenon in terms of displacement activity or repression.[79] In all fairness to Thompson, it does not follow that you must have a faith perspective to research the role of religion in a social and political context, neither does it mean that, without a faith commitment, you would be unable to reach an informed opinion. It could be argued that it is the analysis from outside of a faith perspective that gives the historical study of religion its credibility. We don't think Thompson is offering us some kind of psychology reduction to explain why working-class people joined Methodism but, rather, his approach is sociological in character.

Hempton puts a further argument forward that everything is premised for Thompson upon industrial capitalism. Thus, an example of Methodism in the rural context shows Thompson's analysis to be in error.[80] Here again, this does not seem to be Thompson's argument but a criticism of Marxism in general. For Thompson, Methodism is largely a counter-revolutionary movement that took off when various forms of radical political intervention had already failed. However, he does make an important distinction in the Methodist hierarchy between who, after Wesley's death, wanted a seat at the table of establishment, against those brethren, known as Primitive Methodists, who seemed content with their

77. Thompson, *Making of the English*, 417.

78. Thompson, *Making of the English*, 417–18.

79. Hempton, *Religion of the People*, 5.

80. Hempton, *Religion of the People*, 5–6.

lowlier estate and who were probably closer to the original ideals of this movement. Thus, we have, within early Methodism, two very different class groupings. The ministers and hierarchy of the orthodox connection, who were now part of a rising middle class and, therefore, in potential conflict with the Primitives, many of whom were local preachers and shared the poverty of the working class. This latter group was to make a significant contribution to trade unions and the labor movement.

Thompson offers an example of rural Methodism to support his view that recruitment to the Methodist fold had as much to do with Protestant theology as it had to do with industrialism. He draws our attention to rural locations where Primitives were making their mark. In East Anglia, field laborers converted to Methodism were demanding that the fruits of the earth, as part of God's good provision for humankind, should be equally shared among his people. Thompson comments on how Methodism had been received in rural England and that "next to poaching, it was the gravest of all offences."[81] Sanctions were soon brought to bear on the Primitives; many were expelled from the movement and women were stopped from preaching.

According to Thompson, the Church of England had failed in securing the obedience of the lower orders on account of its limited credibility with the working class. As, to some extent, the Methodist movement had now become the new establishment, it was able to reassure those in authority that it could now effectively manipulate its congregations.[82] Child labor was condoned in the interests of capital, and the actions of mill owners and manufacturers were endorsed by a new, compliant brand of Methodist preaching. Thompson makes it clear that this is contrary to Wesley's teaching, as Wesley had foreseen the greed of the new merchant class.[83] However, this leaves us with an important dilemma, namely, how did Methodism keep not only the support of a submissive working class but also that of their lords and masters, the captains of industry. Thompson suggests that Methodism, of all religious movements, was best placed to do this because of its theology of election, influenced by Lutheran ideas about submission to authority.[84] The universality of God's grace leading to salvation does not fit with any Calvinist notion of election, whereby a predetermined number of people get into heaven. There is,

81. Thompson, *Making of the English*, 437.

82. Thompson, *Making of the English*, 386.

83. Thompson, *Making of the English*, 391.

84. Thompson, *Making of the English*, 399.

in the Wesleyan system of salvation, an equal opportunity for sinners, regardless of economic class. This left Wesley with the problem of good works, which he had already subordinated, to that of justification by faith. But could not such works also be a sign of grace and thus appeal to the owners of industry? Moreover, what of the poor, who were more likely to remain in a state of grace since they had little opportunity to express their temptations? The Wesleyan system would argue that, constrained as they were by the work-discipline of the factory, their limited life-chances had put them in a spiritually privileged position.[85] This is not to confuse this rather patronizing approach with the much later preferential option for the poor.

• • •

So, what about *Adam Bede*?[86] Eliot started work on *Adam Bede* just as her earlier *Scenes of Clerical Life* had concluded their serial publication. She was greatly encouraged by the critical acclaim she had received.[87] It was the first of her full novels and much of her later techniques and approaches are evident in it. *Adam Bede* concerns the story of country folk, harking back to a rural life that was beginning to be seen as idyllic by Eliot's late nineteenth-century audience. In brief, *Adam Bede* tells the story of two young women and how they relate to the world. Both are orphaned and both live on the generosity of their family. Dinah Morris lives in the city and spends her days, after working in the mills, helping the other people around her, who are as poor as she is. She does this by seeking to open their hearts to the message of God's love in Christ Jesus. She is spending time in the country with her farming family, where Hetty Sorrel is a permanent resident. Hetty's duties are light, looking after the much-indulged younger child of her aunt. Unlike Dinah, Hetty is vain and easily swayed by appearance and by fine words. The two young women could hardly be less alike. Hetty is seduced by Arthur Donnithorne, the young squire. Hetty follows the fate of Mary Voce, while Dinah accompanies her to the end. As they are at the place of execution, Arthur Donnithorne rides through the crowd with a document giving a reprieve from the death sentence. So, Hetty enjoys the privileges of fiction and

85. Thompson, *The Making of the English Working Class*, 401.

86. Eliot, *Adam Bede*.

87. Eliot, *Adam Bede*, xiv; Woolf, "George Eliot," 166–76; Sanders, *Short Oxford History*, 440.

does not pay the ultimate penalty, being transported instead. Dinah and Hetty present opposing depictions of womanhood, but it is with Adam Bede that Dinah reveals the contrast between the Church of England, as embodied by Adam, and Methodism, represented by Dinah.

Eliot personifies the tensions between traditional and new religious expression. This is what, from a purely literary point of view, makes the ultimate marriage of Dinah Morris and Adam Bede rather an anticlimax, as Dinah disappears into domestic felicity. Sociologically, the Church of England and Methodism are still at the stage of a long and overtly polite betrothal, in dialogue but not of one mind. It is the differences rather than the similarities between the two denominations that fascinate Eliot.

Throughout *Adam Bede*, there are many layers of juxtaposition permeating the text. The old and the new, the moral and the weak, rural contra city, the Church of England against Methodism. The latter is where our focus lies.

The novel opens with a bucolic scene precisely dated: "the eighteenth of June, in the year of our Lord 1799."[88] Five workmen are busy in the carpenter's shop with a "strong barytone" being raised in hymn singing, the voice of Adam Bede. A detailed physical description follows to commend him to the reader. His brother, Seth, is also described, Seth being a Methodist whereas Adam attends the Church of England. Seth is so occupied with Methodism that he forgets to finish the door he is working upon. The other workmen tease him about this, expressing the belief that Methodism addles brains for the real world. Interestingly, however, "the idle tramps always felt sure they could get a copper from Seth; they hardly ever spoke to Adam."[89] So, right from the very beginning of the novel, the rather aloof Church of England is contrasted with the social gospel of the Methodists. This is further emphasized later when Mr. Irvine was too gentlemanly to press Arthur Donnithorne to reveal his feelings for Hetty Sorrel, being "too delicate to imply even a friendly curiosity"[90] when Arthur is obviously trying to work matters out about his temptation to trifle rather too much with Hetty Sorrel. If Irvine had listened, much of the subsequent tragedy could have been averted. Drawing on the ardent Evangelical Anglicanism of her youth, Eliot writes with a preacher's passion for Dinah Morris. Dinah's long passages are actually moving and show a woman devoted and completely committed to

88. Eliot, *Adam Bede*, 162.

89. Eliot, *Adam Bede*, 10.

90. Eliot, *Adam Bede*, 189.

a religious practice that shapes her everyday life and drives her forward with vocational energy. She consults her Bible before undertaking any enterprise, bibliomancy; she spends hours in ecstatic prayer; she sacrifices her slender resources and jeopardizes her health to aid others.

To this day, for example, with the (in)famous advice to J. K. Rowling to use her initials to cloak her gender, women and what they represent are routinely subordinated to dominant and male interests. One then wonders, as Dinah so very much embodies the spirit of Methodism, whether Eliot was apophatically yielding precedence to the Church of England. As well as the links between Dinah and Adam in their religious pursuits, there are also contrasts between how Rev. Irvine prospers his vocation as opposed to Dinah's method. Irvine is described as a man of good family rather than of means. He remains uncomplainingly single to support his mother and his two sisters. His mental map centers much more upon the Greco-Roman world. He reads Aeschylus at breakfast, as Arthur finds when he arrives unexpectedly. Irvine is tolerant, or is it a more passive *laissez-faire*? He does not evict Dinah from his parish, despite the hectic urging of his verger. It seems that this tolerance springs, therefore, more from the inability to be pastorally vigorous; as earlier cited, he was too gentlemanly to probe into Arthur's obvious distress.

Dinah's sense of vocation is completely different. "I felt a great movement in my soul, and I trembled as if I was shaken by a strong spirit entering my weak body."[91] Yet, Dinah does not meet with lasting success in Loamshire, whereas Irvine does stay the course. Dinah notes, "I've noticed that in these villages where people lead a quiet life . . . there's a strange deadness to the Word, as different as can be from the great towns, like Leeds."[92] Dinah, although she is a fine preacher, is at her finest in hours of great agony, when she throws herself into the service of the one afflicted. She, and she alone, is the one able to soothe the querulous Lisbeth Bede after the accidental death by drowning of her drunken husband, Adam and Seth's father, Thias. Dinah is gifted with a prescient insight, moving into Lisbeth's shadows with a gentle and consoling radiance. Here is manifested no scatter-wit enthusiasms, as Seth was teased about at the opening of the novel. Again, it was only Dinah who could reach out to poor, frightened Hetty and convince her to admit to herself exactly what she had done to her child. Because we hear this through

91. Eliot, *Adam Bede*, 83.

92. Eliot, *Adam Bede*, 84.

Dinah's ears, Hetty's confession is related in a descriptive rather than accusatory fashion, prompting the reader, whatever the mores of their context, at least to empathize, if not to sympathize, with the bewildered young mother. In a long and moving scene, Eliot shows us the two young women as they sway their way through this most terrible of crises; what can focus the mind more than expecting to die at exactly such and such a time and in precisely such a way. "Dinah began to doubt whether Hetty was conscious who it was that sat beside her. She thought fear and suffering might have driven the poor sinner out of her mind."[93] Later, she prays with and for Hetty in such a long outpouring that it has echoes of the highly priestly prayer of the Johannine account of the agony in the garden. Jesus is real and present to Dinah, and she follows his example in her own agony for Hetty. "Jesus, thou present Saviour! Thou hast known the depths of all sorrow: thou hast entered that black darkness where god is not, and hast uttered the cry of the forsaken. Come, Lord . . . stretch forth thy hand . . . and rescue this lost one."[94] All very unlike the more sedate and composed prayers that we can imagine a dutiful Irvine might make when he does appear as the local vicar to escort Hetty to the scaffold. The irony of this contrast between Anglican with Methodist is that if Irvine had but one *soupçon* of the evangelical fervor of Dinah, if he had been able to reach out to Arthur that morning, then Hetty would never have been in that gloomy prison cell in the first place; she may even have married Adam Bede, as planned, and have been happy. So, we can see that, as with Methodism itself, Dinah, despite the ecstatic side of religion, is also pragmatic. Her implicit message was that pains and ills are part of the human condition but that faith and openness towards God and each other can sustain us.

The following very short, one-page chapter depicts the morning of the execution and the journey to the scaffold. "All Stoniton had heard of Dinah Morris, the young Methodist woman who had brought the obstinate criminal to confess, and there was as much eagerness to see her as to see the wretched Hetty."[95] Dinah appears obliviously to the crowds and to the interest in her as well as in the spectacle of the fallen Hetty; again, typically Methodist, she is so wrapped up in her prayer for Hetty as to lose her sense of self and of self-consciousness. Her work continues, even after Arthur arrives dramatically on horseback with a commutation of

93. Eliot, *Adam Bede*, 402.

94. Eliot, *Adam Bede*, 404.

95. Eliot, *Adam Bede*, 414.

the sentence to one of transportation, right up until the actual departure of Hetty sometime after this chapter ends. The narrative does not show what happens to Hetty; she has a few references made to her. The focus now shifts away from Dinah and Hetty back to Adam. Yes, the plot does creak at this point, and the modern reader may well feel that Eliot should have been more concise but, contextually, it works, as we slow our pace back to the rural after the hectic town rhythm of the trial and the last-minute reprieve. Also, we need some respite from the intensity of the emotion that Dinah has expressed.

The whole of the eighth chapter, entitled "A Vocation," records an intense conversation between Dinah and Irvine, in which the vicar effortlessly assumes the role of interrogator, at least initially, in his role as male, upper-class, and established, in every sense of the word. Irvine queries the possible outcomes of people declaring their own vocations in Methodism: "But don't you find sometimes that both men and women fancy themselves channels for God's Spirit, and are quite mistaken, so they set about a work for which they are unfit, and bring holy things into contempt?"[96] Dinah replies earnestly and at some length. "There's a very strict order kept among us, and the brethren and sisters watch for each other's souls as they that must give account."[97] Irvine's role has now reduced to become that of a stooge, a Nicodemus figure,[98] asking questions to let Dinah's account of her vocation flow. Dinah describes how she can spend hours in prayers and how she suddenly felt called to become a preacher in response to the need of others. Irvine has become a function of the narrative. Remember that the title of the chapter was singular; Eliot never intended it to be an equally weighted dialogue.

Ironically, as this conversation occurs between the two religious leaders, a parallel, but deeply mundane one, is occurring in the dairy where Arthur is loitering in dalliance with Hetty. Here we find interesting layers of juxtaposition that make Eliot still an esteemed novelist. So, Dinah, self-destined for chaste service to God; Hetty, destined for quiet married life with Adam; Arthur, the upper-class man playing with the local maiden; and Adam, steadily comforted by a sense of his own importance and rectitude, all presided over by a vicar who can only be described a spiritual effete. There can only be trouble ahead. This contrasting of spiritual/vocational seductions as opposed to the physical/emotional one

96. Eliot, *Adam Bede*, 81.

97. Eliot, *Adam Bede*, 81–82.

98. John 3:1–21.

are part of Eliot's intensely realistic approach to her writing. The reader can skip lightly at the soap-opera end or delve into strong currents where the eddies and flows of philosophy and religion are debated seriously through the fiction.

This approach gives us a rich tapestry of characters, each of whom is emblematic of some aspect of society. Overwhelmingly, the native residents of Loamshire identify themselves with the Church of England as a right and proper thing to do, part of their very Englishness. As Adam remarks in the opening chapter, "I'm not for laughing at no man's religion. Let 'em follow their consciences, that's all. Only I think it 'ud be better if their consciences 'ud let 'em stay quiet i' the church. . . . And there's such a thing as being over-speritial; we must have something bedside Gospel i' this world."[99] Whereas, in Stonyshire (Yes, we agree, surely no modern editor would let a writer get away today with such nomenclature!), people are so lodged in their context, from a modern sociological post-Marxist perspective, they are so oppressed that they can be seized by fervor in a damascene suddenness that truly can transform lives. And where are the Methodists more successful? After the departure of Irvine and Arthur, there is a comic interlude between Dinah and her formidable aunt, Mrs. Poyser. In vexed anxiety about her niece, whom she loves but disapproves of, Aunt Poyser quizzes Dinah about her talk with Irvine. Is there a backstory here? We know that Eliot chronicled social change deliberately. The eventually global spread of Methodism was deeply rooted in the world of work and of the rapidly expanding Industrial Revolution. Is Eliot implying that the old, serene, and unchanging ways of rural life, as typified through the Church of England, are going to fade away as they cannot be kindled?

That Eliot leads us first one way and then another on the question of religious prominence suggests something of the closeness of the two denominations, but also that their differences mean each can reach out to very divergent target audiences in equally different ways and methods. Certainly, Eliot, through Dinah and the other characters, seems to suggest that the slowness of the average bucolic personality is somehow out of step. Is this just part of the essentially English reverence or nostalgia for those mythical good old days of yore? It is this part of the adult George Eliot who found herself in uncharted waters with her personal life, harking back to the secure old days in her childhood Warwickshire, traveling

99. Eliot, *Adam Bede*, 9.

around with her father and visiting widely in the area around Nuneaton and Coventry where she grew up, most of whose citizens would have expressed horror at her romantic entanglements. Is that element why she does not give a judgment of assessment of which religious way is right—has her approval? As a chronicler, she remains neutral, but we wonder. Work is a strong theme throughout *Adam Bede*, with Adam and Dinah sharing a Protestant work ethic despite their very different expressions of it. Adam sees doing a sound piece of work as godly in itself—who sweeps a room but for thy sake—"[Adam's] work, as you know, had always been part of his religion, and from very early days he saw clearly that good carpentry was God's will."[100] In due and decent course, Arthur goes away to the army, the Poysers and the Bees remain in their ancestral haunts, and Adam proposes to Dinah. Seth has given up his love interest in her; yes, you can hear that creaking plot again. She confesses her love, but, with a contrariety that Aunt Poyser would definitely categorize as Methodist, she shows her struggle, saying, "I felt before that my heart too strongly drawn towards you."[101] She sees Adam with his arms out to her, offering a life of ease, whereas Jesus, the Man of Sorrows, also claims her attention. She has been wrestling at her own internal Jabbok and we, the reader, will later see her as wounded, limping in consequence. Dinah sacrifices much for her eventual marriage from the perspective of the twenty-first century. We have to remind ourselves what real bondage and mortal danger marriage actually was for women, with child after dangerous child, year on year.

But Dinah is not thinking of her own internal problematic at all, it would appear. As she explains, "A great terror has come upon me lest I should become hard, and a lover of self, and no more willingly near the Redeemer's cross."[102] Her methodistical ardor has a very New Testament feel to it in its urgency. She is naturally consumed with thoughts and longings about the man she has come to love, a love born out of the agony of Hetty's ordeal, where each looked into the futures they had planned and found them wanting. Dinah is a passionate woman, as we have so often seen, so the overwhelming arrival of Eros into her world is cataclysmic. She explains, "Since my affections have been set above measure on you, I have had less peace and joy in God; I have felt as it were a division in my

100. Eliot, *Adam Bede*, 436.
101. Eliot, *Adam Bede*, 455.
102. Eliot, *Adam Bede*, 455.

heart."[103] She, the woman who knows the Bible so well and who turns to it on every occasion, forgets here St. Paul's compassionate words about it being better to marry than to burn; so, she is not pragmatic, rather naïve, about how she uses the Bible to guide her. Incidentally, Aunt Poyser's take on Dinah's marital prospects, as the wider community begins to debate a possible match between Adam and Dinah, runs thus: "She'll never marry anybody, if he isn't a Methodist and a cripple."[104]

An almost comical example of how other-worldly Dinah is occurred at the encounter between Adam and her some weeks after she had rebuffed him and returned to her old life to think and to pray. Adam, impatient with waiting, went to find her one Sunday, but she had left Stoniton and was preaching in an outlying hamlet. He saw her still talking to a crowd of people and withdrew back up the hill to wait for her. As she, in her turn, duly neared the summit of the hill, she turned to look back behind her. Adam felt she should hear his voice before she saw him. The reasoning is acute if initially obscure. He drew close behind her and uttered her name. "She started without looking round, as if she connected the sound with no place. . . . He knew quite well what was in her mind. She was so accustomed to thinking of impressions as purely spiritual monitions, that she looked for no visible accompaniment of the voice."[105] Smart move on Adam's part! But, glancing at Irvine, it would be hard to imagine the good vicar, dipping lightly into Aeschylus rather than eggs at breakfast, to be so caught up in the spirit. Certainly, his majestic mother would have found it extremely *infra dig* if he had betrayed the slightest tendency towards trance—very ungentlemanlike and certainly not Church of England.

Fortunately, for Dinah and Adam's future marital bliss, not to mention the demands of the plot, as Lewes had desired[106]—this was a novel after all, and novelists do need sales—Dinah now feels "it is the Divine will. My soul I so knit to yours."[107] Eliot now expresses their ardor in spiritual and biblical terms using liturgical language about sorrow and ministering. In depicting Dinah Morris, Eliot was drawing upon a rich seam as, since as early as 1742, women had been appointed as class leaders at the foundry chapel.

103. Eliot, *Adam Bede*, 455.

104. Eliot, *Adam Bede*, 457.

105. Eliot, *Adam Bede*, 475.

106. Eliot, *Adam Bede*, xviii; xxxviii.

107. Eliot, *Adam Bede*, 475.

> By the 1760s, Sarah Crosby (1729–1804) and Mary Bosanquet-Fletcher (1739–1815) had, with John Wesley's reluctant approval, made the transition from "exhorting" to preaching the Gospel. It is not known how many women preachers there were in eighteenth-century Methodism, but contemporary sources indicate that their number was not insignificant.[108]

After the death of John Wesley in 1791, the general attitude towards women functioning in public to mixed audiences hardened until, in 1803, women were permitted only to speak to groups of other women in specific circumstances. Some women, such as Mary Barritt-Taft (1772–1851) could not be constrained and continued to exercise a public ministry, often winning many souls for Christ. The Methodist approach to women had a real pragmatism about it. As industrialization grew, the crying need of the urban poor became unavoidably urgent. In the first half of the nineteenth century, Methodism divided and it was the newly formed churches that maximize the use of their female members. The Primitive Methodists, established in 1811, and the Bible Christians, 1815, were quick to capitalize on the novelty of women preachers and evangelists. They also found that women could venture into areas that were not necessarily open to men.

By 1890, the Wesleyan Deaconess Order had been founded to organize this outreach work. Deaconesses also worked overseas in foreign mission work. The Primitive Methodist, and then the United Methodist Free Churches, founded similar orders by the end of the century. In 1910, the Wesleyan Methodists officially rescinded the ban on women preaching to mixed congregations.[109] By 1918, women were officially granted the same rights and conditions as male local preachers. Of course, all this was against a background of sweeping changes not merely in these islands but across the world. First, in the nineteenth century, the Reform Acts made enormous differences to the lives of everyday people. A concept of society, similar to the one we share, was emerging. Methodism played an incalculable role in placing into the public arena the notion that we are bound to help each other, that the poor are not necessarily so out of choice. Can it be any coincidence that the date of the lifting of the ban on women preaching came right at the end of the so-called Great War? The changes forced upon people radically shifted the concept of

108. John Rylands Research Institute and Library, "Role of Women Within Methodism," para. 4.

109. Lloyd, *Women and the Shaping.*

gender and role. All the old certainties that George Eliot harks back to in *Adam Bede* were long evaporated in the heats of change.

The major Methodist divisions reunited in 1932 to form the Methodist Church of Great Britain. Alongside this, the growth towards equality between women and men quickened. Again, the date can be no coincidence. Against the vast backdrop of the interwar years and the gathering storm clouds of another war looming, Methodism seems to have been able to look past the exterior of a person to see beneath, to the image of God, and to use everyone for those good works they were called to walk in. In 1944, the Women's Fellowship was set up as a full part of the Home Mission Department. The Fellowship has maintained its concern for social issues. The story of Methodism contains many interesting twists and turns, far more complex than the snapshot, or reflection, that Eliot presented in *Adam Bede*. We feel that it was the influence of so many active and increasingly empowered women who made the paradigm shift from the stereotypical conditioning of women to put things right within their own domestic spheres and emerged the ability to bring those skills to bear in a wider field. Like Dinah, these women, driven and sustained by faith and compassion, asked the questions needed to run a good home and our world. Their questions were not ones about status and money. Rather, these women asked pragmatic questions as to food and clothing and their quality of life. Ministry thus becomes deeply personalized rather than institutionalized, based on service rather than establishment. From Dinah Morris up to today, women have had a profound effect on Methodism and have helped to shape it into a church that declares mission as its great imperative in a forceful and an organized way, making it far more mission-shaped than many other denominations.

## Explicit Establishment by Parliament, Monarchy, and State Occasions

George Bell, in his biography of Randall Davidson, quotes the archbishop as saying,

> Bishops, in short, are entrusted, as I believe, with a place in the legislature not only for what are technically called ecclesiastical questions but for whatever things directly concern the moral life and the social well-being of the English people.[110]

110. Bell, *Randall Davidson*, 218.

Archbishop Davidson played a full part in all issues affecting the life of the nation, but it was the funeral of Edward VII in 1910 and the coronation of George V that stand out as signifying the church as an icon of Englishness. Davidson's successor, Cosmo Lang, crowned George VI following the abdication of Edward VIII. The archbishop's diary entry gives us an important insight into how he understood this event in the life of the nation. He writes thus,

> And now the Great Day itself, Wednesday, May 12th—to me I suppose, in a sense the cumulating day of my official life, the day on which the Archbishop of Canterbury fulfils his highest office in the national life, on which through him the Church of God consecrates that life in the person of its King.[111]

Similarly, Archbishop Geoffrey Fisher speaks of the coronation of Queen Elizabeth II in 1952. He comments thus,

> This was the most precious thing that I ever did, in a kind of way.[112]

Archbishop Fisher also presided over royal weddings, baptisms, and funerals. These included the marriage of Princess Elizabeth to the Duke of Edinburgh in 1947 and the marriage of Princess Margaret to Mr. Anthony Armstrong-Jones in 1960. Royal baptisms included Prince Charles's in 1948, Princess Anne's in 1950, and Prince Andrew's in 1960. Royal funerals included that of King George VI in 1952 and of Queen Mary a year later.

So, state occasions continue to require the Church of England. Mrs. Thatcher went to Westminster Abbey, not Westminster Cathedral, to "celebrate" the victory in the Falklands. It is in Westminster Abbey that England buries its ancient and great. This is about secular legitimacy, which is not only exclusively located in the state as a political institution but also one that says the English have a state religion, which is Christianity as it is expressed in the Church of England. It is indeed rooted in that, but it is also to do with a series of cultural sensibilities independent of a legal system. These sensibilities are not just about state apparatus but, rather, shared cultural assumptions about what is natural. Historically, the Church of England had a very particular position to construct Englishness and, until recently, a remarkably high profile was maintained.

111. Lockhart, *Cosmo Gordon Lang*, 417.

112. Purcell, *Fisher of Lambeth*, 240.

Today, while the centrality of the church within the life of the nation has been weakened, it is still possible to argue that the church continues to be an important signifier of Englishness.

The Church of England is more than a national church. It is also a church established by the law of the land with the monarch as its temporal governor. The Chadwick Commission in 1970 defined establishment as "the laws which apply to the Church of England and not to the other Churches."[113] Colin Buchanan, taking up this definition, tells us that an established church is one in which the state can exert a measure of control that is somehow different from the influence it would have on similar organizations.

Thus,

> I believe the most helpful use of the word "establishment" is in relation to those laws (and sometimes conventions) which bring from the state upon the Church actual control in a way that it is not brought upon other Churches.[114]

Buchanan accepts the Chadwick definition in part but takes issue with it for not allowing for degrees of establishment. His argument on this point is that other churches are governed by laws specific only to them but are not established churches because of such legislation.

John Habgood talks in abstract of terms about an Anglican ethos and how the English church was there before the English nation.[115] He argues that establishment at the governmental level before the Reformation of the sixteenth century was not imposed but rather evolved through a historical process. Establishment at ground level was about providing a comprehensive system of pastoral care to a whole nation of people. This also included the implementation of social justice work at the local level, and he cites a series of church reports to support this. Finally, Habgood maintains that the Anglican expression of the Church is to be found in its locality.

> The life of the Church is not primarily expressed in meetings of bishops, valuable though these may be. Christ is present wherever two or three people meet together in his name, in the worship and work of the local church, and in the individual lives of those who love him and try to serve their fellow human beings.

113. Chadwick, *Church and State*, 2.

114. Buchanan, *Cut the Connection*, 3.

115. Habgood, *Church and Society*.

> Issues of Church and society are frequently most real, therefore, when they are most local. They need to be identified and grasped at the local level by those who care about the kind of society in which they live, who are both committed to it and critical of it, and who are faithful to our Lord's prayer Thy kingdom come."[116]

Wesley Carr makes an important distinction between what he calls "high establishment," which is about the historical and legal relationship between church and state, and what he terms "earthed establishment," which is about having a vicar responsible primarily for the cure of souls within a geographical area, known as a parish. Thus, the parson is not a chaplain to a congregation but rather a vicar to the whole parish.

> This is an acknowledgment of an assumption about the nature of the Church, as a body with frayed edges, which encourages association as a means to ministry rather than membership as a means to belief.[117]

For George Austin, establishment is not only a safeguard against what he calls the strange doctrines and iconoclastic tendencies of the General Synod but is also a means of keeping the church within the mainstream of the political life of the nation.[118] Thus, the sacred and the secular are not separate zones but rather they are linked to their mutual benefit. Furthermore, the Church of England has an important role as a folk-region, offering an open membership to those who require baptisms, weddings, and funerals. For Austin, there is here a spiritual dimension that could be lost with disestablishment. Buchanan is extremely aware that there may be conventional Christians, that is, those who identify with the church as a matter custom rather than a faith commitment. These people feel that the church, in some way, is able to sanctify important occasions in their lives.[119] However, it is Parliament, not public opinion or folk law of potential church members, that regulates the institution of the church, where the Crown is the supreme governor.[120]

Buchanan's argument for disestablishment of the Church of England is largely political rather than biblical or theological in nature. His thinking here is that the essential nature of the church institution is not

116. Habgood, *Church and Society*, 40–41.

117. Carr, *Say One For Me*, 8.

118. Austin, *Affairs of State.*

119. Buchanan, *Cut the Connection*, 62.

120. Buchanan, *Cut the Connection*, 62.

doctrinal, as it takes its direction from a secular state.[121] He does not believe that theology and morality can go under the radar of state control. In this type of governance, the Church of England is unique in that no other church in the Anglican Communion operates under such state control by a secular authority. Clearly, if the church is to be taken seriously, it should be free to make its own decisions on the appointment of bishops. Buchanan is advocating a disestablishment from monarchy and Parliament in which the church's chief pastors are no longer appointed by the Crown. Under the establishment system, the prime minister of the day can choose between two candidates given to them by the Crown Appointments Commission and can ask for other names if they don't like them. For Buchanan, an Episcopal church should not be controlled and regulated in this way by a secular state. He comments that in the early days of the Commission, the members probably thought that they were selecting bishops, but the reality was that they were short-listing a field of choice for the prime minister. Buchanan disagrees with those who say this is the price the church has to pay for having bishops in the House of Lords. Interestingly, we are only talking about a handful of the Lords Spiritual. For what we get from that suggest, Buchanan, the price is too high. At this point, he does make a theological point quoting Bishop Mark Santer, who talks about how the church is undermined by looking for foundations for its apostolic ministry in other than Christ and his apostles.[122] Buchanan objects to the very weak argument that the state system allows exceptional people to be appointed as bishop who would otherwise be overlooked by church structures. He points out that colonial systems may have ideas about senior appointments but that after decolonization, such opinions are irrelevant.

Having placed the church in the English context of privilege, Buchanan goes on to a critique of John Habgood's earlier book *Church and Nation in a Secular Age*.[123] Buchanan dismisses Habgood's arguments not only as a preoccupation with a waning folk religion but also as lacking any consideration of biblical models in the relationship between church and state. Buchanan is referring here to the prophetic role played by Jewish and, later, Christian leaders in both the Old and New Testament. Furthermore, so far as Buchanan is concerned, Habgood's book does not

121. Buchanan, *Cut the Connection*, 61–62.

122. Santer, "Freedom of the Gospel," 133–34.

123. Habgood, *Church and Nation.*

adequately address the issues in the establishment/disestablishment debate as they were at the time of writing.[124]

> Clearly, he is not handling the full weight of the case against the establishment, but choosing only medium-weight charges to resist. There is not treatment of whether a Christian Church ought to be answerable for its spiritual life and organization to a secular State, no discussion of what I have called Old and New Testament models, no recognition of the widespread collapse and end of even wispy Christian folk religion.[125]

Buchanan is setting out arguments that challenge not just those who claim that we live in a Christian country but also those establishment advocates who accept we now live in a secularized and religiously pluralistic context.[126] The former commend establishment to both church and state, claiming that we have a role to protect our inheritance. Here, establishment and Englishness is often synonymous with a notion of the national, or something found in national life, and this can include its past in a way that can be independent of the present. In other words, the past has been reconstructed to suit the needs and false arguments of the present. Buchanan is noticeably clear that disestablishment would not communicate to the English nation the idea that the Church of England was repudiating the Christian faith.

Following Buchanan, our commentary on the Letter of James advocates the abolition of the establishment system, which operates in the Church of England. Buchanan's argument, which we support, is that although the Church of England has gained its place in English society as a result of its establishment status, it should now sever its connection with the English state while, at the same time, it should celebrate the benefits of that connection, even if we want our cake and eat it. However, for us and Buchanan, at the end of the day, these strengths should no longer be associated with establishment, even though they come out of that situation.

Similar arguments to those of Wesley Carr are put forward by Martyn Percy and Elaine Graham, writing nearly two decades later in a collection of articles on the establishment of the Church of England.[127]

124. Buchanan, *Cut the Connection*, 66.

125. Buchanan, *Cut the Connection*, 66–67.

126. Buchanan, *Cut the Connection*, 65.

127. Chapman et al., *Established Church*.

Martyn Percy is a pro-monarchist, establishment theologian. He draws our attention to royal funerals, rituals, and protocols as occasions for social cohesion in English society and the reinforcement of democratic freedoms, and where monarchy represents something metaphysical.[128] Another familiar argument is that of nationhood, which is seen as intertwined with ecclesiological concerns. For Percy, this is a socio-sacramental paradigm, which involves volunteering and other charity work.[129] We are told by Percy that the Church of England is able to provide a "National Spiritual Service" because it is an organic part of our national identity.[130] Thus giving to the nation a symbol and sign directing the English beyond themselves to the common good.[131] In all this, Percy wants an earthed establishment where the Church of England, supported by the monarchy, would protect our national freedoms. Elaine Graham contributes to the debated-on church-state relations by relating religion and citizenship to national identity via the concept of cultural pluralism. Her focus is the promotion of social cohesion and the role of the established church to achieve this desired condition.[132] Following Norman Bonney, British society is seen as a coexistence of both a multi-faith pluralism and also a context for societal secularization.[133] This idea of society calls upon the term *post-secular*.[134] A lot of sociological terms are listed here, including multiculturalism, but it is far from clear how they are being deployed or how relevant they are to a book on the Church of England.[135] So, is multiculturalism about being nice to people of global majority heritage while ignoring the cultural plight of the indigenous white population? For all its failings, multiculturalism as a concept is complicated and requires serious analysis that goes beyond a consideration of social capital.[136] The contribution of Elaine Graham is centered on the earthed establishment of the Church of England, which takes place at the local level. We, then, are left wondering what this has to say about the things that happen at the national level, where clearly considerable institutional power resides.

128. Percy, "Opportunity Knocks," 30.

129. See Isiorho, *Faith in Unions*, 47–52.

130. Percy, "Opportunity Knocks," 31.

131. Percy, "Opportunity Knocks," 33.

132. Graham, "Establishment, Multiculturalism, and Social Cohesion," 124.

133. Bonney, *Monarchy, the State and Religion*, 199–200.

134. Keenan, "Post-Secular Sociology."

135. Grahan, "Establishment, Multiculturalism, and Social Cohesion," 126–30.

136. See Isiorho, *Faith in Church Newspapers*, 50–53.

## Faith, Cosmos, and Social Reality

So, what of the wider context? Well, once you accept a faith system as the one by which you seek to shape your life, then an important issue is how you demonstrate your recognition of that system to the rest of the world. At the heart of the Christian faith are two important questions. Why do we live? Why do we suffer? The Letter of James is very much about those questions. We do not live in isolation from a world of disorder. We have obligations about how we live in such an environment. We know that we are faulty and imperfect in our being and our doing. This leads us to a consideration of the special place of God's beloved, the poor and helpless. Also, the righteousness of protest against a situation that contains injustice—and what human situation does not contain injustice somewhere along the line?

The Epistle of James has a core text. "Has not God chosen those who are poor in the world to be rich in faith?"[137] This comes after a depiction of how to receive people with no discrimination between rich and poor. This text has a deep resonance with those of us who feel marginalized. We feel that our faith and our marginalization are holy aspects of life that can feed our desire for justice and grow our faith. Perhaps the Christian gospel serves to make us always aliens in whatever culture we are born into as we seek to live by the values of God, not by the world that hoards a passing treasure.

For Peter Berger, the construction of social reality and the dialectic process of society is one in which religion has a distinctive role.[138] The construction of a world that has meaning for humankind has historically involved a process of religious cosmization. Secular or non-sacred approaches to cosmization are relatively new. Cosmization involves humankind in a process of self-examination, in which reality is infused with human meaning. Intrinsic to the religious enterprise is a division of reality into the sacred and the profane, which are contrary terms. Humankind is offered protection from the chaotic world of the profane through

137. Jas 2:5.

138. Berger, *Social Reality of Religion*, 26. "Religion is the human enterprise by which a sacred cosmos is established. Put differently, religion is cosmization in a sacred mode. By sacred is meant here a quality of mysterious and awesome power, other than man and yet related to him, which is believed to reside in certain objects of experience. . . . The cosmos posited by religion thus both transcends and includes man. The sacred cosmos is confronted by man as an immensely powerful reality other than himself. Yet this reality addresses itself to him and locates his life in an ultimately meaningful order."

its inclusion in the ordered world of the sacred. In sociological terms, we are saved from *anomie*, the ultimate abyss of meaninglessness.

Following John Bowker,[139] we can argue that a sociological account of the dichotomy between the sacred and the profane does not rule out the possibility that human understanding of a world other than the one in which we inhabit could derive from sources of meaning other than those associated with the social domain. In other words, the discipline of sociology does not lose orthodoxy by keeping an open mind as to how people ultimately obtain a sense of God. For Bowker, Berger is trapped in a fundamental dilemma in that his dialectical structure, on the one hand, has people who are formed socially and are a product of society. On the other hand, they have an individuality or creativity as seen in the internal appropriation of social values, which is not only independent of society but is responsible for the creation of these social realities.[140]

We would argue that the claim that people produce society, and that society produces them, is nineteenth-century in origin. It is not necessarily contradictory if we accept, as Berger puts it, "the inherently dialectic character of the societal phenomenon."[141] However, if we accept that the sociological frame of reference is concerned with the reality that individuals confer on the external world, the question still remains: Are there resources of meaning that are not encompassed by Berger's sociological orthodoxy? In his later book, *A Rumor of Angels*, Berger does not preclude the possibility that if we pour meaning into externality, then externality could pour meaning into us.[142] He suggests parallels between a formalist/Platonist conception of mathematics and religious imagination. Thus, religion does not have to be a human projection; it could be a

139. Bowker, *Sense of God*.

140. Bowker, *Sense of God*, 33. "On the one hand, individual behavior must be able to be explained by the laws which operate through history in the forming of societies; on the other hand, it seemed important to be able to say that individual actions transcend those laws, since otherwise, it would be difficult to attribute worth or merit to moral efforts or altruistic behavior."

141. Berger, *Social Reality of Religion*, 3.

142. Berger, *Rumor of Angels*, 64. "Put crudely, the mathematics that man projects out of his own consciousness somehow corresponds to a mathematical reality that is external to him, and which indeed his consciousness appears to reflect. How is this possible? It is possible, of course, because man himself is a part of the same overall reality so that there is a fundamental affinity between the structures of his consciousness and the structures of the empirical world. Projection and reflection are movements within the same encompassing reality. The same may be true of man's religious imagination."

human response to an external reality.[143] Thus, Berger is here seeking to invert and reformulate the religion-as-projection thesis. In this, Berger does not lose his sociological orthodoxy; it is enhanced. He argues that the Feubackian idea of religion as a projection and the Hegelian idea of religion as a reality beyond this world are not necessarily different propositions. They can coexist simply because the projection could contain a reality reflected by our "religious imagination." Thus, even if religion now occupies a category of exception, in which sense, experience has a part to play in the construction of reality, we still gain most of our ideas about the world in which we live from other people, and it is from them that ideas about the world are made plausible. Thus, all reality is linked, in some way or another, to social processes.

Just to recap a theory of reality ostensibly linked to social processes leads us to a concept of objective knowledge as interpreted and understood by society. Berger now accepts the premise that society is both the product and the producer of human activity and consciousness. Human beings do not have a given but an ongoing relationship with the world. Thus, they give shape to the world by their human activity and, in so doing, the world gives shape to them. It is in coming to terms with what it is to be human that we express ourselves in our human existence and produce a world. Berger describes the process of world-building as consisting of three moments, or steps, and these are 1) externalization and society as a human product, 2) objectivation and society as a reality *sui generis*, and 3) internalization and humankind as a product of society.[144] The activity of world-building is, by definition, a process that involves changes. The totality of our products, known as culture, is continuously produced and

143. Berger, *Rumor of Angels*, 65. "The theological decision will have to be that, 'in, with, and under' the immense array of human projections, there are indicators of a reality that is truly 'other' and that the religious imagination of man corresponds to a reality that is superhuman and supernatural, then it seems logical to look for traces of this reality in the projector himself."

144. Berger, *Social Reality of Religion*, 61.

1. Externalization and society as a human product: "the ongoing outpouring of human beings into the world, both in the physical and the mental activity of men."
2. Objectivation and society as a reality *sui generis*: "the attainment by the products of this activity (again both physical and mental) of a reality that confronts its original producers as a facticity external to and other than themselves."
3. Internalization and humankind as a product of society: "the re-appropriation by men of this same reality, transforming it once again from structures of the objective world into structures of the subjective consciousness."

reproduced by social beings who are engaged in a collective enterprise. However, the same society that is the phenomenon of externalization is also the phenomenon of objectivation and internalization. Thus, society is more than a product of humankind. It has an objective reality, in as far as it stands, as something independent of human activity and even in opposition to it. The concept of objectivation explains how the product, society, can reset the producer, human beings, and confront them as a facticity outside themselves. Furthermore, these structures and concepts return to the individual where they are internalized and become part of our human consciousness.

For Berger, our engagements with language are linked to the same dialectic of socialization. Language stands in relation to the individual as an objective facticity that can be changed and modified by the human condition from which it derives its existence. Its purpose is "linguistic interaction," and, unlike religion, it does not have a special category status linking it to a transcendent reality.[145] Language, then, is how society stores and structures its knowledge, and this knowledge becomes socially objectivated knowledge through the process of objectivation. In the main, this knowledge consists of pre-theoretical schemas, or interpretations, about the world we inhabit. We can live in the world because we know something about it. Thus, social interaction is possible because we share many assumptions about society. These assumptions empower society to impose an order or *nomos* upon its participants.

So, what does the sociology of symbol and sign tell us about the theological enterprise known as Anglicanism? Does Berger's "common order of interpretation" shed any light on the appropriate reading strategy for the Letter of James? Does the sociology of transcendent reality, which included human beings as the product and producer of society, have implications for reading the New Testament in the language and structure of the Anglicized edition of the NRSV? If we treat the Letter of James as a product of human society as well as the inspired word of God, we can ask what is the relationship between these biblical utterances and their sociocultural context. John Bowker, writing in *The Church Times* in the late 1990s, says that religion is programmed into our being, and we

145. Berger, *Social Reality of Religion*, 12. "Any particular language is the result of a long history of human inventiveness, imagination, and even caprice. While man's vocal organs impose certain physiological limitations on his linguistic fancy, there are no laws of nature that can be called upon to explain the development of, say, the English language. Nor does the latter have any status in the nature of things other than its status as a human production."

should not be surprised that it brings out the negative and destructive in people as well as the good.[146] For Bowker, religious systems protect information, code this information, and transmit it from one generation to another. This information has great value for the human experience and people become precious about it, which explains why religious people are often involved in conflict, especially when the boundaries between these systems come under threat. Christianity, like other religions, reaches out beyond this world for a sense of salvation. Furthermore, we realize this through a liturgical and linguistic process often involving art, music, poetry, drama, and dance. Thus, religion gives humanity meaning and hope.

We think this would be a good point to ask the question, what is this thing called Christianity or what is it to be called a Christian? Unfortunately, the word "Christian" has come to have a loose descriptive use apart from its real meaning. When people talk generally of leading a good Christian life, for example, or describe someone as a real Christian, this is often no more than describing a way of life that is based upon being kind to others. But if we are looking for an answer to the question of what is it that sets us apart as Christians, it is not sufficient to say that we try to be good and look out for our neighbors. So, what, then, is a Christian? Someone who believes in God? Well, yes, so far as this goes, but so do people of other faiths. Someone who lives a good life after the example of Jesus? Again, this should come into the definition somewhere, but it isn't the main thing—many live exemplary lives that are honest and kind and generous but make no claim to be Christians.

A Christian is first one who believes that Jesus is God, who accepts the revelation of God that Jesus gave us, and recognizes the Holy Spirit of God, whom Jesus promised to send to be with his disciples always and guide them. All sorts of things follow, or should follow, from this faith, but it is the faith that is distinctively important. The important thing about being a Christian is how we make sense of Jesus. It isn't enough to think of Jesus simply as an exceptionally good man who lived in Palestine at a certain point in history—leaves too many unanswerable puzzles—things he said, things he did, his birth, his death, and resurrection. The only answer that makes sense in the record is to say that he was God and a human being.

This is our Christian faith. It isn't a neat, scientific answer—it is itself a mystery. But the mystery is inescapable. No other statement does justice

146. Bowker, *Church Times*, Mar. 14, 1997, 11.

to the facts. It is not easy to understand the mystery that Jesus is God and a human being; scholars have tried to work out explanations. The trouble is that all these explanations finish up by ignoring either Jesus' humanity or his divinity. Thus, saying in effect that Jesus was not God but just an exceptional person, or that he was not a human being but a sort of ghost, or a human being with a divine soul. These explanations won't do because they don't square with what the New Testament tells us. Our creeds originated as tests of right belief, summarizing some of the most relevant facts from the New Testament, which, unless we feel we can choose for ourselves that we will accept and what to reject, compels us to believe that Jesus is God and a human being. If Jesus was only human, then it should be possible for anyone to be perfect by their efforts, without any help from God or religion. When we realize that Jesus, who lived the only perfect human life, was also God, then we recognize our own great need for God's grace if our lives are to be pleasing to God. What we believe affects our attitudes and actions, whether we realize it or not, and this is a particularly good reason why we should believe the truth if we can find it.

## Preaching James and the Pauline Tradition

This commentary is about how we understand the Christian message through the lens of the Letter of James. But first, let us consider its relationship to that of the theology of Paul. So what about authorities and subjection? St. James asks us to question governing authority while St. Paul, in Romans, at a first reading, seems to be saying the opposite. "Let every person be subject to the governing authorities."[147] St. Paul could have had no idea of just how much trouble the section of Scripture known as Rom 13:1 was going to cause. If we, the authors of this book, had a fiver for every time that verse has been quoted at us, usually in an attempt to gag us, then we would be laughing all the way to the bank. Subjugated peoples for the last two thousand years have had this verse thrown at them, and if we had followed this text out of context then, we would still be an overt slave trading nation and the apartheid regime in South Africa would still be in power.

So, let us take a closer and more prayerful look at what St. Paul was actually saying and the context in which he said it. St. Paul was writing to the early church in Rome. The Christians there lived in the shadow

147. Rom 13:1.

of great and terrible peril, for they lived right at the heart of the Roman Empire, where the cult of emperor worship was at its strongest. The early Christians represented many nations, cultures, and languages. Many of them were poor, and many of them were slaves. Their declaration of the doctrine of the one omnipotent God was perceived as treason since, increasingly, Roman emperors wanted to be treated as gods and have sacrifices offered to them. It would not be long before the emperor Diocletian killed Christians in their thousands on this very issue. Perhaps, St. Paul was writing to an endangered and beleaguered band of people who needed to be warned against the impetuous recklessness of the zeal of the newly converted. St. Paul counseled them with the tactics of survival. It is very possible that he had Matt 22:15–22 in mind and the question of taxes to Caesar; there are echoes of it in the passage from Romans. This is how we understand Rom 13:1 in the light of the Letter of James, and we invite you, the reader, to join us in that application. At a deeper level, Jesus is asking what does belong to Caesar. It was certainly not the loyalty of the subjugated peoples of the Roman Empire. And in the end, what could belong to Caesar? What had Caesar ever made? Nothing, for everything comes of thee, O Lord.

To complete this section of the introduction, we look now briefly at the parallels and contrasts between James 2:14–26 and Paul. We don't know if the Letter of James comes after the Letters of Paul or before, so any suggestion that one is correcting the other is not the focus of our commentary. Clearly, these traditions have different definitions of faith and works, which is due to the different context of their writing. This does not mean that James and Paul were preaching a different gospel. These New Testament writers have quite different starting points. Paul is offering some kind of Alpha course for new converts, who are not expected to earn their forgiveness from God but must rather accept it as a free gift. James, on the other hand, is running an Emmaus course for seasoned Christians, who need to be reminded of the tenants of the faith, which is expressed in Christian deeds. Let's be clear from the start that Paul's teaching, like that of James, is ethical and about actions that believers should take.[148] What makes it different from James is the emphasis placed on faith as a means of justification. The good works for Paul are not the Jewish law, which is no match for faith in Christ Jesus.[149] So, both writers

148. Rom 2:6, 13:12, 14:12; 1 Cor 3:8; 2 Cor 5:10; Col 3:9.

149. Gal 2:16.

are saying the same thing but from different directions. Thus, Christians cannot be saved by works alone, nor can they be saved without them, and the same goes for faith.[150] It is probable that Paul's teachings were known only by report to James and his readers.

• • •

Preaching is a strange thing because when you start preparing for a sermon, you may have fairly clear ideas about the sort of thing that you are going to say. And then you start to look at the passages of Scripture that are set and you end up somewhere quite different. A few years ago, we started to prepare a sermon for the fifth Sunday before Lent. We were going to talk about our duties as the witnessing community of God on this earth, picking up on the gospel theme of our faithfulness as the salt and the light of the world. We were going to mention the way that Isaiah saw people doing their witnessing as righteousness, and about how St. Paul stood up in public and gave a brilliant witness to the faithful. Would that more of us were so gifted. In other words, we started by wanting to talk about how much we have to do for God in this world, giving focus to our sense of mission. We, David and Linda, had been in parish ministry for thirty-five years and have seen many diocesan mission initiatives and strategies come and go often, with little to show for their urgency. We ended up preaching that God does not need any kind of help from us to be God. It is not God that needs rescue or help of any kind. God is not lost. You know those people who say they have found Jesus. God has not made us to compensate for some lack in the divine composition. We are not some species of cuddly toy for a God, lonely in eternity, nor are we experimental subjects for a scientific monster engaged in a grand exploration of the potential of matter.

One of the reasons that the early church formulated the doctrine of the Holy Trinity was to try to express the self-sufficiency of God. The God who is three in one and one in three lives in a communion that is deeper and fuller than any communion we can ever know on this earth. God is God's own company, self-sufficient and self-fulfilling and self-reliant. We should have this huge idea of God, the source of all power and life and breath and of all things that we can conceive of. We catch a glimpse of God, who is busy about concerns that we cannot even begin to guess at. A God who is full of energy and purpose that we cannot comprehend. A

150. Barclay, *Letters of James and Peter*, 85.

God who is almost beyond our knowing, let alone beyond any witness that we can give to this world. So, how can we have any special knowledge to impact this deity of immense cosmic vitality? And what use is a God who is supposed to be full of power, yet who seeks our company? But let us not leave it here. Can we go on to say something about why God made us so that we might look towards him? But why did God have to visit us in our flesh and undergo death?

We find God because the God who animates all of creation is near enough for us to find and delight in the divine presence. To put it another way, have you ever wondered why Jesus died? It is a deceptively easy question. If you read again through the four Gospels, you will see what we mean when we say that we don't think that Jesus' death was necessary from God's point of view. God made the world without our knowledge or our cooperation, and God can restore our meddling without informing or consulting us. Surely, the point of Jesus donning the frail life of the flesh was to demonstrate to us that God had not left us. Jesus died because he was saying, "No matter what you say, no matter what you do, I would not leave you." The service that we do for God is not for God but on God's behalf, to witness to the life, death, and resurrection of Jesus Christ. That's all. We don't know the whys and wherefores of it all. So, we just have to accept that God wants us. God could command an order but not so; God invites and walks alongside and stays with us. This does not make life easy. There is no special insurance against disaster written into this. Jesus suffered and so do we. And as Mother Julian of Norwich wrote, "I should not be greatly distressed for no manner of thing: for ALL shall be well."[151] We don't prove to the world that God exists, and that divine love is real and free by having immaculate lives unmarked by sorrow and pain.

Our job then is to begin to let everyone know that perfect love casts out fear, as mortal humanity struggles through the darkness and terrors of this world. If just for one fleeting instance, you can manage to help someone glimpse the love that pours out all its fullness to each one of us, then you are doing service indeed. You have become a small partner of God in the greater act of service being conducted in this cosmos. That is what we call "Christian witness," as it exceeds the righteousness of the scribes and Pharisees.

• • •

151. Julian of Norwich, *Revelations of Divine Love*, 71.

The church is often criticized today for interfering in matters that, allegedly, should not concern it. Some politicians say we should not concern ourselves with politics, even though such issues affect the poor and the powerless in our inner cities and in the developing world—and more in the safe and leafy shires, whose well-planned pensions or whose high-flying jobs no longer seem so secure. Our critics say we should concentrate on saving people's souls and safeguarding their morality. We are accused in the newspapers and on television of putting forward the view that it does not matter what you do in bed as long as you have the correct political attitude. This is set in opposition to those in our church who do want to legislate what consenting adults do with each other. We are then accused of being obsessed with sexuality to the exclusion of other aspects of the human condition.

Jesus never took a political party position, but this did not prevent him from being at the heart of the political and social issues of his day—asking the questions that people would rather he did not ask. Why else did he stir up the power factions of his day so much that they wanted him dead? Jesus was a powerfully compelling man who was more than capable of taking direct action when it was appropriate to do so. A man who could not help drawing all kinds and conditions of people to his warmth and his loving wholeness. For ourselves, we need to remember that the gospel was written down by people increasingly anxious to survive the hostility of the authorities. Even in that context, the robust, liberation-focused Jesus shines through.

As Christians, we must be concerned about all issues of social justice in the community in which we live. This is God's world and as human beings, we are set in it as stewards, with a mandate to love God and to love our neighbors as ourselves. Our concern should be for the wholeness and fulfillment of all people, since all are of equal worth in the love of God. As Christians, we are charged with the responsibility of loving each other and challenging injustice. The Letter of James constantly urges us to remember that, as Christians, we are called to a radically different way of life that should betoken the full kingdom of God. We must remember the commands that our Lord himself gave us. First, we love God; then, we love as we are loved. So, we can stand in a stance of radical suspicion of every human institution as Christians. For we are the voice of truth and right and justice in the world. The role of the church and of the individual within the church is to be a prophetic challenge to all human institutions is clear. Remember our Lord in the temple. He didn't say, "I must be careful not to upset anyone now because I am in a holy place." He used his love of God and his knowledge of Scripture in a profoundly iconoclastic way. So, he was not gentle Jesus, meek and mild. This is the Jesus who knows how to kick some ass. He overturned not only tables but ideas revered like idols.

Sometimes we, too, are called to revolutionary action but always through the love of God. So, we start to bring this introduction to its conclusion with a call to prayer. Our prayer is that we may bring healing to a broken world. That all our works and words will bring the kingdom a little nearer as we pray for our Lord's return saying, "Come, Lord Jesus, come." Our prayer here is that God will help us to rely more on the divine will. So that we can lead more people into the grace-filled presence of Jesus' love. We pray, then, that God will hasten the time when none shall live in contentment while they know that others have a need—that we will be inspired with people of all nations by the desire for social justice: that the hungry may be fed, the homeless housed, the sick healed, and a just and peaceful order established in the world, according to God's will.

• • •

In this introduction, we have tried to make some sense of the relationship between Englishness and Anglicanism within the contemporary context of the Church of England. As an icon of Englishness, the Church of England continues to have an influential role within the life of the nation simply because it is able to represent England to the English. This is shown clearly in state occasions in which national loyalty is combined with implicit religion. It is also seen in English literature, which engages its readers in nostalgia for a probably fictional past. However, one writer, Susan Howatch, linked some of her fictional characters with the historical figure of George Bell, who had opposed the terror bombing of German cities during the Second World War—a past that was not such a deep England.

Colin Buchanan was right to say that John Habgood's argument to maintain establishment was not based on any Bible foundation. However, *Cut the Connection* does not deliver on biblical analysis despite its criticism of others for failing to do so. *Faith in the Letter of James* uses an explicit biblical model to support a call for the disestablishment of the Church of England. So, what does the Letter of James tell us about our relationship with a system of privilege, such as the British monarchy?

James tells us not to bow down to the wealthy and to treat them with the respect denied to the poor. Furthermore, it was the rich and powerful that worked against church members in the first century. Many parables of the kingdom emphasize the small, almost insignificant signs of its presence. However, we must not forget that it is the kingdom of God who stretched out the heavens and the earth and gave life and breath to all within it.[152] It is through the cross and the resurrection of Jesus Christ that the door is opened to us. That Christ has died, Christ is risen, and Christ will come again is a fundamental part of our Christian faith. Through the Gospels, the Christian tradition, and our own experience, the first two are familiar and have been realized. The third is yet to come, and the manner of it is beyond our knowing. That it will happen is our Christian hope. "And when these things begin to come to pass, then look up, and lift up your heads; for your redemption draweth nigh."[153] It is not a sign of a lack of faith to say we do not know how or when. Jesus tells us it is not for us to know the times or the seasons that the Father has fixed by his authority. It is therefore presumptuous to threaten those whom we would bring to Christ with all kinds of retribution. We can only put our hand in his and say, "Jesus, 'remember me when you come into your kingdom.'"[154] And those with whom we would share our faith, Jesus said, "I am the resurrection, and the life: he that believeth in me, though he were dead, yet shall he live."[155]

So, how do we apply the theology of the Letter of James to our twenty-first-century context and promote the disestablishment of the Church of England? Through the chapters of this commentary, we hope to have conveyed to our readers a clear understanding of how structural inequality is embedded in the laws of English society. The disestablishment of the Church of England would allow us to think again about how we respond to God's call. How can we not give ourselves to Christ's ministry in the hope of that new context. God meets us in ways that we can bear and understand and gives us tasks to do that we can achieve. We must explore the biblical themes of respect of all people, gratitude, and generosity as part of our ongoing review of how we disestablish the Church of England. It is an invitation to test the reality of our commitment to Christ Jesus.

152. Isa 42:5.

153. Luke 21:28.

154. Luke 23:42.

155. John 11:25.

# Chapter 1

# Doers of the Word

## Introduction

But be doers of the word, and not merely hearers who deceive themselves.

—James 1:22

So, HAVE YOU EVER been left hanging around during a game? We have, and we can speak from our personal experience. Those with power are choosing who is going to be on their side, and we are the last ones to be picked. If you are also in this situation, how does that make you feel? Have you ever been somewhere where everyone is discussing a party that they're all going to? They are all excited and talking about what is going to happen. It sounds really good, but you don't know anything about it. You aren't sure if they're talking about it in front of you because they assume you're going, or if they are doing it to make you feel bad for some reason? No one likes to be left out, do they? Fortunately for us, God doesn't play games, and God doesn't leave anyone out.

So, why this discussion about inclusion and being left out as we attempt to discuss what the Letter of James means by "doers of the word"? Well, maybe you need access to the power structures of this world to be able to take some action for the common good, but power corrupts. The majority of people who become bishops and archdeacons are unlikely to change anything because they got those positions by supporting the establishment. We, the authors of this book, in our professional lives, did not have the power to change very much in terms of church structures, but we are able to speak *power to truth* through this commentary.

James wants his readers to embrace the Christian faith not just in the words they hear in church but, most importantly, in the way they live their lives. So they, like us today, must live out the faith by turning those words into action. If people are not willing to do that, then there is no point in them hearing the word of God in the first place.[1] For James, we cannot adequately talk about the love of God without speaking about God's truth, and not do so would make us hypocrites. It would also involve the denial of the realization that everything must be undergirded with the power of prayer—of quiet, listening as we seek to hear God's voice, the prayer of confession for our past failures, and the confident prayer of intercession as we ask for God's blessing in everything as doers of the word.

## Advent, Lent, and *The Book of Common Prayer*

So, what of Advent when we focus on judgment—when we consider how we will give account of ourselves and what we have done or not done to work for the kingdom? The season of Advent is the time of the church's year when we look to the second coming of Christ. The readings of this season remind us that the price of faith is vigilance. We are to be ready, and Advent is the time when we check this out. So, are we ready? If you are like us, part of you says "yes" and longs for that day to come while another part shrinks into a corner and wants to hide because the second coming sounds like very big stuff indeed, and we are so small and fragile.

The Advent wreath is here to help us with all that. The Advent wreath is traditionally associated with the following four themes: the patriarchs, the prophets, John the Baptist, and the Blessed Virgin Mary. Why these particular four? What is the church trying to teach us from these choices? It is reminding us that God works in human history and works through human beings. It is making us remember that there is a progression going on even though we may not be able to discern it. We are reminded that God is a God of intervention and surprise. Let us think and imagine for a moment of a world where God is like some kind of giant who can reach down and zap us. What if we asked God for help and we got help coming down in a monstrous arm the size of half the sky? Why, every contact

1. Barclay, *Letters of James and Peter*, 61.

would be a cosmic disaster. The world would be shaken to its foundations and unmade in every molecule and atom and microparticle.

The Advent wreath tells us that God comes to us in ways that we can tolerate and profit from. Not that the meetings with God this wreath recalls have been light and easy matters. It was no joke when Abram was called to up sticks and journey out of Ur.[2] It was not easy for Jacob to wrestle at Jabbok's shore and to bear being the father of the nation.[3] But they did these things because, although it is a terrible thing to fall into the hands of the living God, it is also a matter of great joy, releasing huge quantities of energy that flow into creative action all around the lives of those people whom God has so especially called. And what about the prophets? Who are your favorite ones? We think of Jeremiah and his tortured relationship with God, who made him angry and, yet, who could not walk away. Or Jonah, the only book in the Bible that ends with a question mark.[4] Jonah himself is a character who is unreliable, shifty, and arrogant, but that doesn't stop God, who uses him and speaks through him. Then, there is John the Baptist with his dietary program of locusts and honey. He was the wild man in the desert eating high protein, high-energy food and emerging like a whirlwind to call people to repentance. And our Mother Mary, the unmarried woman who thought for herself and had the courage to answer God in the affirmative. She was not broken by her contact with the angel, nor was she cowed into submission; but out of a prayerful and pure heart, she said that "yes" that God aches to hear. And at the foot of the cross itself, she still said "yes." So, this Advent wreath, all dressed in evergreen and decked with light, recalls us to the joyful fact that we can cope with God because God meets us in ways that we can bear and understand and gives us tasks to do that we can actually achieve. Thanks be to God.

• • •

And now, for Lent. Sometimes, particularly in Lent, in churches that do not usually have a responsorial psalm, the psalm is used instead of the Gloria,[5] which is traditionally omitted during Lent because of its trium-

2. Gen 11:31–32.

3. Gen 32:22–32.

4. Jonah 4:11.

5. This is an introductory rite in the Anglican and Roman Communion Service, a hymn in which the church praises and give glory to God.

phant tone. And so it is from our psalm that *doers of the word* hear: "The fair beauty of the Lord."[6] In the Roman Catholic Church in Indonesia, there is a custom of making a mantra for the Mass. This is a fusion of cultures, taking the Hindu notion of a mantra, a short phrase that can be chanted over and over, and placing it within the context of the Christian tradition. Mother Linda first came upon this years ago when she was in the College of the Ascension preparing to go to Zimbabwe under the auspices of the United Society for the Propagation of the Gospel. A priest from the Society of the Divine Word, a Roman Catholic missionary order, celebrated the mass and invited her and another Anglican to lead the service with him. They took the mantra from the psalm set and she still uses it: "*For God alone, my soul waits in silence*," especially useful in times of trouble.

We do have in Christendom the tradition of chanting, but repetitive chanting is more Eastern Orthodox than Western Catholic. For example, the Greeks have given us that wonderful prayer known as the Jesus Prayer. *Lord Jesus Christ, Son of God, have mercy on me, a sinner.* There is a specific technique to use when chanting. We do have a taste of that in the Church of England when we chant the psalms and observe the colon—you know, have a pause between lines. What this regulated chanting does is control the breathing, which has a huge physiological effect. When using a chant or mantra on your own, this quiets the body and frees the soul. Your mouth or your mind is focused on sacred words, and, after a short while, a profound effect can sweep over you. When chanting in the company of others, the united pace of breathing brings about a deep sense of communion with others and, therefore, with God. Buddhists know a great deal about this phenomenon. With the Jesus Prayer, the idea is to breathe in as you think the words "*Lord Jesus Christ*." You then hold your breath before breathing out to "*Son of God*." Pause slightly before breathing in again to "*Have mercy on me*." Pause before exhaling to "*a sinner*."

• • •

As *doers of the word*, what we want is more hell—fire preaching, a stricter and more serious approach to religion. No, what we want is something less demanding, the sort of religion that caters for the likes and dislikes of ordinary people. Too strict or too soft? Do we, as *doers of the word*, know

6. Ps 27:4.

what we want? Can you choose your religion tailor-made to suit your ideas? The only real criteria is the truth of God, and this is too great to be tied down by our current ideas. It is always possible to attack, to ridicule, to criticize, to find excuses for rejecting any and every approach to God, if this is what some people have made up their minds to do. On the other hand, if we have spiritual insight, if we desire God and take God seriously, then all life is relevant; nothing is incapable of witnessing to the truth and the glory of God. This is not to claim that it does not matter what the church teaches and practices—that it does not make any difference if the form and language of our services is unintelligible. We must always be searching to express more adequately the truth about God, in our worship, our praise, and most importantly, in our preaching as *doers of the word*. We need to make it easier rather than more difficult for people to see the relevance and importance of the Christian gospel, but always with the truth about God and the greater glory of God as our aim. To try to make religion popular, in the sense of giving people what they want without regard to the greater glory of God, is a fruitless exercise. If people have made up their minds that they want nothing to do with God, they will find fault with any and every approach. And anyway, if we look at things in this way, we shall quickly lose sight of what we are trying to do.

So, how do we understand our Christian faith as *doers of the word*? If we are convinced of the importance of a Christian faith, if we have glimpsed some vision of the glory of God, we shall want to pass on our faith to others. And we shall legitimately use every gift that God has given us to achieve this end. The downside to all this is to cry your heart out and fail to get a single tear of sympathy. We must never underestimate the danger of disillusionment and disability to deflect us from our purpose. Our zeal for the gospel is indeed tested, but at the end of the day, nothing can separate us from the love of God. Whatever we have to face, God is there with us—Christ has been through it before us. Only we have to make this truth our own and feed upon it until our faith and trust in it is strong enough to support us in action. And this we can only do through prayer. If we are to keep and maintain our spiritual insights as *doers of the word* and persevere wholeheartedly in trying to convince our generation of the truth and importance of Christianity, surely, we need to pray earnestly and in that faith.

• • •

> Ye that do truly and earnestly repent you of your sins, and are in love and charity with your neighbours, and intend to lead a new life, following the commandments of God, and walking from henceforth in holy ways; Draw near with faith, and take this holy Sacrament to your comfort; and make your humble confession to Almighty God, meekly kneeling upon your knees.[7]

In *The Book of Common Prayer*, these words are said before the confession of sins at the Holy Eucharist. These words do not appear in the modern service. It is taken for granted that we are in love and charity with our neighbors and intend to keep God's holy laws. And it is on this understanding that our sins are forgiven, and we are able to share the peace.[8] So, what can we say about these commandments, and why are they so important? When the Old Testament book of Deuteronomy was written, not everyone believed in the one and true God—the God of Israel. They believed in many gods. Today, the problem is not that people believe in lots of different gods but that they refuse to affirm their faith in anything. Most people believe there is a God but do nothing about it. To believe and trust in God is to love and obey him and bring others to know him. In the days of Moses, the idols that people worshiped were often gold figures of animals and birds. Today, people are sophisticated. Today, people worship fast cars, fast food, and fast money. Yet, we are all called to put nothing in the place of God. The Old Testament prophets tell the rich and the powerful that they must stop oppressing the widow and the orphan. We continue to live in a violent and greedy world. Yet, we are all called to have respect for the life God has given us. We must bear no malice, prejudice, or hatred in our hearts.

The Bible tells us not to commit adultery. In many of our soap operas, extra marital affairs are presented as the norm. We are sure this reflects something about the attitudes of our society, even if it does not reflect reality. We have all been called to use all our bodily desires as God intended—that is within a relationship of love and commitment. Our sins are forgiven in the church through baptism and confession, both of which involve prayer. It is by prayer that the bond between our souls and God can be strengthened. In fact, prayer is essential. Without it, our vision of God would soon fade away. It is not only essential for us to pray, but it is natural to us. Our souls were made by God, for God, in order that

7. *Book of Common Prayer*, 270.

8. Church of England, *Common Worship Services*, 175.

we might have communion with him. So, when we pray, we are doing that for which we were made. From God comes all that makes life good and glad. We sin when we seek our good apart from God or look to God's gifts alone. But God has reconciled us to himself through his son Jesus Christ. It is for this reason that we, who are in love and charity with our neighbors and intend to lead a new life following the commandments of God, can meet in Christ's name and share his peace.

• • •

Stir up, we beseech thee O Lord, the wills of thy faithful people.[9]

So the church prays on the last Sunday of the Christian year. There are different kinds of stirring, aren't there? In Advent, we think of the stirring of Christmas puddings—for this kind of stirring, we need to have just the right ingredients in exactly the right amounts, and mix them together thoroughly so that each contributes its part in the finished product. This may have something to teach us about the way God works. There has been a lot of stirring up lately, influential people causing a stir by their statements and comments on subjects like faith and morals—deliberately trying to shake us and quite rightly so. John the Baptist did some stirring. So did Jesus. And so did the Holy Spirit working in the disciples after Pentecost. We might think of stirring with a stick in a muddy pool. Before stirring, it all looks lovely and clean, the mud is lying undisturbed at the bottom. We often think about our world in this sort of way—as long as everything looks nice and clean, even though we know there is a good layer of mud underneath, it is much easier to leave it undisturbed. It is a serious business, stirring up. There are times when we need to be shaken out of our set ways of thinking, made to think for ourselves, reminded of the things we would much prefer not to have raked up.

As Christians, we have to come to terms with the past, the present, and the future. We can't live in the past—dwelling on the past glories of the church and wishfully thinking how nice it would be if things were still the same. Nor can we rest on our laurels in view of what we have done in the past. Certain historical events are of vital importance—events like the incarnation of Jesus, when God became a human being and walked in our flesh. This is vitally significant because of what it means for us now. The saints are important not merely as historical figures but because we share the same faith and they are a cloud of witnesses encouraging us,

9. Collect for the Sunday next before Advent, *Book of Common Prayer*, 220.

urging us on to follow in their footsteps. The past is important, but we can't relive the past—we must live in the present, and we must look always to the future. Our eyes must be fixed on Jesus who will come again, as the season of Advent reminds us, to judge the living and the dead. We must run with patience the race that is set before us, looking unto Jesus.

The Communion collect for the twenty-fifth Sunday after Trinity prays, "Stir up, we beseech thee O Lord, the wills of thy faithful people."[10] God does not make us run this race—nor is he constantly chasing us if we slacken off. The end of the church year is a good time for stocktaking. Look unto Jesus. How far have we kept our eyes on him, trying to line up our wills with his will? None of us really like being stirred up. There are plenty of things we could do—there is plenty of potential. But it's much more comfortable to carry on at our own self-appointed pace. The post-Communion collect hits the nail squarely on the head when it says, "Stir up, we beseech thee O Lord, the wills of thy faithful people."[11]We want, as *doers of the word*, to take our Christianity seriously, and no amount of preaching will make any difference. *O God, stir up*—let's pray it and mean it and be prepared for the influx of new life that God's stirring brings.

## The Gifts of God, Passiontide, and Slavery

Every generous act of giving, with every perfect gift, is
from above, coming down from the Father of lights, with
whom there is no variation or shadow due to change.

—James 1:17

God's gifts can only be good because the Creator of the lights of heaven is consistent in that goodness. Here, James gives focus to the unchangeableness of God, whose purpose is that humanity should be reborn through the word of truth, which is the Christian gospel.[12] In the city of Jericho, a blind beggar called Bartimaeus was sitting by the roadside, asking the passers-by for money. Jericho was Palacios and called the "city of palms," with the baths, theaters, and the palace of Herod. What a condition to be in, begging and blind. Bartimaeus was poor in the context of much wealth. Jesus was common knowledge to the people at this point in Mark's

10. *Book of Common Prayer*, 220.
11. *Book of Common Prayer*, 220.
12. Barclay, *Letters of James and Peter*, 60.

narrative. When people knew where Jesus was, they would assemble in expectation that something wonderful would happen. There was real hope and faith that Jesus was the Messiah, the chosen one of God. Hope was something that Bartimaeus had lost years ago, that is, until he heard about Jesus and that he was coming to Jericho. So, Bartimaeus shouts out, "Son of David, have mercy on me."[13] Bartimaeus had heard about Jesus' love for the common people and that he would do miracles for them. So, hope comes back for Bartimaeus and he is healed. The word of the gospel does not bring hope without conditions. For action needs to be taken, and Bartimaeus was ready to act. He stood up and went to Jesus for healing. The big question for us is this: Are we willing to get up in the hope that the call of Christ arises in our hearts? We, too, like Bartimaeus, must "take heart"[14] because we can only do this by action.

• • •

So, what, then, of our commitment as *doers of the word* as we consider Passion Sunday, marking the start of Passiontide, the last two weeks of Lent? This calls us into what was done in the past, what we are now doing, and where we might be called to be tomorrow. And in our remembrance of our Lord in his human anguish, it is so appropriate that the UK should commemorate the 200th anniversary of the abolition of slavery, recalling our deliberate torturing of our brothers and sisters. Suffering, as the cross teaches us, is unnecessary and against the joyful freedom that God's love calls us all into. A few years ago, there was a service at Westminster Abbey to mark the bicentenary end of the slave trade in Britain. Tickets were like gold-dust, as the great and the good, not so good and the downright wicked would be there. This group included the secretary general of the United Nations at the time, Tony Blair, and even the late Queen—and also, yours truly, the authors of this commentary. The service was the official occasion at which Britain and the Commonwealth gave focus to the murder of thirty-five million enslaved Africans. This took place over three centuries and left an ongoing legacy of colonialism, whose economic exploitation is the origin of UK's wealth and prosperity. In the end, the slave trade imploded through the weight of its sinfulness and suffering. Yet, many sermons were delivered from Church of England pulpits encouraging slavery, while many slaves made links between Exodus and

13. Mark 10:47.
14. Mark 10:46.

their own context and drew some comfort from these texts. How could anyone possibly claim that slavery was compatible with Christianity? However, wicked things happen in all generations and there are always reasons, or should we say "excuses," for wrong behavior. We have only to think of the atrocities that have taken place in Gaza.

Some defenders of slavery argued that the Bible sanctioned slavery, even though they were unhappy with the violence of the plantation system. Well, it is amazing, historically, how some white people want their cake and eat it. The first part of their contention could be found in the Epistle to Philemon, which clearly shows that Christians owned slaves and that slaves could be Christians. These verses advanced what some call a "pie in the sky" theology among slaves, which suggested that they would obtain their share of good things, the pie, when they go to heaven, the sky, their reward for being none-complaining Christians. This belief resulted in hymns, choruses, and spirituals as well as sermon materials that are still used today to justify black disengagement. Many of us are aware that the Bible inspired many of the original abolitionists to take a stand against slavery and African exploitation. What is less well known and accepted is the fact that the same spiritual source was also the basis for African exploitation and dehumanization. So, let us think again about our gospel as we seek to make a connection between slavery and the oppression experienced by the descendants of slaves.

• • •

On Passion Sunday, we traditionally think about what our Lord must have gone through, knowing exactly, it would seem, what was going to happen to him. The word "passion" means suffering. So, this is the season when we particularly recall the sufferings of Jesus as he approached his death. Passion Sunday makes it clear that Jesus was aware that he was entering into a time of suffering that would cost him dearly. Passion Sunday is one that we, the authors of this commentary, struggle with. If Jesus had asked us if we wanted him to die, we would have said "no." Over the millennia, there have been many attempts to explain why Jesus had to die. One explanation that appeals to us is that, actually, he didn't have to. What he was doing in truth was staying with us, whatever it took, and that is quite a different slant on it. He said he would come to us and never leave, and he kept to his word. It turns the cross from an altar of shame and triumph to a place where love was revealed. The God of power and might surrendered to callous human hands. Conversely, the cross shows us exactly how helpless we are as we contemplate our Lord in his agony.

The cross also reflects to us the profundity of human selfishness. It is a constant challenge to us to learn how to surrender in order to survive. On Palm Sunday, we have the whole cycle of the passion read as the Gospel. When you hear the entire story in one go, as opposed to the tiny little morsels that we often try to feed ourselves with, then the saga of the passion becomes almost overwhelming. We can enter into the physicality of the man Jesus, suffering in his flesh. But what can we understand of the wounded urgency of the love that reached out to save those so lost that they did not even know they were astray?

In the mystery of the uniting of God and flesh that was the life of our Lord, what a terrible anguish assailed him as he prepared for what his body knew would be something perilously like the end. So, how did this happen? How did Jesus fall into the hands of sinful men? Well, one evening Mary poured an expensive jar of perfume over Jesus' feet.[15] Judas believes this to be an expensive waste of money, but Jesus says that Mary has done a beautiful thing. For Judas, this was the last straw. Utterly disillusioned with Jesus for what he perceived as favoritism towards this woman, he decides to betray Jesus for thirty pieces of silver. Mary anoints our Lord as a preparation for his death. All this can be related to the washing of his disciples' feet, and although it looks, at times, as if Jesus lets people walk all over him, he actually was on a specific mission and was in the process of successfully accomplishing it. It is a question of discernment, of learning to see when it is appropriate to let others call the shots and when it is right to stand up and take action. We must not forget that the Lord, who washed the feet of his disciples, is the same Lord who overturned the tables of the money changers in the temple. The washing of the disciples' feet is not unlike the baptism through which we become living members of the body of Christ. In Jesus, the *doers of the word* have a tremendous freedom at a tremendous cost. The cost, to us as it was to him, is the price of total obedience. This is the cost of service, which Mary understood and Judas did not. The cost that the abolitionists embraced and the slave traders could not comprehend.

15. Matthew 26.6–13; Mark 14.3–9; Luke 7.36–50; John 12.1–9.

## The Glory of God

And the word became flesh and lived among us, and we have seen his glory, the glory as of a Father's only son, full of grace and truth.

—John 1:14

So, what, then, is the glory of God and what does it have to do with us, *doers of the word*? As a common word, glory means anything vaguely pleasant. A glorious summer's day, for example, just means one with congenial weather. We heard a woman once talking about her daughter's glorious wedding dress. Some kind person once told Mother Linda that her laugh was glorious. All these uses are tepid compared to the glory of God—they are but a shadow in comparison with God's glory. In the Old Testament, the word "glory" does not refer to the reputation put on someone from the outside, where others reward a person with fame and honor. Glory is primarily the real value of something, like the weight of gold to its intrinsic worth. Thus, having a sense of the glory of God is the process by which we begin to know God in the fullness of the beauty, holiness, and bright majesty that belong to God alone. Now, light is not the absence of anything, whereas darkness is the absence of light. In the obscurity of darkness, we are afraid; in light, we are both enabled to see and to move freely, but we are also exposed. So, the glory of God is both more wonderful than the softest dawn after the longest, darkest night in a wild mountain place, but it is also the most blinding flash of reality.

In the radiance of God's glory, we see, for a second, as God sees. And that gives us some insight into the terrible pain that is God's, whose vision is never clouded. That is why God, in love and wisdom, never fully reveals his glory. Moses was instructed to hide his face in the rock; Elijah cowered in a crevice of the mountain. Revealed and concealed, God reaches out to the world and to his people in love, clarity, and majesty. In thinking about God's glory, we begin to see how the boundness of the power of God's glory has been both celebrated in its immensity and, yet, made small enough for us to bear. The smallness we refer to is our Lord incarnate in our flesh, as one of us in order to reach out to us. All the way through the New Testament, this is the theme, the glory of God as revealed in Christ Jesus—God made little enough to live alongside us so that we can bear it. God is the one who knows us from the inside, yet still loves us for what we are. The closeness of God to us and of us to God is like a Christmas present that has been scarcely unwrapped and put away somewhere in a cupboard, unappreciated. We need to take this present out and look at it again.

We persist in imagining an immense distance between ourselves and God, heaven and earth separate and alien to each other, but this is not how the early Christians saw it. The spirit of Jesus was in their hearts; Jesus was with them and, therefore, so was God. No wonder that they expected the second coming at any time. They felt it was upon them. So, remember, as *doers of the word*, we are not lost. God is not distant but beside us. God's glory has been and is being revealed. It is being revealed here in this commentary on the Letter of James. We are, each one of us, part of that revelation, and that is part of the work we are called to do here in our own context. We are lights, then, for the world because Christ is the Light of the world and we share in God's glory. Our light is a reflection; it is not ours in this moral state. The glory of the church is God's glory, seen as it were, in a mirror. Christianity is the world's major religion, and the international date system is based on the incarnation. So, as you pray and work for the kingdom, rest in the warmth of the glory of God and delight in your part in it through the abiding reality of the glory of the incarnation, which is when God became a human being in Christ Jesus. So, as we pray and work for the kingdom, may we always know that God is with us because Jesus is with us. And Jesus is the Prince of Peace.

• • •

A life in tune with Christ is one sustained by faith, and that increased awareness will involve some kind of sacrifice and a way of seeing things, which only faith as a *doer of the word* makes possible. Coming to the end of this chapter, we ask, then, what does sacrifice mean for a *doer of the word?* The root meaning of sacrifice is "to make sacred." A sacrifice is something offered to God. This meaning we come across over and over again in the Old Testament in the sacrificial rituals associated with the worship of God, which took place in the Jewish temple. There are long and detailed instructions telling us how to make a variety of sacrifices for a variety of purposes. The rules are elaborate and time-consuming. Sacrifice is not something undertaken in a hurry, not something done lightly. The essence of making a sacrifice is in its costliness—the animals offered in sacrifice had to be without blemish—one could not offer to God anything imperfect or valueless. And the heart of the person offering had to be rightly turned towards God. Look at the story of Cain and Abel, when Cain offered a sacrifice of real value materially, but his heart was not in it. However crude this manner of worship now seems to us, at least the making of costly offerings to God reflected in some way the worth of God—how much those people thought of him. They wanted to recognize that God is in every part of life. God has created all things and should be acknowledged in all things. That is the basis of Torah, the Jewish laws. From this root meaning, the word "sacrifice" has come to refer more generally to giving anything up that costs us something for the sake of something good. One example that springs to mind is the sacrifice made by parents so that their adult children may go to university. Or we might think of a family making sacrifices in order that they may have a good holiday together, or of an individual making sacrifices in order to help some worthwhile organization. So, we talk of small and great sacrifices. We can only make sacrifices under the compulsion of love, or devotion, or duty.

No one would make sacrifices unless he or she had ideals and principles that mattered a great deal. In any sacrifice, self is subordinated. The symbol of the one perfect sacrifice is the cross—a constant reminder of the complete selflessness of our Lord, whose example we are pledged to follow. The opposite of sacrifice is selfishness and greed. It is obviously true to say that there is a frightening amount of selfishness and greed to be seen in the private and public life of the Western world. We may sometimes be baffled to know how we can help to put an end to racial oppression. How can we alleviate the lot of the underprivileged and undernourished in this world? It is baffling—we see needs, we have the urge to do something, and somehow, we feel frustrated and powerless because we do not know what to do. Whatever we do will involve us in sacrifice. If we are to do something to help the hungry and needy of the world, we shall have to be prepared to forgo something ourselves. Even to wrestle with these problems, to bring our uncertainties before God in our prayers, to ask God's guidance as to how we can do something in practice, even this will involve us in the sacrifice of time that we might prefer to spend in other ways. And in the end, we won't do any of these things unless we have faith in Christ Jesus. It is a dreadful thought that it may be necessary, for us who are pledged to follow the example of our Lord, that we ask ourselves whether our ideals have grown cold—whether we still have the will to practice what we believe.

## Endnote

As we contemplate this chapter on *doers of the word*, these words from Ps 27:4 kept coming into our mind: "the fair beauty of the Lord." And into our mind and heart came dreams of what it will be like when we stand ravished with awe and wonder before God—our restless, chattering souls, at last, stilled into peace before "the fair beauty of the Lord." And we dream of the days when the new earth would, at last, be healed and "the fair beauty of the Lord" revealed for all to dwell in. What will the fair beauty be like when we meet it in full? It will be beyond any dream of paradise that anyone anywhere at anytime has ever depicted. It will be beyond bliss. And to that perfection we are called. So, as we travel through the austerities of our faith, let us never lose focus on our destination, held within the arms of the one whose fair beauty patiently and steadfastly is working towards the day when all will be put right for the *doers of the word*. Until then, may the fair beauty of the Lord captivate and uphold us all.

We, the authors of this commentary, promised not to pack this book with a load of Greek words. However, there are always exceptions to the rule, and Linda persuaded David to consider the two Greeks words for "time." One, *chronos*, is about the normal ebb and flow of the steady stream of time—a timeline approach—time with a beginning, a middle, and an end. Another word for time, *kairos*, can be used of a season or, in some theologies, has been applied to mean a moment when time is transfixed, if you like, a marker upon the *chronos* that changes it forever. When we are aware that we have lived through one of these *kairos* events, then we can begin to ponder again upon the mysteries and the meaning of the cross. Jesus never said there is no pain; he showed us how to live and die as creatures of the light. Our symbols in church today bespeak deep cosmic events that should reassure us, even as they almost overwhelm us in their magnitude. So, look at the small flicker of our mortal flames and see that held by the enduring light of the cross, irradiated with the saving love of God.

Very few people today see the world as an uncomplicated place. Most of us feel sometimes that it is difficult to see where we are going. Light is a great help and a great comfort; and this idea of light is one that crops up time and time again throughout the Bible. This light is associated with God's salvation. For the *doers of the word*, the light of the world is Christ. For us, the authors of this commentary, the light of Christ is like a magnet drawing people to God, as the Epiphany star drew the wise men. But we who bear Christ's name, who are his disciples, are also the light of the world. So, as *doers of the word*, how bright is our light? Is it so dazzling that other people see our good works and glorify God? Or do we sometimes let our lamps go out for want of oil? Clearly, our lamps are kept alight through our contact with Christ, who is the source of all light. This light will be reflected but the intensity of the reflection is something we may be able to do something about.

Reflectors are useful things, and they make a real difference to a car headlight. But if you take out the reflector, or if the reflector is dirty or rusted, it becomes useless. We have got to get near enough to God's light so that God's light will be reflected through us. Reading the Letter of James, we must be blameless and above reproach; we are to be without blemish, faultless, where all around are warped, crooked, and perverse.[16] It sounds a formidable specification, and it sounds like the sort of description we reserve for a very few especially saintly people, but is this is what God intended, or as St. James understands it in this letter. Surely, God's will is that all Christians should aspire to this standard. In that sense, we are all called to be saints, and it is the vocation of every one of us to be as lights reflecting the truth and glory of God to those in this world whose perceptions are warped by sin, who need a light to lead them back to the source of all light.

So, reading the Letter of James, there is no room for any artificial piety. This is what he means when he talks about the difference between accepting the word and actually doing it. So, Jesus bids us showing like a clear, pure light. But we can't decide just like that how we shall set about shining today. We can't make our own light, nor is moral goodness the only thing that matters. We may try so hard to be good in our own strength that we get in the way of God's light. The only way we can fulfill this vocation is by welcoming God into our lives through Christ, inviting him to come closer and closer with the intensity of the divine light. As *doers of the word*, we can fulfill this vocation by asking God to take away our sins and imperfections so that we can become genuine vehicles for his light.

16. Phil 2:15.

# *Chapter 2*

# Faith That Needs Works

## Favoritism

My brothers and sisters, do you with your acts of favoritism really believe in our glorious Lord Jesus Christ?

—James 2:1

FAVORITISM IS CHALLENGED IN both the Old Testament and the New.[1] So, clearly, James is questioning the faith of Christians who treat rich people with favor and the poor with contempt. Faith is required, not partiality. In this, he is standing in the tradition of the eighth-century Old Testament prophets. God spoke to our forebearers through these prophets. From a Christian perspective, this revelation was one that ushered in a new age, a new covenant, a new relationship with God and the poor. The prophets of the Old Testament were people of God who, each in their own generation, tried to interpret God to their contemporaries. These prophets came to see and tried to convey the loving kindness of God as expressed in faithfulness towards a concern for all of creation. They came with new truths and understandings, which did not easily commend themselves to others who had grown up with the idea that God was the national God of Israel, who was expected to protect and prosper the fortunes of the Jewish nation and destroy their enemies. It was a slow process of discovery and

1. See Mal 2:19; Lev 19:15; Luke 20:21; Mark 12:14; Matt 22:16; Acts 10:34; Eph 6:9; Col 3:25.

education, and it was far from universally successful. The prophets tried also to interpret the covenant relationship between God and his chosen people, and they came to see clearly that there were two sides to any covenant relationship. That God was faithful, but faithfulness was called for on their part, too—hence, the many prophetic calls for moral renewal and the denunciation of selfishness and wickedness. The prophets were not popular with everyone. It was an uphill struggle for them in the course of Old Testament history. The national moments of renewal were short lived. The prophetic consciousness came to look for a new initiative from God. They could go no further without this.

• • •

In the fullness of time, Jesus was born as God incarnate, and for some, the Messiah expectations were realized. Even though there were only a handful of people who were prepared and ready at the event, we may say that Christmas Day marked the end of an era. Thus, centuries of expectation had reached their climax. For Christians, the old covenant became the new and they looked at the history of God's redemption of the world from a different point of view. The kingdom of heaven had come amongst them.

Most of the first Christians were Jews. Judaism was already an ancient religion. The Jews had been called into existence by the word of God. Abraham journeyed in faith and had waited childless for half a lifetime before the promise that he would be the father of the nation could even begin to be fulfilled. After Jacob's son, Joseph, had been betrayed by his own brothers, the whole tribe had followed Joseph into Egypt in search of food. When Joseph was alive, all went well, but he died, and there arose a king who knew not Joseph. Then the harsh, unwalled prison of slavery came upon the Jewish nation in Egypt. So, they groaned aloud and wept in their travel. Moses arose as a great leader to take the Jews out of Egypt, to the promised land of milk and honey.

They waited in the desert, that strange in-between kind of place, a place of chaos and wonder. Out of the chaos, they emerged with the law of God, set in tablets of stone as the visible proof of the covenant that God had made with them. They entered the promised land just after the death of Moses. They settled down under no king in a state of freedom, where prophets functioned as directors. They fell into sin and worshiped false gods. The temple was built in the era of the great kings, and for a time, stability seems to have been achieved—and then vanished as the

Jewish nation became, again, the prey of invading potentates. The temple fell into decay as the Jewish nation languished in exile. In time, they were allowed to return, and some semblance of ordinary life was painfully and painstakingly restored. And always, through it all, the call and the promise of God's steadfast covenant love could never be shaken. And so, they adored God in songs of praise, prayers, and devotion. In a world of barbaric practices, where integrity often counted for little, the Jewish nation shone as a light of morality. This is how Jesus came to be born a Jew. At that time, no other nation was fit to bear the flesh that housed the holy one of God. In this world of division and pain, the undivided spirit of Judaism shouted to the Lord in triumph, that God is good and that his mercies endure forever.

There are those who claim that we live today in a post-Christian era and imply that the teaching and example of Jesus is all we have—that to be a Christian is simply to live a good life for an example of his life. But this is to ignore a vital truth of the Christian faith we discussed previously in this book, that Jesus not only lived in history but he is alive now in glory and in the hearts of those who are in his glad service. In Isaiah, Jesus is foretold to come along with his just and gentle rule. This is a long-term process guided not by the standards of Isaiah's day, nor by those of the twenty-first century. We are talking about justice and peace and how creation in the future shall be ordered. Into this context, John the Baptizer was the last of the prophets who tried to prepare the world for the coming of Christ. The story of John the Baptist is well known. Out of the desert, full of energy from his high-protein, high-sugar diet, sweeps the prophet and causes absolute mayhem. He has people rushing from one end of the country to the other to see and hear him. So, why did the proclamation of the kingdom of heaven attract such large crowds and what would they understand by it? The bulk of the people came to hear John because of their hope of deliverance from the Roman Empire. The country itself was on its knees, subjugated to brutal Roman rule. So, John's message was more than thrilling; it had implications for freedom and liberation. There was also the personal appeal of John's call to repent, which echoed so strongly with the cause of the prophets of old. They cried for repentance and promised that contrition would bring deliverance. This New Testament prophet baptized the people on the understanding that they were sorry for their sins and would seek to amend their lives accordingly.

So, John's preaching was blunt and practical. John preached that the Jewish nation must repent and demanded a conversation attitude. In other words, a rebirth of outlook was called for—a return to the ancient understanding of justice. Clearly, he reminded the people of Elijah, that prophet of ancient justice who had denounced the mighty for robbing the poor. If John's teaching had been a preaching of personal kindliness, the government of the day would have left it alone. If it had been the urging of the rich to share to some extent with the poor, he would have got away with it. But the encouragement of good works as a preparation for the coming of a world that could only be established on the ruins of the present order terrified those in positions of power and authority. In this new world, the first could find themselves last and the last could be first. John did not claim to be the Messiah but his forerunner, whose sandals he was unfit to tie. He makes it clear that there would arise one mightier than himself, who would know the very secrets of the kingdom of heaven. Thus, John the Baptist is the herald who comes to announce the approach of the king and warns the people to clear the road. Clearly, John refocuses our attention from the messenger to the message. John's baptism in water spoke of external cleaning, but the baptism of fire that Jesus would bring is the transformation of life itself. John's baptism of preparation pointed on to something beyond itself. In the desert of Judea, John spoke as God's voice that went before Christ to warn of the Messiah's coming, so that people would make ready to receive him. The voice of John the Baptizer still warns us now to wait for Christ. If we forsake sin, the Christ of faith will come bringing salvation. Those who obey the call to repent shall hear Christ say, "Believe the gospel and I am real for you."

Whether he willed it or not, John's message was highly charged politically. If enough people were baptized for the forgiveness of sins, maybe the nation would once again be free. Into this heady maelstrom steps Jesus, whom John recognizes. So, here's the question: Can the Gospel accounts of Jesus baptisms be trusted? And what was Jesus doing by insisting that he be baptized? This has challenged the thinkers of the church ever since. The story figures in all four Gospels, so we can be fairly certain that something happened of universal significance. Our own feeling is that Jesus was not baptized but anointed. But whatever happened in the Jordan on that day, it was a marker of the beginning of Jesus' public ministry. So, what was Jesus' mission? We see it as one of being, living in solidarity with us in the perilous frailty of our human flesh. We see it as a mission of enacting, doing the life of faith in order to be a real pattern to us, thereby breaking the old habits of our sinful choices. We see the anointing of Jesus as doing two things. Firstly, assuring us that Jesus was the Christ and that the love and Spirit of God was truly within him. Secondly, providing one of many opportunities for people to recognize Jesus and call him Lord. But the hardness of the human heart drove us to test Jesus to the very end and beyond. Through Christ's persistent love, embodying the covenant of love of God from of old, Jesus showed us that his way of life is real and that his promise to be with us is true—for no matter what we did to him, he would not go away until his job was done.

In the descent of the Holy Spirit upon Jesus in his personal Pentecost, maybe we see the start of the final unifying of heaven and earth, the inhabiting of the world by the One who made it. That Spirit is here now, and so we live in the echo of that affirmation so long ago, both by the pattern Jesus set and by our own baptism. As we meditate upon the mystery of God's love in Jesus, let us recall with joy his obedience and his faithfulness. May we work for justice and peace; may we, too, know the fullness of God's love in our hearts and, encouraged by the letter and witness of James, show that love in our lives, to Jesus' praise and glory.

In the early days of the Christian church, from the day of Pentecost on, the apostles preached the gospel with an urgency that was compelling. It is possible, from the Letter of James, to build up a picture of the message they proclaimed. This was a message that empowered those who heard it to action. So, what was the content of their preaching? Well, the prophecies are fulfilled, and the new age had started with Christ's birth from the seed of David; and this Christ was crucified by the sin of humanity, died, was buried, and came back to life on the third day, according to the Scriptures. Jesus then ascended to heaven to sit at the right hand of God the Father and will come to again to judge us all.

• • •

The first Christians worshiped at the temple and in the synagogues, but that left them with a great problem. To account for their experience and their understanding of Jesus, of what he stood for and of what he had done, the first Christians could not stay within their Jewish tradition. Pious Jews were horrified at Christians when they claimed that Jesus was the Son of God incarnate. How could that possibly be true when God had said that he was One, the Holy One of Israel, the One whose name was too huge to be encompassed within a single word. Yet, how else could the Christians describe all that Jesus meant to them, and how else could they begin to explain the leadership of Jesus together with his ministry and his love? So, the first Christians expected the second coming at any time. Jesus had promised that he would return in power to judge the earth. They thought that this would happen within their lifetime. That gave urgency to the call to mission. It also meant that they had to work out a way to show both that Jesus did come out of the covenant love of God to the Jews and also that, in Jesus, through God's great grace, a new age had dawned. This new age was an age of reconciliation with God for all humanity.

For New Testament writers like James, Jesus was the author and finisher of the Christian faith—from one point of view, the completion of the expectation of the Old Testament—from another, the beginning of a new era. The New Testament does not end neatly at the end of a story. It breaks off just as the story is really getting underway, and in one sense, the story is still being written in the church of Christ. The Old Testament people of faith looked to the future, and so must we, still pressing on always towards the goal, our eyes fixed on Jesus, on whom our faith depends. He who was, and is, and is to come; as it was in the beginning, is now, and ever shall be; world without end.

• • •

In the Anglican lectionary, the Letter of James is related to a complicated Gospel reading from Mark. In the story of the gentile woman, we are confronted by what looks like unwillingness on the part of Jesus to respond kindly to a case of human need and distress. An unwillingness on the part of Jesus to heal this woman's daughter is expressed in what appears to us, initially, to be harsh and unsympathetic. However, before we accuse our Lord of pastoral insensitivity, we must look for a more profound understanding of this passage. The remark that helping this woman would be like feeding the children's food to the dogs is a test, and a severe one at that. The woman gives the only possible answer she can. She is not one of the chosen, nor does she have any idea of becoming a disciple of Jesus. She relies entirely on her own needs and on the fact that no true household of faith can exist unless it provides for more than its children. Jesus now responds to the woman in her faith and in her need.

So, let us look in more detail at Mark's account through the lens of James. Let us look first at the context in which we find this story. This woman was probably a Syrophoenician. The community from which she came was associated with false doctrines and pagan behavior. The dogs referred to in our reading are more like household pets than savage beasts who roam the hillsides. They are poodles, not rottweilers. The gentile woman had asked Jesus for help concerning her daughter. There is an important gap between the request that this woman made and the response that was given. The delay can be said to correspond to the interval between the ministry of Jesus and the time the gentiles were admitted to the church. Jesus tells the woman that he was sent to the lost sheep of Israel. In Matthew's Gospel, we see that Jesus sends out his disciples, warning them not to go to the gentile districts or the Samaritan cities. Surely, these limitations were not meant to apply for all time. We can interpret our reading to mean that the matter is one of priorities. The first, but not the only, task of the Messiah is concerned with Israel. Other people are not excluded, but their needs can best be met when Jesus' mission to his people is completed. So, the immediate task was to create a community of faith within Israel, and that this faith would transform the world. St. Matthew's Gospel ends with an explicit instruction to the apostles from the risen Lord to go and make disciples of all nations. Jesus was born and lived on earth within the bounds of the Jewish church, with its Scriptures, laws, sacrifices, and rites. In his divine person, Jesus gives them a fuller meaning and a new power to serve and to lead the souls of all people. For those of us who are apostolic Christians, the old sacrifices are fulfilled in the sacrifice of the Lamb of God on Calvary and its continual appreciation in the Holy Eucharist.

## Finding Faith in Our Poverty

> Listen, my beloved brothers and sisters. Has not God chosen the poor in the world to be rich in faith and to be heirs of the kingdom that he has promised to those who love him?
>
> —James 2:5

From what has been said so far, the saints and the great people of faith of past ages are important not merely as historical figures but, because we share the same faith, we continue to build on the foundation they laid down. They are a cloud of witnesses encouraging us, urging us to follow in their footsteps. However, for some people, religious faith is seen as a last resort in times of trouble. When the bottom falls out of their world, and they can do absolutely nothing about it, in desperation, they turn to God—perhaps, somehow or another, God can help. When our faith in ourselves is completely shattered, then we find the humility to turn to God. How often, when the crisis is past, do we turn back to self-confidence and forget about God? It happened repeatedly in the Old Testament and throughout the history of Christianity, too. True religion means giving God the central place, not merely using him to fill the gaps when all else fails. Sadly, religion is often seen as an end in itself and church-going as a destination rather than a place that equips us to practice our faith in the world.

So, is Christianity an interest that keeps us busy all the time or a hobby among other hobbies for our spare time? Nothing more needs to be said, we think, to amplify this. But it is an idea held by many people and is behind the often-repeated assertion, "I haven't got time to come to church." How many times have you heard people say, "If this is what you get for being a Christian, it isn't worth it." "I've always gone to church, and yet, look what I have had to suffer—while other people, who have never bothered, seem to sail through life without an anxious moment." "If so-and-so goes to church and calls themselves a Christian, I'm not going to have anything to do with it."

We must cling to our faith through thick and thin, confident that God is there and will support and save us. We should pray that our faith in God might be strong enough and real enough to withstand any hardships and misfortunes that may come our way. Persecution has often renewed and purified the church—not that we won't suffer for its own sake. It has brought Christians face to face with their true priorities and inflamed their faith in God and his kingdom. In more comfortable times, we always seem to lose this sense of urgency, and with it, our sense of the priority of God's place in our lives. So, how strong is our faith? Do we give full expression to our faith—that Jesus is Lord? Surely, we ought to thank God that we can openly profess our Christian faith and practice it without fear, and be all the more concerned to take full advantage of our freedom—to profit by hard-won insights of those who were faced with quite different circumstances in which to witness to the love of God in Christ Jesus. All this is easier said than done. But there are so many excuses and reason for not believing in God, or for ceasing to believe—some of them trivial, some of tremendous personal weight. God is there with us in all our trials and tribulations. Jesus has been through them all and triumphed. God will give us strength to triumph if we will only believe and ask for his help.

• • •

There is something deep in human nature that prevents us from being genuinely good, selfless, and loving to all at all times. We can do it selectively but not reliably and universally. Yet, at our best, we know that is what we need to do if we are to follow the pattern of Jesus as the pinnacle of human perfection. So, we need to go on calling on the Lord to help us, and we need constantly to acknowledge our faults before God. And that is not always easy. That is why our focus is not the simple act of remembering the first coming but a calling out and a crying out and a longing for the second coming. So, we watch and pray, trust in Christ our King, strive to be his faithful representatives now, and yearn for the future when he will come.

So, the task in our context is how to rediscover the Christian gospel. We have to realize the relevance of the good news for our age and then boldly preach the gospel following the guidance of James and the New Testament in the power of the Holy Spirit. Salvation is a term we come across very often in the New Testament, as well as in the prayers and hymns and writings of Christian people. It isn't confined to the Salvation Army or those Christians who are sometimes referred to as the saved and happy variety. As we said previously, we may find it disconcerting to be confronted with the abrupt question, "Are you saved?" Now, this may be an overtly simple approach for some people, but we can't be Christians without the assurance of salvation. It is a concept we could well think about a great deal more than we do. A starting point might be to ask the question, "Salvation from what?" This really is a basic question. So, to talk about salvation, to ask the question "Are you saved?" without defining saved from what is meaningless. We can't assume everyone knows what we are talking about. We may discover, when we begin to think about it, that we are far from being clear ourselves. The Christian faith is, in its deepest sense, the answer, but it is not the immediate, self-evident solution to every single problem. We need to teach its relevance by trying to appreciate something of the purpose and will of God in the whole of creation. The Christian faith can give a satisfactory understanding to life in terms of God's purpose. Our need, then, of salvation is ongoing. Our calling on the name of the Lord must therefore be the continued building of a growing and deepening relationship with God through Jesus Christ. So, the gospel of God's salvation and the Christian faith as understood by the Letter of James are relevant and important—indeed, essential—for life as God meant it to be. All this we must accept first for ourselves and constantly be deepening our own relationship with God, and then, by word and example, by the very quality of our lives, we should be able to communicate this faith to other people.

## Faith Without Works

> What good is it, my brothers and sisters, if you say you have faith but do not have works? Can faith save you? If a brother or sister is naked and lacks daily food, and one of you says to them, "Go in peace; keep warm and eat your fill," and yet you do not supply their bodily needs, what is the good of that? So faith by itself, if it has no works, is dead.
>
> —James 2:14–17

Again, a claim to faith must be put into action.[2] For James, faith without works just isn't faith. Clearly, he is thinking about what we read in Matthew's Gospel about feeding and clothing the poor.[3] For God chose to enter this world from the position of the poor and that is how God calls us to live, as hidden, potent, and faithful icons of the Lord, who made the universe and who reentered it as helplessly as we do. What else could possibly demonstrate to us the essential and basic goodness of creation? If it was safe enough for the Son of God, then its original goodness must still be there, though cloaked. A major part of the new creation is about how God interacts with his world. No longer is God the outsider, the one who comes in from above, the transcendent God. Now God is immanent, Emmanuel, God with us. Now, God intervenes in each human heart, and, through Jesus, God cries out to us individually and personally with all the longing that our Lord expressed when he yearned over Jerusalem like an overshadowing and protecting mother hen. And so, the cosmic dialogue continues, God to us and we to God, through the great intermediator, Jesus Christ. God's word empowers and consoles us; our words to God urge and implore. For we call the same call and sing the same song: that of redemption, of restoration, of life made whole again, justice and peace. And so, the kingdom comes nearer, year on year, until that day dawns, when all our pleas shall be answered. For this reason, we cannot live complacent lives, but we must be stirred up, restless for

2. Barclay, *Letters of James and Peter*, 86.

3. Matt 25:34–36.

God, restless for the best for our fellow creatures and for our universe. As Christians, we believe God is the Creator of all things and that God had a purpose in creating the world. There is a supreme purpose in life; this life is incomplete in itself, and it will find its completion in the fullness of eternal life with God.

• • •

But someone will say, "You have faith and I have works." Show me your faith without works, and I by my works will show you my faith.

—James 2:18

In terms of faith and practice, what is true discipleship? It is what we believe in sincerely and act on appropriately. An Evangelical friend once asked David, "Have you accepted Jesus as your Lord and personal Savior? And when were you saved?" David said, "At about 3:00 p.m. on Good Friday two thousand years ago." David could have also added that he was saved every time I demonstrate that faith in a practical and tangible way to those who are in need. As baptized members of the church, we have been called to live a holy life in the service of Christ. When we are baptized, we join the family of the church, which is Christ's body here on earth. The church, then, is the saints on earth and the instrument by which Christ continues his work in the world. It is a body by which Christ makes himself known. So, what is the nature of true discipleship? And what is faith? Because what we believe about Jesus is important. Jesus was more than just a nice man who went around doing a few miracles. He was the Son of God. The second person of the Blessed Trinity, of the Father, the Son, and the Holy Spirit. Not only does he tell the truth, but he also *is* the truth and the creative power behind the universe. True discipleship, then, is to respond to Jesus by putting the principles of his gospel into practice. The church James is talking about is a genuine religion where money is raised for the care of the needy and the sick. In Britain, where the welfare state is on the decline, the work of the Christian church among the poor is important. That is real religion.

• • •

For just as the body without the spirit is dead,
so faith without works is also dead.

—James 2:26

Can we assume that the majority of people reading this commentary come from warm and comfortable homes? Well, we hope that is the case. We make this point not to make anybody feel guilty but rather to focus our minds on the plight of those who are homeless. However, the question has to be asked: How comfortable can any of us be when others have no such comfort? Most of us have a home with food for sustenance and furniture to rest our bodies. We have a door to open to friend and stranger and a door to shut when we need our peace. At Christmas, church congregations are asked to hold in their hearts the people who have nowhere to call their home. We want to say a bit more about the concepts of home and homelessness. *Home* is an interesting word. It means as many different ideas as there are people who associate with the Church of England and the worldwide Anglican Communion, but there are some common threads. Home is the place where you feel safe and special. For a homeless person himself, Jesus had several interesting things to say about home. On one occasion, he remarked that "God is love, and those who abide in love abide in God, and God abides in them."[4] On another occasion, he said that if we call, then he and the Father will come and make their home with us.[5] So, God seeks to be with us.

At this point in the Christmas Day sermon, most congregations are quietly asking themselves, "So, what has all this got to do with Christmas?" After all, the story of Christmas is a lovely one and we all enjoy it. A baby, a young mum, and her partner. The animals in the cattle shed. The angels singing. The star shining. The shepherds watching. The wise men bringing gifts. And what is the Christmas story? Is it just mistletoe and mild wine? Jesus' family had to up sticks and travel through the harsh winter to Bethlehem in order to fill in a census form. And then, threatened by King Herod, they had to flee to Egypt. Just before the congregation gets completely restless and anxious to get home for Christmas Day lunch, we usually ask if anyone is looking forward to a traditional family Christmas? We then remind the congregation that Jesus came into this world with no privilege or status and is presented to us as an asylum seeker.

In the Church of England, Harvest Thanksgiving is another time when we naturally think about the poor and the needy, for the abundance of God's goodness should be for all. People rarely choose to live in poverty. So why, then, are people poor and needy? In some countries, the soil is hard and there is little rain, so people built greenhouses and raised earth

4. 1 John 4:16.

5. John 14:23.

platforms to grow their crops. In some parts of the world, there is not enough rain, and in other parts of the world, there is too much. Annual floods are good for the soil, but when there is too much rain, flooding can bring death instead of life. So, people in the so-called third world have been building raised earth platforms on which houses can be built—trees and vegetables can also be planted out of reach of rising water.

Some so-called third world problems are created by the rich world. Sometimes, people are hungry because they grow too much tea and coffee for the West instead of wheat for local consumption. We continue to pay a pittance for their harvest and sell their governments arms to suppress the people. For a number of years, now many Christians have bought fair trade products. The problem is not that we are lacking food in this world. We are, however, lacking the good will and generosity to distribute that food equally. Governments, to save thousands of lives, could use hundreds of tons of food that are kept by the rich nations in cold storage. Our giving is important but is small in comparison with what governments could and should do. Governments, have at their disposal, the means to make all the hungry nations capable of feeding themselves. To be able to feed yourself is better than receiving handouts, especially if that aid comes with political strings and can stop at the whim of self-serving sociopathic politicians. This is what Christian Aid Week is all about—helping people in poorer countries to help themselves. The money collected during Christian Aid Week is used to help people grow food. It is also about providing blankets and shelter when there are floods and earthquakes. Following the Letter of James, how do we put our faith into action? What are the means of channeling our love and respect and service for God and our neighbors? The apparatus of organized religion—church buildings, church services, prayer and sacraments, clergy, parochial church councils, and churchwardens—are these the means of building up and maintaining real faith and commitment that is needed to realize the teaching of the Letter of James? Is the Church of England a serious part of that process and means of channeling to us the love and power and presence of God that leads to righteous action?

• • •

In a Gospel reading from John, the people were hungry and the responsibility for meeting their need lies with Jesus and his disciples. But his disciples claim that they are not able to feed the people. So, who were these disciples and why do they think they have no resources adequate to meet the demand that is made on them? More to the point, how did they understand Jesus? Well, they are the sort of people who get into a boat with two packets of crisps, row to the other side of the lake, meet up with five thousand other people, wait until they know all the shops are closed, and declare they have nothing to eat. They are just like us, then, or is this just a literary style to get us thinking? All the way through the Gospels, these same disciples are to be amazed by what Jesus has to say. But how much more amazed must Jesus have been by them? Christ's followers were hungry for bread—the bread of life. This is the teaching and self-offering of Jesus himself. For the bread of life is the food of eternal life because it comes from God who is in heaven. The bread of life is a new relationship with God in which our hunger is satisfied. Jesus is able to give us the bread of life because he is the bread of life. And if we want to receive the gift of real life from Jesus Christ, then we must put our trust in him.

So, what is going on here? Well, Christ's followers were wearied and in want. Christ knew what he could do and was meant to do. In his question to Philip, he asked for faith, not bread. The disciples had to trust him to give them the true bread by which their souls might live. The bread we are talking about is the spiritual food that is able to sustain life, not only in this world but also in the world to come. The life we are talking about is life with God beyond death in the resurrection of the dead. Like the disciples, we are tempted to say that we have no resources adequate to meet the demands that are made on us. But we are a work of God's creation, and he continues that work through our labors. He demands are participation in the creation of a just society. Thus, to know God is to love God. To love God is to do justice.[6]

Clearly, St. John has the Eucharist in mind when he records the story of the feeding of the five thousand. The sacraments are the outward and visible sign of the truth that God has chosen to reveal. But God does expect us to do our bit as well. There is something that human hands must supply—bread, wine, and water. Simple things like the barley cakes and fishes that St. Andrew persuaded the lad in the story to offer. The disciples were charged to gather the people to the feast. It is not a mere crowd but an organized community that sits down in ranks on the green grass.[7] Disorder and confusion have no place in the divine purpose. The early church had a common form of eucharistic worship in which

6. See Isiorho, *Faith in Church Newspapers*, 5–6.

7. John 6:10.

social class was abolished and the rich and the poor sat down together as equals. In the early church, there was a real sharing of resources and living conditions—where the care of the needy was taken seriously. Thus, our witness teaches us that it is not sufficient to give to the poor and keep them dependent upon our charity, but rather it is also necessary to change the unjust structures of society that cause poverty. The Letter of James teaches us that it is no privilege to be rich when others are poor. It is a burden, which weigh upon us and prevents us living the Christian life. If we come to the Lord's table in penitence and in faith, then we must also recognize that God has a preferential option for the poor and the oppressed. The Letter of James points us to our relationship with God and how it relates to our relationship to the rest of humankind.

So, what did Jesus mean when he said, "I am the living bread that comes down from heaven."[8] Clearly, he meant something radically different from the conventional understanding of the words "bread" and "life." The bread we are talking about is the spiritual food that is able to sustain life, not only in this world but also in the world to come. The life we are talking about is life with God, beyond death in the resurrection of the dead. Jesus promised that he would raise us up on the last day. Here, we are following the Pauline tradition, and there is no reason to think this was not also common to the readers of the Letters of James. So, when Christ appears again, there will be a general resurrection of the dead, which will be followed by the end of the world. As for the nature of the resurrection body, it will not have the same characteristics as the body we have now. But the identity of the individual will be preserved in spite of the change. We shall acquire a new instrument for our personality, which will be nevertheless a proper successor to the present body and will actually be linked in definite continuity with it. The new body will be immortal, the final victory of life over death. In heaven, we will live with God forever.

• • •

The foundations are constantly being shaken by the traffic of materialism. But we do well to remember that Christ is the same yesterday, today, and forever. The rock cannot be shifted. Those whose faith is really founded upon the rock of Christ are the true pillars of the church. We need to nourish and maintain our spiritual foundations. We can only do this by living a Christ-centered life. And there are no short cuts, no easy ways

8. John 6:51.

out—we can't put this job out to contractors—we've got to it ourselves. A Christ-centered life is one that involves regular prayer, reading the Holy Scriptures, penitence, and feeding on the body and blood of Christ in the Holy Communion. There is no substitute for these practical means of grace for those who really wish to make Christ the center of their lives—the rock on which their faith is grounded. So, how do we make sense of things through the lens of the Letter of James? Well, Jesus Christ did not burst in on this world from a position of great strength and power; he was born in the humblest of surroundings, and out of death on a cross came the supreme manifestation of the creative power of Almighty God—the resurrection. Thus, the Christ baby of Christmas can be found in the arms of Mary, his mother, who is also there in the pain of the Good Friday cross. At the Holy Eucharist, the priest proclaims Jesus' glorious resurrection, and we are reminded of the circumstances of his death. From everlasting-to-everlasting, Jesus puts a choice before us: Are we with him or not? He will not force us but begs our friendship with words of love and deepest understanding.

So, the Christian faith is for the whole of life, in every conceivable circumstance—not just an insurance against misfortune. It is a great pity that this later impression has often been given, and many people think of God only in times of trouble. When things are going well, it is all somehow irrelevant. But the Christian faith is relevant at all times, in prosperity as well as adversity. And we must take care not to forget this. In the introduction to the marriage service, Christian marriage is spoken of as "signifying unto us the mystical union that is betwixt Christ and his church." If the relationship between Christ and the church can illustrate the relationship of marriage, we can perhaps turn the illustration around and be helped in thinking out our relationship with Christ. For better for worse, for richer or poorer, in sickness and health, but not till death us do part. Rather, till death unites us perfectly in the life that is to come. We live in an age in which faith is not easy.

## Endnote

We end this chapter with the words of the *Nunc Dimittis*.[9]

> To be a light to lighten the Gentiles.[10]

9. *Book of Common Prayer*, 53; Luke 2:29.
10. *Book of Common Prayer*, 53.

These words which we sing at the Anglican service of evensong sum up a particularly important aspect of the Christian faith. Jesus came to bring the light of God to the gentiles and to God's people Israel. It's worth spending a little time thinking about this subject. So, who were the gentiles? Quite simply, all those who were not Jews. We need to start with the very beginning of the Jewish faith. We know that the Jews worshiped the only true God, the same God whom Christians worship. But the earliest Jews didn't know as much about him as we do, through the revelation of his Son, Jesus Christ. Jacob and Moses and Abraham had hugely different ideas about just what God was like from those of the prophet Isaiah. The Bible as a whole is the story of the gradual revelation of God's true nature, as God's chosen people came to know and understand him as the God of mercy and loving-kindness, who would forgive the sins of his people if they repented. It was a slow process and not everyone shared exactly the same ideas. It was the prophets especially who came to understand and tried to explain these new insights. God the Almighty, who had made the whole world, was interested in all people, Jews and gentiles alike. This understanding of God and his purpose for humankind was terribly slow to emerge. It is this truth that the book of Jonah is all about.

Jonah was thrown into the sea, and was saved by a large fish or whale that swallowed him, and then, three days later, deposited him on dry ground. Well, can you believe that in the literal sense of what happened? Here's the answer: you don't have to because this is not what is being asked of us. This is a theological and psychological narrative with plenty of meaning, and we should think of it as parable, an earthly story that conveys a heavenly and complex understanding. Jonah was told by God to go to Nineveh, a great gentile city, and warn them that God was going to punish them for their dreadful wickedness. But Jonah didn't like the idea of this task, and tried to run away from it, taking instead a boat going to Tarshish. However, he wasn't to get out of his errand so easily. God sent a storm, as a result of which, Jonah was thrown overboard by the sailors and brought back to land by the whale. Then, God spoke to him again and said, "Now go to Nineveh, and give them the message that I gave you." And this time, Jonah decided he had better go. When he got there, he delivered the message. Surprisingly, these wicked gentiles, when they heard what Jonah had to say, didn't just laugh it off, but they believed God, proclaimed a fast and cried mightily to God, and turned away from their former ways.

And God saw their repentance and had mercy on them. But it displeased Jonah exceedingly, and he was incredibly angry. He was of the firm opinion that the progress of God's kingdom was marked by the destruction of the gentiles. He felt he had wasted his time coming all this way to warn them. He had come to announce the wrath of God, and now God had gone soft and forgiven them, and Jonah probably felt he had been made to look silly. He went out of the town and sat down and sulked. God had lessons to teach him. God caused a leafy plant to grow to shelter Jonah from the great heat of the sun. And Jonah was extremely glad of the shade. But the next day, the plant died, and Jonah fainted from the direct rays of the sun. He missed it tremendously and was angry that the plant had died.

But God reasoned with him. Jonah was sorry that the plant had died, and yet he hadn't had anything to do with making it grow. So, how should God feel about destroying Nineveh, a great city containing more than sixty thousand human beings? The writer of the book of Jonah was trying to make his fellow Jews face up to these ideas. Wasn't the God they worshiped rather more wonderful than they imagined? As the Creator of the entire world, wasn't he interested in more than just showing particular favoritism to his chosen people—weren't all people just as much God's people? These are some of the ideas contained in the book of Jonah and relevant to our understanding of the Letter of James. They weren't, by any means, widely accepted by the Jews, but they show that at least some people were thinking deeply about the nature of God. Even when Jesus came, the distinction between Jew and gentile was very clearly marked. And within the early church, there was a division of opinion among the apostles as to whether it was necessary to become a Jew before one could become a Christian. And for some time, the Christian church was divided into two: the Jewish Christians and the gentile Christians. But before the end of the Acts of the Apostles, it had been clearly established that there is no room for any distinctions on any grounds within the church. Jesus came to the chosen people—he also came to be a light to lighten the gentiles. He came to break down all barriers and to establish the truth that all people are the children of God. We should always be aware of this truth, remembering that it is God's will that not one of his children should perish—that Jesus Christ came into the world to save sinners and that there is joy in the company of heaven over one sinner who repents, more than over ninety-nine righteous people who don't need to. The church exists to worship God and to spread the good news of the gospel as widely as possible. The church is never justified in being inward-looking and exclusive in regarding those inside as the chosen people and those outside as beyond the pale. If we ever catch ourselves jealously resenting the comparative outsider who has not done nearly so much for the church as we have, or if we feel like the prodigal son's elder brother[11]—then, perhaps, the story of Jonah will remind us of that God, who made all things, loves all his children.

It is our Christian duty, while not forgetting the preferential care for the poor, to make the gospel accessible to all people, including the rich and successful. Evangelism is not only about bringing the good news of Jesus Christ to those who have not heard it but also about building up our own faith and that of one another, so that we may effectively make his ways known on earth and his saving power among all nations. We are warned that the kingdom will come suddenly when we least expect it. Opportunities to make God known also come unexpectedly, and our evangelism has to be so much part of our way of being that we can respond to those sudden opportunities in ways that make the message of the gospel accessible to those with whom we share it. Change is coming, the values of the kingdom are not the values of the world. It is for all people. Even the celestial powers will be shaken, whatever that means. But clearly, we are to seek the kingdom of God as our first priority, and then everything else will also be ours.

11. Luke 15:28.

# Chapter 3

# Wisdom, Righteousness, and the Theology of the Cross

## Introduction

> Who is wise and understanding among you? Show by your good life that your works are done with gentleness born of wisdom.
>
> —James 3:13

WE START THIS CHAPTER by praying for the humility of our scholarship, that our teaching will come out of a genuine desire to build up the faith in Christ among the faithful. In this, we want to teach the truth with gentleness and not selfish ambition.[1] In the light of these considerations, we continue this commentary with the book of Ecclesiasticus, one of the books of the Jewish tradition that takes as their topic the subject of wisdom. From this, we want to look at two points. Firstly, where does wisdom come from? And secondly, can wisdom explain the presence of wickedness in this world? In other words, is wisdom any use in building the Christian kingdom?

Those of us with an interest in the myths of European tradition may recall the story of the birth of the Greek goddess Athena, who personified wisdom. She sprang fully armed from the head of Zeus, the king of the gods. She was associated not only with the cleverness of skillful handicraft

1. Barclay, *James and Peter*, 105.

but also with insight and prudence. She was wisdom in her person, in vigorous action. Her origins were nonhuman and were directly from Zeus. Greek thought developed until ideas concerning wisdom became the direct forerunners of some of our modern notions of what science is about—a human inquiry into the nature of the universe together with the resulting understanding of the truth that emerges from that quest. Various books in our sacred tradition deal with wisdom. They take up the debate on the connection between truth and wisdom, reality and understanding. The book of Proverbs presents wisdom as something that can be gained after a quest involving patience, endurance, and prayer. Wisdom is seen here as the right understanding that enables the enquirer to grasp the sense that underlies the created order. In other words, the comprehensible and explicable within the cosmos. So, for the book of Proverbs, wisdom is essentially a human quality. By the time we reached the end of the wisdom writings, we find Jewish thought has actually gone the opposite way to Greek philosophy because wisdom is God's and God's alone.

So, what about our second question: Can wisdom explain wickedness in the world? Or to put it another way, how can a good God allow bad things to happen? Going back to the history of our religion helps us because there is now the emergence of a link between the Old Testament and the New Testament in Christian thinking. Many early Christian writers and teachers understood Christ as the Word of God, which is an important theme in St. John's Gospel. Wisdom became the word, and the word became flesh. Suddenly, here is our link—God is not distant but Emmanuel, God with us, to the point of fleshly brotherhood, family relationships. I passed a church the other day that had a garish poster adorning its door announcing Jesus is the answer. Now Jesus, as the divine wisdom incarnate, as the word made flesh, never said, "I am the answer." No, he said, "I am the way, the truth and the life."[2] Jesus is saying that wisdom is a process, not a finished statement but a way of living. What, now, is the answer to our second question: Can wisdom explain wickedness in the world? Well, actually, no! So, what are we left with? We are left with the most wonderful thing of all, that invitation into the divine process that is Jesus. We are left with the example of our Beloved as he lived his life of obedience to the Father's will. For if we yearn for good, how much more does God? If we want peace and healing, how much

2. John 14:6.

more does God? And if we want righteousness, this can only be realized in his glad service.

## The Knowledge of God and God's Righteousness

And the fruit of righteousness is sown in peace of them that make peace.

—James 3:18

We continue this commentary by looking at some of the ideas contained in the Old Testament book of the prophet Ezekiel. The emphasis here is on the sovereignty of God to choose and order the world as God wills. The theme is God's will and capacity to revive and to restore; this leads us to an understanding that we can live under God's direction by being responsive to his love. Taking our steer from Ezekiel, let us explore this theme through the symbolism of trees and fowls within God's creation. Thus, the flower on the tree should turn into fruit, and by their fruits, ye shall know them. The aim of the Christian life isn't just to produce beautiful flowers but also the fruits of the Spirit. Remember the seed that first fell in our hearts and started off our growth in Christ Jesus. The flowering and the fruit of our lives ought all the time to be sowing the seeds of grace in the lives of others. The kind word, the loving action, the way we live. Later on in the book of Ezekiel, we hear God say, "A new heart I will give you and a new spirit I will put into you."[3] For the people of Ezekiel's time, the word that we translate as "heart" referred to that part of their makeup that made its own decisions. It was in the heart that sin occurred. "Mind" or even "salt" might be a better translation today. Here, we have the powerful but loving God who recognizes our difficulties in turning Godward and offers the remedy. The Creator God who enters into our humanity, infusing us with divine strength, this is the God of continuing and making. Not the technician God, who made the world and then went off somewhere else and absentmindedly forgot us. The people of the Old Testament, who were exiled in Babylon, were under this impression as they longed to return home. Some thought that God lived in Jerusalem, even though the temple had been destroyed. Ezekiel makes it clear that God is everywhere. That is what Ezekiel's vision of a family of dead and dry bones is all about. God does not have to travel from Jerusalem to breathe new life into his people. God is already there and ready to

3. Ezek 36:26.

connect these bones together. To put skin on them and breathe his life into them, Ezekiel likens the exiles to these dry bones that would receive new life and, as a consequence, would return to their own land, so God intervenes. This is the point that Jesus is making through his parables. And Jesus tells us that if we have faith the size of a mustard seed, it could grow into a great faith and love for God. This is an earthly story with a deeper, or heavenly, meaning and is a very powerful method of communication. When Jesus adopted this means of talking to his followers, he was following in the tradition of the rabbis. Jesus' message is clear, and in the most potent demonstration of that, Jesus came into where we are so that we might come into where God is. Jesus was the living, breathing, dying, rising proof that God is real and active in our world.

• • •

So, how do we talk about wisdom and righteousness in the love of God? How should we live in society and how should it be organized? We need to talk about the faith of the church and what this means for us who live in a world of disillusionment and unbelief. So, what, then, is this thing called "faith" anyway? True faith is what God has revealed, but we have the task of discernment. So what do we understand to be the knowledge of God? We need to distinguish more clearly than we usually do between religious knowledge—knowledge about God—and knowing God himself. This last is the heart of what is meant by "the knowledge of God." It means taking the truth about God, particularly in the Scriptures, and quietly meditating on them until we really get to grips with the "knowledge of God." It is a process that never ends in this life. We shall know God perfectly only in the life of the world to come. But we can make some progress. What the Bible says is important. What the church says, and has said, is also important. There is a great contrast between the two halves of the Christian year. The first half contains the great festivals commemorating the facts of our redemption—Advent leading up to Christmas, the Epiphany, Lent leading up to Holy Week and Easter, Ascension, Whitsun, and then, to mark the turning point, Trinity Sunday—a glorious summary of all we know about God. The second half, the Sundays after Trinity, apart from saints' days, is less exciting and the color is quiet green. But this is not meant to be a slack period reflecting the fact that the weather is fine and people are away on holiday.

The truths to which the great festivals draw attention are always relevant and important. We say the whole creed every Sunday. Christmas, Good Friday, Easter, Ascension, and Whitsun are important every day. This second half of the year is a great opportunity to assimilate the truths about God that we consider at the festivals. It is an opportunity to deepen our knowledge of God in the light of all we know about him and all that he has done. The Trinity period is also a time of testing. God is unchanging—the same forever—ever faithful, ever sure, all-knowing, almighty, perfect love. We know that we could never be as faithful as he is. However, there are questions we should ask about our faith. Do we know him so well, appreciate and trust him so much that we find it impossible to be distracted away from him? Or are we still inclined to forget about him or push him into the background when something else crops up? Is God an interest in our lives among many others, or the root and source of our very life itself? What, then, is the reality of our knowledge about God? God's favor and love don't come and go—Christ died for us—just as we are. God knows perfectly well the best and worst in us—and he is not going to change his attitude or withdraw his love—his unchanging love. And didn't he promise the power of the Holy Ghost? The knowledge of God brings faith and trust. And there are no short cuts or easy ways to gain this knowledge—no amount of crash courses, refresher courses, or lectures can guarantee anything. In the end, there is no alternative to meeting with God and getting to know him better. We can do this in our prayers, in the sacraments, and as we quietly meditate on the word of God.

• • •

We look now at a parable from Matthew that relates to the theme of wisdom and righteousness. A parable likely to have been familiar to the readers of James.

> What do you think? A man had two sons; he went to the first and said, "Son, go and work in the vineyard today." He answered, "I will not"; but later he changed his mind and went. The father went to the second and said the same; and he answered, "I go, sir"; but he did not go. Which of the two did the will of his father? They said, "The first." Jesus said to them, "Truly I tell you, the tax-collectors and the prostitutes are going into the kingdom of God ahead of you."[4]

4. Matt 21:28.

We say it often enough—we are committed and want to follow out our commitment—but do we? How often are we like the son who said "yes," but then, for whatever reason, don't? And we aren't told in the story why the son didn't—whether he was on his way and then something else cropped up, whether he bumped into a friend and forgot, whether he didn't feel very well, or whether, in the end, he just didn't feel like it. *Thy will be done.* I am sure it is true to say that more than half the battle, and often the most difficult part, is discovering just what is God's will. This is not to say that God deliberately makes it difficult for us or hides his true wishes from us. It is rather simply to underline the fact that we cannot easily and readily assume that God's will is always obvious, and if we don't do it is simply because we choose not to. It cannot be that simple, if only because God's view of things; God's plans and hopes for the whole universe are on an infinitely greater scale than we can ever imagine

God sees all clearly. Our picture is, to some extent, always blurred and indistinct. To us, indeed, God often appears to move in a mysterious way, his wonders to perform. If sometimes we find that we are too readily jumping to oversimple decisions about what God's will is in a particular situation—or if sometimes, we are distressed because no obvious solution seems to present itself to a particular problem that we have to wrestle with, then we might do well to think of Jesus in the garden of Gethsemane, wrestling in prayer with an intensity that caused the sweat to fall from his brow like great drops of blood. It is inconceivable that Jesus should not have done his father's will. He had, first of all, to thrash out just what that was. If we are committed to doing God's will, we are committed also to searching it out. And we can't always lightly assume that it will be obvious or that it will be the first thing we think of. *Thy will be done.* There is no substitute for prayer, Bible reading, worship, study, and discussion if we are to keep closely in touch with God, and so, be able to have a chance of interpreting his will in our own lives. Jesus was in perfect communion with his Father, and yet, God's will for him was not always crystal clear—he needed to go into the wilderness for forty days, to go up onto the hillside in the early morning, to spend hours alone to think out, in the presence of the Father, the implications of his chosen way of obedience.

Conscience is an important tool, but it is only as good as the care we take of it. It needs to be maintained in good working order, fed with up-to-date information above all, not to become rusty for lack of use. The more relevant the information with which it is fed, the better the guidance it will be able to give us. And of course, it will be only guidance—the decision to act according to our conscience is one we have to make for ourselves. Our conscience will function to a limited extent on the basic information we assimilated from early childhood about the will of God. Our early teaching about the ten commandments, for example, will probably ensure that we are in no doubt about the wrongness of such obvious things as murder, adultery, and open theft. But conscience should be a more delicate instrument than this. Not all moral decisions are so clear-cut, and there should be a positive side as well—not only what God does not want me to do, but what he does expect of me. Not only individually but also corporately, what does God want us to do as the church? We will gain increasing insight as we pray, as we study the nature of God through the Scriptures, and as we come to know him in our worship. *Thy will be done.* If we are committed to this, we are committed first to discovering as perfectly and completely as we can what is God's will. This is the essential first step, a continuing and developing process from which we can't opt out and still claim to be doing God's will. At each turning point, each moment of decision, we receive our directive to do God's will and our willingness to be faithful is tested.

• • •

Staying with the Gospel of Matthew, let us consider the text.

"For many are called, but few are chosen."[5] The guests have been given advance notice of the dinner. But when the servants arrived to tell them that everything was ready, they made last minute excuses. They prefer occupying themselves with their own affairs. They are like people who say that they have no time for religion. If they carry on their own business honorably, what more can God expect of them? Such people are not opposed to religion. They quietly leave it on one side. Jesus calls us to love God with all our hearts. So, what are the things that you and I love most? What are the things that we think about and worry over? We are not perfect people. We have are worries and preoccupations. Jesus knows we need many material things. We also need the love of the Living God. Human beings are made to love and worship him. Human life is not like a shallow pond where stagnant water cannot escape. Think of it more like a river that is heading to the sea. If we choose to live as if there were no God, we become locked within ourselves. And in the parable, our Lord shows how this attitude is an insult to God.

5. Matt 22:14.

So, what does the host in our parable do? Other servants are summoned and sent out into the streets to call in anyone who may be found to take the place of the original guests. So, they drag in the poor and destitute. And then, because there are still empty places, they bring in those who live outside the city, the most extreme dropouts. At this point, the king suddenly enters the hall where his usual guests are all assembled, and his attention is at once taken up by the appearance of one particular person who is not wearing proper wedding dress. He had made no effort to be worthy of the honor that had been shown to him. Like the earlier invited guest, he "made light of it."[6]

So, what was Jesus trying to teach us by this parable? God's invitation to us to enter into fellowship with him is an unconditional invitation, but when a person has accepted it—when they have come into the visible church—they are pledge to a definite effort to walk worthy of their calling. It is God's will that every human being shall learn to know, love, and obey him. However, he will not deal harshly with those who have little or no chance of hearing the Gospel of Jesus Christ. If they die ignorant of his love, they will be given fresh opportunities of learning about him. But what about those who have had the privilege of true and regular teaching and, yet, have turned away deliberately from it in open disobedience. The man in the parable was among the many called, but not among the few chosen. The wedding robe had been offered to him, as to the other guests. He chose to come in his own clothes. Speechless and shamed, he did not say how he came without the wedding garment. It was too late to put it on, too late to ask for mercy. So, was the one man cast out of the feast typical of many that would apparently accept the call but, in the end, be rejected?

As Anglicans, we have to believe there is such a place as hell. As Christians, we, the authors of this commentary, would find it difficult to believe that God, in his great mercy, would allow anyone to go there. For it is not part of God's plan that we should be separated from his love and face everlasting torment, but rather that we should enter the blessed condition of unending happiness in his presence. Our Lord does not picture the church as a society of righteous people. Christianity is for sinners and offers them forgiveness. This is why we are within the Christian fellowship with all its benefits. It is not by any virtue of our own but because God has called us into it. Like the people in the parable, dragged in from

6. Matt 22:5.

the highways, we were made to come in. One way or another, it was the message of Jesus that pulled us in. For this reason, we must have faith that the love of God that called us will keep us ever in his presence. And we must pray that we will be counted not only as one of the many that are called but to be numbered among the few that are chosen.

## The Kingdom of God and Equality

> He has shown the strength of his arm; he has scattered the proud in their conceit. He has cast down the mighty from their thrones and has lifted up the lowly. He has filled the hungry with good things and the rich he has sent away empty.
>
> —Luke 1:51–53

Mary's song, the Magnificat, is an amazing piece of Scripture. It is about God's intervention in the human story. However, we are still waiting for the proud to be scattered, the mighty brought down from their thrones and the poor fed. The answer would seem to be that we thought God would do this for us and that we had no part in bringing it about. We sing the song but very few of us want to change anything. We continue to support an established church controlled by a state apparatus that oppresses the poor. The Letter of James challenges the proud and mighty who have increased their wealth by robbing the poor. The Magnificat draws our attention to the role of Mary the mother of our Lord and the theme of the virgin birth. This last is a topic that is debated from time to time with varying degrees of intensity. As authors, our natural inclination is to interpret the virgin birth in this way: you cannot be partly a virgin; it is a human condition that is absolute in a world where blurred edges are commonplace. Pregnancy is the same, you either are or you are not pregnant. So is holiness, you either are or you are not holy. Through the offering of the virgin birth, Mary expressed, and the Gospel writers maintained, the absolute commitment to God that is necessary for the state of holiness to be lovable. Therefore, virginity is a metaphor for holiness and is also its concrete articulation.

A special birth presupposes some type of special conditions and persons. And, of course, we find it personally no problem that the virgin birth is true. This is God's world, and God can order it in any way that suits the divine purposes, although the great kindness of God lets us usually have fairly predictable events to try to come to terms with. For some people, our viewpoint might seem like a fudge, as if we are blurring edges that are meant to be sharply defined. If you are one of those people, then you will be very relieved to know that there is a scientific explanation for the virgin birth. The scientific term for virgin birth is "parthenogenesis." It is common in other species but not known in humanity apart from the occasion maintained in the Christian tradition. If parthenogenesis occurs, then the offspring of the process is invariably female because she will have received all her chromosomes (XX) from her mother and will be female.

Now, our wildly feminist side at once said, "So, Jesus was a woman and that is why she never married and why so many of the men of her day hated her!" No, that doesn't work, does it? It seems there are other possibilities but no, that seems to be too much science for a Sunday morning. What we are trying to do here is to demystify the notion of the virgin birth. And having given some focus to this, let us now think about Mary. Like each one of us who encounter the power and the majesty of God's purposes, Mary, in her faith, asks, "How shall this be?" She is not ready to be a mother, let alone to cradle in her womb the Son of the highest. And yet, as the angel paints in more detail, Mary takes the risk, not knowing what, in tangible, everyday terms, lies ahead for her, and says "yes." The Mary of the Gospels is different from the painted statues that so often provide the focus of Marian devotion. She is the handmaiden. The kingdom is proclaimed, the word is spoken, the messenger is sent—but all depends on the simple "yes" of the handmaiden, humbly, even if fearfully, spoken, with no sense of her own importance: "Behold the handmaid of the Lord, be it unto me according to thy word."[7] She is the willing and, so inevitably, the suffering servant—patient, obedient, present, attentive.

Only once is she center stage—her window of opportunity was terrifyingly narrow, but all history and all eternity turned on her answer. By the time she visits her cousin Elizabeth, she is already turning attention from herself to the God who has done great things, not just for her but throughout all generations—"holy is his name."[8] We, then, are called to be handmaidens, and that includes men and women, because we are as messengers seeking the divine will and ready to play our part in the bringing in of the kingdom of God. In preaching Christ to others, therefore, we

7. Luke 1:38.

8. Luke 1:49.

need always to be pointing beyond ourselves to the Lord, whose ambassadors we are and in whose ministry of reconciliation we are invited to share. The spirit of God, that same spirit who overshadows Mary, is sent to strengthen and to empower us for his service. When we are challenged by the powerful in this world, we shall know what to say. No one promised it would be easy for us. Mary was warned that a sword would also pierce her heart. We are called to be obedient and faithful. On the feast of St. Mary, the Blessed Virgin, we should think about the impact of female liberation upon the traditional methods of reading Scripture and upon our understanding of church tradition.

We, the authors of this commentary, want us to be struggling towards a more inclusive view of humanity and the Christian faith. It is interesting that in most novels and soap operas, and the Bible is no exception, all the best parts go to male characters. Are we to believe that Jesus chose only men to associate with and to authorize them alone? As a young woman, Mother Linda was told she was too clever for her own good and that once she married and settled down to motherhood, it would all make sense. You may perhaps like to imagine Mother Linda's reactions to that kind of patronizing platitude. Then, someone gave her a photograph of an icon that was from Jerusalem of Mary, queen of heaven. She was beautifully and cruelly encrusted with gems, eyes downcast, hands folded, very traditional. And as she reread Luke, she realized the men had got it all wrong. Well, they often do! To have stood in the presence of God and to have said, "Be it unto me according to your word,"[9] were not the actions of a pussycat. Clearly, this was the response of a stout-hearted and deeply loving woman who went knowingly into dangerously uncharted waters in the ark of faith. So, let us look into the language and the origins of some of the terminology. There is, for example, an argument that says that the term *virgin* derives from a feminized version of the Latin, which refers to women who were in charge of their own lives and not subject to any particular male authority. That certainly gives a new slant on the Virgin Mary. What we need is a new working through of what it means to be a woman in a male-dominated religion that needs rescuing from its own entrapment.

So, let's raise some dangerous but interesting questions. Can a male savior rescue women? Is the Church of England too masculine? Why are all its religious symbols male? We speak of Father and of Son and of brethren,

9. Luke 1:38.

but never of Mother, daughter, or sisters. Is there any basis for feminine symbols in Christianity? How can women find a place in the church? These questions have caused some women and men to look at teachings about Mary with new eyes. Maybe there are some positive elements for us in Mary, who is so esteemed by other branches of the church. Let's look more closely at Mary. It is often said that she is a survival of the goddess figures of Ancient Near Eastern religion. Such statements are often taken to discredit teaching about Mary as a true part of Christian teaching. But many biblical symbols and festivals were also common to the Ancient Near Eastern cultures. For example, the idea of the Messiah had its roots in the age-old concept of the god-king. The king in those societies was understood as a representative of the gods to the human world, and also a representative of society before the gods. Such a king was understood to be a savior. Later in the development of Jewish thought, in the wisdom literature, another dimension of feminine symbolism appears. The figure of wisdom as a female personification of God appears in writings such as the Old Testament book of Proverbs. Not unlike the Christian concept of the word, wisdom is written about as though it were a second "person" of God, who acts as a delegate of God the Father. In the wisdom tradition, however, this second "person" of God is not male but female. She is not a divine "son" but a divine "daughter," Sophia.[10]

As we move then to the New Testament, we find it does not include much on the figure of Mary, the mother of Jesus, either as a historical figure or as a theological symbol. This suggests that Mary had not become linked with the theology of the church. And where did she go after the ascension? She must surely have been an object of particular respect, given her relationship to Jesus. It would not be fanciful to suggest that she had a major role within the early church in those first days. The texts are silent. And we should ask why? There is historical evidence that the actions and influence of women was actively suppressed, yet the use of feminine symbols was not unusual in the Old Testament or in Judaism. Our scholarship has shown that images such as Israel as God's bride, Israel as a mother, and God's wisdom personified as a feminine being were quite traditional. The early Christian church inherited these feminine symbols and continued to use them. At first, they were adapted and developed in the New Israel, quite independently of teaching about Mary as an individual. So, why do we have these feminine symbols of the person of the mother of Jesus?

10. A feminine aspect of the divine sometimes identified with the Holy Spirit (Prov 8); Silva, Trinidad, "Naming the Wise"; Steiner, *Isis Mary Sophia*, 50.

Is it possible, then, to think of the image of Christ and the church in a liberating way, where reconciled relations to God are expressed through reconciled relations to one another? In her ages-old role as the representative of faithful love, Mary can help us reach out into a new expression of what it means to be Christian and liberated. In her courage and selflessness, she does show us the way. Without her, nothing would be as it is. She could have said "no," God would not have forced her. Wherever you come from historically and culturally, Mary has a unique place. Mary, in her womanhood, shows us what persistent, insistent love can achieve. So, with an open and Anglican heart, we can still say, "Hail, Mary, full of grace, the Lord is with thee. Blessed art thou amongst women and blessed is the fruit of thy womb, Jesus. Holy Mary, mother of God, pray for us sinners now and at the hour of our death. Amen."

• • •

So, what was the kingdom of God and how would it be understood by the readers of the Letter of James? The kingdom was the coming of a new age in which Israel would be out of the clutches of the Roman Empire. So, they waited for a universal king who would help them to promote righteousness and peace. Now, Jesus sometimes speaks of the kingdom as though it were a process going on in his own time and connected with his ministry. Wherever people begin to accept his teaching and live by the laws of the kingdom, he seems to say the kingdom is already beginning. The two ideas of the kingdom—that it is a future event to be anticipated and a present reality in the process of arriving—are not necessarily contradictory. Jesus speaks of first one aspect and then another. But underlying both is the firm assurance that God's will must finally prevail. It may be that Jesus expected the perfect realization of the kingdom only in the future, and used future language to describe it, but also taught that even in the present age, people could apprehend its coming and enter into its anticipation. Often, there is a conflict between the demands of the kingdom of God and the wishes and desires of our hearts. This type of conflict is an ancient theme and much of the Bible is based upon it.

We have only to think of the story of Noah and the great flood. We cannot say for certain what happened. But something must have taken place, for the story grew out of an upheaval that threatened the foundations of the world. The creation that God had made was washed away with all the mud and ugliness of a flood. A drenched and weary world awaited a second creation, another chance to get things right. In the Christian gospel, we see how it was confirmed that Jesus was the Messiah. But how was he to carry out that role? Jesus' newly revealed relationship with God is followed by the temptations in the desert, Jesus had to be aware of all the power and love that was within him. This was a time of testing and working out how he would establish the kingdom. Jesus fasted forty days and forty nights. There is no way of knowing if Jesus went completely without food or merely the privation of living on what little could be found in the wilderness. But it was sufficiently serious to cause real hunger. The Son of God was not exempt from human physical needs. But Jesus did not need to be hungry. He has the power to satisfy physical needs by miraculous means. Later miracles prove this to be true. But Jesus recognized in his hunger and experience designed by God to show that his mission was to be one of continued privation, for the sake of his ministry of the word of God. As the Son of God, he could surely claim with absolute confidence the physical protection that God promises. The Son of God can live only in a relationship of trust that needs no test. What was tested was Jesus' loyalty to his Father, even when it meant renouncing the easy way out of allowing the ends to justify the means. The Son of God refused to compromise his loyalty. Jesus' rejection of the temptations in the wilderness shows that the purpose of the kingdom of God was to establish the spiritual rule of God in the obedient heart of people set free from sin.

So, Christianity confronts us with two basic truths of our existence. Firstly, we are created by God's deliberate design and with God's great care. Secondly, we are sinful. For reasons that we do not know and cannot really guess at, God made us in such a way that we are heedless, tending to do what we want, when we want to, regardless of the consequences. The Holy Bible is about the tension between these two basic facts. The whole of our lives is about these two facts. These facts are the mystery at the heart of our religion, and they are the joy and the anguish combined. They help us to understand the mission of Christ incarnate in Jesus. We feel angry at our failure to resist sin. We know the horror of sin and the wickedness that is sin and its desire to unmake, to tear apart, to destroy; this is our pain. So, let's focus, then, on our Lord's pain as he passed through the test of our suffering? We see him for forty days in the desert. The desert is a strange place where the light prevents vision in its blinding heat. Vegetation is scarce. The very landscape shifts and changes in the winds that blow the sands relentlessly, endlessly around; the desert is like a nightmare where reality is warped and frightening alone. You face yourself, your own inner self, and learn to pray. Jesus prayed, and his prayer was the battle that he waged against sin. That is what prayer is; that is exactly why it is so blasphemous to take the holy name in vain. Jesus was tempted to prove his own identity. He was tempted by worldly power. All these temptations make sense. And all of them tell us what ways we, too, are tempted; perhaps, the root of sin is the desire to have all our needs and desires fulfilled, and all at once, just as Adam and Eve did in the garden. We want satisfaction, we want security, and we want control—and we want it all now. Those are very potent and dangerous desires to have. St. Augustine was the person who, more than any other, developed the church's doctrine of sin. We don't always agree with him, we have to say, but he is a fluent and elegant writer with a memorable turn of phrase. He wrote that Adam was able not to sin, while we are not able not to sin.[11] Clearly, because Jesus was not able to sin, one day, we will also become not able to sin. What we need to remember in Lent is the way in which Jesus forged his human nature into that blessed state, it didn't just happen. There were temptations along the way, but Jesus fought until his human nature was not able to sin. That is what the desert story is all about. It was the divine aspect of Jesus that made it possible for him to overcome sin. We cannot, in our present state, achieve this freedom. But we can follow Jesus' pattern in the way in which we resist it. For what Jesus did was draw on his knowledge of Scripture. Now, Jesus had other knowledge of the Godhead that we do not have. But he used the intelligence that we have. In his humanity, Jesus used our stubbornness, our cleverness. These attributes are, if you like, the positive sides of the very qualities that cause us to sin. The only difference is that Jesus was more stubborn, more clever, and more versatile than we are. But the pattern still holds true for us. So, locate your stubborn, clever, versatile self and develop it. Train it up and feed it with study and with prayer. But the great mercy of God is that our judgment will rest on our intention, not fully on our record. It will depend on what we tried to do and the struggles we have had to undergo, rather than a dismal record of our many failures. So, take heart and continue to trust in the Christian faith.

• • •

11. Augustine, *City of God*.

Let us look at something in the Christian gospel that would have led the readers of James to think very seriously about equality issues and their place in an unequal world. I refer to the parable of the vineyard workers.[12]As authors of this commentary, we have to confess to considerable sympathy with the disgruntled laborers who worked all day, yet did not receive more wages than those who had just arrived and done just a few hours work. So, some of them had worked all day in the blazing sun; others had hardly done five minutes work. All got the same wage. Whatever happened to differentials and seniority? The gospel story seems a strange one. A winegrower hires some workers who were standing around hoping for work, as was the custom in those days. They agreed to a wage for the day's work. Then the winegrower hires some more workers and agrees to pay them their whack. In each case, there was agreement between the employer and the workers, and all seemed fair and square. The trouble only arose when the workers got together and started to make comparisons. Then the first group of workers decided that what they had previously agreed was no longer okay. You will notice that it was the workers who changed their minds about the deal. *Why?* They changed their minds because they did not like it when other people got in on the deal that they thought was a private and exclusive arrangement with the employer. Each set of laborers was anxious to preserve their own sense of being special. That was why they accepted a fair wage. The complaint that the first group of laborers made was fair enough, but the motivation behind their complaint was selfish. Yes, both groups of workers got the same pay, and yes, the first group had to work for a considerably longer period. But the first group of workers were unable to find a source of gladness in the good fortune of the second group of workers. Like the elder brother in the parable of the prodigal son, their attitude was ungenerous.

As we are all too sadly aware, God's standards and our own are by no means always the same. So, what Jesus was talking about here was a means of judging that takes God's point of view into account and not the limited human one. Of the laborers hired later, we are told that their idleness was due to lack of opportunity, not unwillingness to work. Thus, their pay was not based upon what they had done but rather upon what they would have done, given a further opportunity. In judging other people, we have always to remember the things that would hold others back

12. Matt 20:1–16.

from realizing their full potential. The religious people of Jesus' day did not believe in the conversion of sinners and tax collectors. Jesus, however, refused to regard any group of people as beyond hope. What really gets up Jesus' nose is the hypocrisy and smugness of the upright and respectable. Jesus makes it clear to them and to us that he did not come into the world to live with good people but to find the sinners who needed his help. Well, does this get us any further forward in trying to understand the parable in our Gospel reading from Matthew? Yes, I think it does. It teaches us that we are not special at the expense of others but that God, in God's mercy and justice, has made each one of us to be equally beloved. No one can say, "I am better than he is, or I don't deserve what she deserves, I am not good enough." That has some very tricky implications for Christian living. It means that we really are not free to judge people's worth. It means that we can make no distinction between even people we like as opposed to people that we find it hard to like. They all have equal claim on us because we all have equality under God. So, the story that Jesus told here is focusing our attention on God and directing us to look at and treat each other from God's point of view.

## Conclusion

We have now reached the conclusion to chapter 3, which gave focus to the knowledge of God, righteousness, the kingdom of God, equality issues among the faithful, and the theology of the cross. In this, we have taken the opportunity to reflect upon how we use the Bible to understand the concept of wisdom with a particular emphasis of how this is understood by the Letter of James. We never come cold to the Bible. There are always things within our own lives that help us to connect to the Scripture that direct and address our own concerns. Many of us, over the years, have turned to the psalms for consolation and to find a voice to express the storms and tempests of our emotions, doubts, joys, and despairs as we travel the road of faith home to God. At times, a feast, and at times, a famine, the psalms can put into words what we feel, can reassure us that it is okay to feel like that, and that we are not alone. As in so many places in the Bible, all the frailty of our human nature is acknowledged. In the end, we are small and we hurt, but God's love is there and is solid. But if our life chances and experience have taught us that there is little we can depend on, how do we know that God is there? It is exactly when we are at the point of greatest desperation—when we reach out in longing to God, feeling that there has simply got to be some reason, some hope, some comfort. Feeling that God is our last and our only hope, then, at that point, God's reality is declared. For God's concern is to care for those who cannot care for themselves. Once we are beyond our strength, then God takes over. And let's face it, we all need God's help.

Wisdom tells us that experience is valuable—we can learn from the past. But we can't alter the past. It's the future that matters now, and we have a real chance to shape that. It can be wasteful to spend time and energy trying to preserve things as they are or were—to recreate the past. It can't be done. There are many that dread the future because it appears empty, or because there are no landmarks, and they long for the security of familiar things. It isn't clearly mapped out because it hasn't happened yet. The Christian is to press forward—there can be no going back. And the future for those with faith is not empty. It is full of hope and opportunity, widening beyond this world into the life of the world to come. If there are no maps, there is, beckoning us on, the light of Christ who has gone before us. There is no going back once we have taken up the cross. Following one of our Anglican prayers, let us put aside what is behind and press on towards the goal.[13] It's an important piece of advice for us in our individual lives as Christians and collectively as a church community. A pilgrim on a journey has to travel light. In terms of worldly cares and possessions, this mean that if these become a huge burden, we shall never get anywhere. But the worst burden is the burden of sin, of a heavy conscience. We have to learn to let go—to accept Jesus at his word, to accept God's forgiveness, to believe that when we have humbly and honestly sought and received forgiveness for our sins, that is that.

We forget what is behind and work for righteousness and peace. And we have to learn to be forgiving—there is no load heavier to carry, no weight more guaranteed to prevent us from taking advantage of our opportunities, than the burden of grudges against others that so often we won't let go of—things that people have said or done to us. As Christians, ready to do our Lord's will, we need every day to pray: forgive us our trespasses as we forgive those who trespass against us. We must try at the end of each day to draw a line under it in the ledger—to lay aside the burden of sins we have committed and the things others have done against us, so that we don't start off the next day with an even heavier load. This ensures

13. Collect for the eighteenth Sunday after Trinity, *Book of Common Prayer*, 209.

that we aren't hanging on to any unnecessary burdens that prevent us from pressing forward or provide us with an excuse for not doing so. If all this applies to us as individuals, it applies to every group of which we are a part—as family, as a congregation, as members of the Church of England, as Christians in the widest sense of the whole church, as citizens of the United Kingdom and of the world. Forget what is past, look to the goal, the ideal, to Christ. Our prayers are a vital part of our life if we are to achieve anything. And as we have already said in all this, we shall need God's help. And this is our prayer through Jesus Christ our Lord.

This brings us to the wisdom of the Christian understanding of the incarnation, when God became a human being but remained God. What we believe about Jesus is important. Jesus, on two different occasions, asked the question, "What do you believe about me?" He asked the Pharisees, "What do you think about the Christ? Whose son is he?"[14] And he asked his disciples, "Whom do men say that I am?" "Whom do you say that I am?"[15] He faces us with this same question, and on the day of judgment, we shall have to give account of our answer. The Pharisees replied that Christ is the son of David—in other words, a man. However, this is not the complete answer. It is not enough just to believe in Jesus the man who lived in Palestine, and as we have considered in a previous chapter, this is not being a Christian. It is true, but it is only half the truth. Peter is in no doubt that Jesus is the Son of God.[16] He also knew that Jesus was a real man—as all his disciples and all those who live and worked with him during those busy years of his earthly ministry knew that. They had seen Jesus tired and hungry, sad and happy, sympathetic and sometimes angry. Peter never doubted that Jesus was a real person, but in this God-given flash of intuition, he saw that Jesus was also truly God. Mary, his mother, knew this; doubting Thomas, among others, came to realize it after Jesus' resurrection. We, too, must believe this. We believe and confess our Lord Jesus Christ as God and human. Perfect God and perfect humanity. The Apostles' Creed places these two truths side by side. We believe in Jesus Christ, God's only son, our Lord—and then, in the next breath—who was conceived by the Holy Ghost, born of the Virgin Mary, suffered under Pontius Pilate, was crucified, dead, and buried.

Jesus' conception was miraculous, but his birth of a human mother was perfectly ordinary. He lived a normal human life, and he suffered at

14. Matt 22:42.

15. Matt 16:13–16.

16. Matt 16:16.

a particular time in history that we can date by looking up the records of the Roman governor Pontius Pilate. He was crucified, dead, and buried. He really did die, like any mortal man—his side was pierced on the cross and there flowed out blood mingled with water. So, why is it so important that we should believe that Jesus was both truly God and truly human? First of all, because we need to know the truth about God as far as we can, so that we can worship him in truth. And also, because wrong belief about Jesus affects our belief about humanity and the world. The fact that Jesus became truly human means that the world really does matter. If God so loved the world that he gave his only begotten son to share our human experience and save the world, then Christianity can never be escapism from the world. That Jesus was both God and man isn't essay to understand. It cannot really be explained. This is one of the mysteries of the Christian faith. It is only by accepting both of these facts together that we can make sense of the account of Jesus in the New Testament. The Christian faith is wonderful, and the more we can think about our creeds and use them in our prayers, the more deeply we shall comprehend the wonders and the glory of God and the greater sense we shall be able to make of our own human life. The book of the Revelation of St. John the Divine is also known as the Apocalypse. It is one of the least preached-on books in the Bible at the moment because it is so difficult to understand, or so say many modern preachers, but not the authors of this commentary. No one really writes in this sort of way anymore—or do they? We would suggest that the writing of apocalyptic material has shifted from the holy to the mundane areas of life. The word "apocalyptic" means revealing things to do with the end of the world. Our newspapers and journals are brimming over with all sorts of things about the future. We are warned of the greenhouse effect, then that there was a mistake and it is not happening. We are warned about the destruction of the rain forests. Quite soon, I expect that new experts will claim that was scaremongering. At an individual level, those of us who have gone to great lengths to alter our diets to lower our cholesterol intake learned in the last few years that this is to no avail. Some cholesterol is good for you. So, eat butter, drink milkshakes, and be merry, for tomorrow they'll change the guidance anyway.

When we were in our early twenties and thirties, the apocalyptic of our time led us to join the Campaign for Nuclear Disarmament. We genuinely believed that without the urgent petitioning of governments by concerned citizens, we would be annihilated in a nuclear conflict between the two great powers of the northern hemisphere. So we went on marches, organized local protests, and camped out for weekends at Upper Heyford and Molesworth peace camps. Where is the might of those superpowers now? The Soviet Empire crumbled into ruins and into near chaos, stalked by the twin threats of economic disaster and starvation. The empire crumbles, states fall apart, and small people suffer untold and unguessable agonies of pain. The Soviet Union has been replaced by something far worse, in which sovereign states have either been taken over or invaded. And what of the other superpower? In the early 1990s, campaigning for the presidential elections had begun with a scarcity of candidates to run for nomination. Why? The problems that faced the US were so immense, and while capitalism crowed over the demise of so-called Communism, the grim reaper of recession cut swaths of alarm and dismay in the stock market and banks. The current American regime has gone so far to the autocratic right, it is unclear if there is any democracy left in the country. And some people say that what St. John wrote on the island of Patmos two millennia ago is hard to understand?

We face, as we have always faced in the perilous nature of our flesh, secular disintegration of such magnitude that we should be scanning St. John's writings to see what we can learn. For when St. John writes of the end of all things, he does so in terms of the glory of God. Juxtaposing passages of light with dark, St. John depicts the end of all things as being ultimately in the destiny of all creation to reflect the glory of God. And the beauty of the visions given to St. John on that tiny island of Patmos—the vision of the city that is God's proper abode, where God's servants shall see him face to face—can't you just feel the yearning of generations of people hungry for God who have found comfort and strength from St. John? To see God, face to face, in all the richness of his glory. For John, this city represents all the inhabited earth. We are not lost. God is not distant but beside us. God's glory has been and is being revealed. That is part of the work we are called to do. We are part of that revelation. As we pray and work for the kingdom, let us join St. John in saying, "Amen, come, Lord Jesus." And in our endnote, let us consider our Lord's passion and the theology of the cross.

We further conclude this chapter on wisdom with a consideration of the theology of the cross. But first, we ask the question, did Jesus have to die and why do some people think it was inevitable and even necessary?[17]

17. Isiorho, *Faith in Church Newspapers*, 115.

If humankind had taken on Jesus' teaching and used it to build a world of justice and peace, would there have been a need for the death of Christ? Humankind rejected the Lord of life and instead embraced greed and strife. Jesus was not crucified for our sins but died because of them. He was not a blood sacrifice to appease an angry God, but rather, he gave his life willingly, just as a soldier would die for their country. The important thing here is that we do not have the last say because in him, as an individual, the universal consequences of sin were annulled. His humanity hurt, the wounds were real, and he still bears the scars today. But his divinity was enough to stop the chain of cause and effect, the chain of sin and death.

Christ Jesus has overcome death. He has done this for himself and for us all. He is alive and can be found in prayer, in times of doubt and distress, bereavement and sorrow. He is also to be found in times of hope and gladness. At a funeral, we meet together to pay tribute for the faithful departed, to thank God for our loved ones who have gone on before us into the heavenly realms. We have already commended them in trust to God, but we seek now further consolation. For it is in God that we find the strength to go on. God sent his only begotten son Jesus Christ to be in solidarity with us and to share our suffering. When we turn to him to ask for consolation and courage, we are not asking a distant God to take pity on us. We are talking to the intimate God, whose entry into our human frailty and sorrows was complete. It is the suffering and death of Good Friday that makes Easter Sunday realizable. Without the cross, there would be no empty tomb to bear witness to the resurrection. For Jesus truly died, was buried, and rose again to eternal life. Jesus is alive. This is the essential message of Easter and of the Christian faith. But what does this mean to the sad and the lonely, those mourning the death of a loved one? Where was Jesus during your bereavement, when the pain was most raw? The answer is that Jesus is there in your suffering, feeling what you feel. So, what are we doing in funerals and memorial services for the faithful departed? What we are doing is not praying for our departed loved ones as if we can save them by our efforts, for we know that we are only saved through the mercy of God offered freely to all through Christ Jesus. So, what we are doing is very different. We are here to bear witness to God of their goodness and of their precious individual worth. We do this with sorrow that we no longer see them and touch them and embrace them, but we also do this with confidence in our heavenly Father, who yearns over all creation until all are returned to him in the fullness of his glory. Surely our testimony that we, in our turn and in our fallen human way, have loved these people is powerful witness to God of all they did for the kingdom while they walked in flesh under the yoke of time. Liberated from the burden, they now walk as children of light in closer communion with God. We, too, are in communion with them because we are in communion with Christ, and we, too, are inhabited by the Holy Spirit. And for some of us, the wound of separation is too raw to revisit unless very gently. For we are filled with fear at the thought of death and full of anger that those we love are denied us until the fullness of God's purpose is revealed. The resurrection of our Lord Jesus Christ is our pledge from God that there is life beyond the grave. It is also a pledge of what that life will be. Heaven is where God is and heaven is being with God. We are inheritors of the kingdom of heaven, which is the goal of our pilgrimage here on earth.

The readers of the Letter of James, like those of Paul, would understand that when Jesus Christ appears again, there will be a general resurrection of the dead, which will be followed by the end of the world. As for the nature of the resurrected body, it will not have the same characteristics as the body we have now. But the identity of the individual will be preserved in spite of the change. We shall acquire a new instrument for our personality that will be nevertheless a proper successor to the present body and will actually be linked in definite continuity with it. The new body will be immortal, the final victory of life over death. God, who made the heavens and the earth, is still a loving God who knows all his children. So, God sees all, forgives all, and heals all in the fullness of eternal life. God sent his Son Jesus to live in our flesh and to suffer all the troubles and the pains of human life, so that we might become as he is, perfect and loving, bringing good to all. For through faith in Jesus and what he has done, we can find the strength to face bereavement. Through faith, we can trust and live freely in this life and the next; through this faith, we can pray and surrender into God's gracious keeping the souls of our loved ones.

So, in this, we ask that the bereaved be comforted and have strength. Give thanks to God for letting us know our loved ones. And offer their prayers to God for their rest in his everlasting arms. For God loves us and has prepared a place for each one of us in heaven—to be with him forever—for all eternity. The faithful departed reminds us that we need to fix our values on the eternal values of heaven. The Christian faith teaches us that death is not an end of all things but a beginning. Yes, it hurts that we should have lost someone, but they are not lost to God and so they are not finally lost to us. So, leaving the faithful departed to God, and giving thanks for all that they meant to us, let us go forward in faith and in trust and love. And all this in Jesus' name as we draw near to God. Our proclamation of Jesus' death and our faith in his resurrection tells us that our powers and our decisions do not have the last word. It tells us that God is underwriting the universe with redeeming, restoring love. He calls us urgently today, as he has always called. And what response does he want? God is no dictator but an inviter. He says, "See, I have shown you the way. You are free to come. I do have work for you and joy for you to look forward to. There is purpose and reason and effectiveness in your being alive; come, please come." Yes, God wants us in all the frailty of our human freedom that leads to so many crocked choices. He wants us to turn to him and to return the invitation, to say "*yes*" in answer to his call. The same "*yes*" that Jesus said, despite his dying anguish. That is a profoundly radical and fundamental "*yes*" to life. God yearns for our response of "*yes*" to him. That "*yes*" has consequences. That "*yes*" calls us into struggle. For how can we be at home with God and see our fellow human beings suffer? How can we know the peace that only God can bring and not want to see that peace abroad on the earth? In our individual inner lives, that "*yes*" brings peace and certainty. In our outer, social lives, as members of the human race, that "*yes*" calls us into the same redeeming, restoring work that Christ himself was engaged in. And that is the challenge of the Christian faith. Jesus was ready to go all the way for us. Are we ready to go all the way with him, listen to James, and disestablish the Church of England?

## Endnote: The Theology of the Cross

Our Lord's resurrection from the dead will be the subject of our next chapter and how we draw some wider conclusions as we try to understand the implications of the incarnation. But first, let us focus on the earthly reality of the events at Calvary. We know the Bible story so well that we sometimes forget how real the pains and agonies that our Lord endured were. So, let's just get the picture in our mind's eye for a moment. Imagine the scene: three bedraggled, beaten men being crucified, hung up in public shame to be an example and a warning to all. A standard

Roman capital punishment, and a very long and slow way to die, basically dying of exposure and dehydration.

• • •

We concentrate on the elements of wood, iron, flesh, blood, and heart present during the crucifixion. Let us be still in the presence of God. Let us think first of all of the wood, the actual, physical material on which our Lord was crucified. Wood: that most homely of all substances, the warming crackle of a good wood fire; the comfort of an old wooden rocking chair; the strength and beauty of a polished oak dining table; the dark wood of many secrets of a bed; the security of our familiar pews in the local Church; the sad wood of our last resting place, our coffin. But that is tamed wood, manicured and domesticated. What about wild wood? The savage force of trees that sunders rocks; the wood that breaks your back to hew it down; the wood that splits your finger as you saw it; the wood that splinters and penetrates your flesh as you plane it; the rough wood, the wild wood, that our Lord knew so well from the carpenter's shop of Nazareth. Feel that wild wood, rough-cut with harsh, unfinished angles, sharp as sorrow, jagged with splinters—cruel-edged wood made by God, mismade by humanity. And the weight of it—world-heavy weight of the cross as our Lord carried it to Calvary, with its unyielding rigidity, as his slight human frame was nailed to it. And how it was as undisturbed as the Son of God cried his last cries of agony on it. How it went on being wood unchanged, untouched in its nature when the crucifixion was over. Wild wood, grown strong in soil of sin and death, embraced by Christ because of us, becomes the tree of life.

• • •

The second element is iron. The most widely used of all metals is remarkable for its obduracy, hard as nails. Iron tortured in furnaces and contorted into fantastic shapes, bent, shaped, forced into our service. And for what? Iron chains and iron bars; iron grubbed out from the earth where the Creator laid it in darkness; iron used on the cross, the three nails that pierced our Lord's hands and feet, the spear that pierced his side. Harsh, unfeeling iron entering the beloved flesh of our Savior, hurting him. Feel the hardness; feel the cold into the warmth of his living flesh, that slight resistance as the elastic skin at first refuses entry to the deadly intruders. Think of the careless force of the soldiers as they push the iron into flesh.

We think about the many screaming pains unleashed by this attack of our Dear One's body. Iron hidden in the earth by God, rifled from the depths by greedy people, anxious for power and wealth. Iron as inflexible as human pride, hard and cold as death.

• • •

The third element is flesh. Yes, he was real; his flesh was just daily flesh like ours. Dark eyes, the tanned skin of open-air life. The hair, the sweat, the hunger, and the need to wash, just daily flesh like ours. This, then, the final anguish on the cross is not just the nightmare of acute pain, the drying death of slow exposure that crucifixion brings, the pulling from the joints of aching arms, but the shame of nakedness held high for all to jeer at. Jesus was a man passionate for God, a man reclaiming what God once made and saw that it was good, at what a cost? We are like drunkards in the sinful reeling of our flesh, stumbled far from God's way. We lurch out of our own control. The good we would do, we do not do, and the bad that we would not, we do. But Jesus, his straight back wilder than unbending wood. His soft flesh harder than iron set on God. He fought like an addict against the lure of sin. For he was tempted in every respect as we are, and he could yet have said, "*No*," but like his mother, he would not.

One by whom and for whom all things were made. Word made flesh, you died calling on God. It was the dying of your old humanity that cried, "My God, my God, why hast thou forsaken me."[18] And Jesus' new humanity could declare it is accomplished. Your death was ours, because of us, but not on behalf of us or instead of us. For you had no need of death, you who are Life itself.

• • •

The fourth element is blood. Bright red blood of artery; dark, tired blood of vein-pulsing life force. Visible carrier of our inward nutrients, bearer of our genes, our inner fingerprint: blood. Blood so incorrigibly liquid, blood running with all the exuberance of life, blood that draws carrion feeders by its stench; blood that dries as we wither into death; blood from the thorns that mocked the noble brow of the sovereign of the universe; blood from the hands outstretched in love; blood from his feet, walking a mission to save; blood and water, from the riven side all flowed.

18. Matt 27:46.

Mysterious words: "Drink from it, all of you, for this is the blood of my covenant, which is poured out for many for the forgiveness of sins."[19] See where Christ's blood streams in the firmament; it is above, it is below, it enters every nook and cranny where depravity and filth of sin lurk. It is triumphantly bloody; it cannot be stopped or stemmed, dammed up or cornered. How can you hold it to check it? It runs as urgently as a mother's love bringing life, health, peace.

• • •

The fifth element is heart: not vulgar pink heart, pulsing with sentiment, puffed with self-important romance and story, but heart, the essence of a person, the seat of thought, of deciding. The heart's the place where we fall short. And the heart's the place where we turn away from God. For the heart can be deceitful above all things and desperately corrupt. Hearts of stone, cold hearts consumed with pride, self-satisfied and dying with the glamor of ego. The inward heart is deep, but who can search it out but God? But the heart of Jesus beating faithfully and truly towards God. The heart of Jesus, yearning over the children of this world, bleeding yet defying death for the daughters and sons of Eve. He walked in our flesh to restore our hearts. Heart calls to heart across the depths of time and space. It is the heart of Jesus that speaks, "Come unto me, all who labor and are heavy laden, for I have won you rest and peace and joy."[20]

19. Matt 26:27b–28.

20. Matt 11:28–29.

# *Chapter 4*

# Draw Near to God

## Introduction

Draw near to God, and he will draw near to you.

—James 4:8a

THERE WAS ONCE A man who was very devout as a Christian. He was forever in church and always reading the Bible—that kind of thing. Eventually, he applied to join a very strict monastery. After a suitable period of novitiate testing, he was fully professed and donned a complete habit. He already knew what the rules were: complete silence except for a meeting with the father abbot, which would be held once every five years. At this meeting, the monk would be allowed to say two words.

Well, the first five years went by, and the man was sent for to see the abbot. "Now, my son, remember you have only two words, so choose wisely." Living such an austere life was not turning out as the monk had believed. He was cold and uncomfortable all the time and could not really settle as he thought he would. So, he looked at the abbot sitting in his big, cushioned chair and he thought about the wooden seats that the rest of the ordinary brothers had, and he snapped, "Hard seats." The abbot looked taken aback but he blessed the monk and sent him on his way.

Another long five years ground by and the monk was next in the father abbot's study. Same ritual until the moment came for him to speak his two precious words. It was beautifully warm in the abbot's office, with a good fire burning cheerfully in the hearth, the only warm room in the freezing monastery. The monk snarled, "Too cold." The abbot sighed and the monk departed.

Picture the scene another five years on. Same abbot, same monk, same occasion. This time, the father abbot inquired, "And what do you have to say for yourself this time, my son?" The monk looked at him with an expression where loathing and exhaustion were evenly mixed. "I quit!" he announced. "Thank goodness," responded the abbot, "You have done nothing but complain ever since you got here."

We started with personal testimony in the form of a narrative about misplaced holiness. So, why bother with this joke? Well, because some people approach the Christian faith in this kind of begrudging spirit. They give stuff up expecting to feel extra holy and all they experience is a lowering of the spirit and a species of spiritual withdrawal symptoms, maybe even physical ones. This is because the offering is not from the heart. It is also because the abstinence is not accompanied by something to put in its place. And what should be put in its place—prayer, Bible reading, and self-examination? This leads us into reflections from the Old Testament and the presence God in this world and the world to come. This chapter of our commentary will be concerned with the concept of resurrection as we think it might be understood by the readers of the Letter of James. So, it will include an examination of the early Christian Easter tradition focusing on the appearance of the resurrected Lord and discovery of Jesus' empty tomb. An evaluation of the work of Pannenberg, Bultman, and Ricoeur will draw upon these themes, making explicit their particular understanding of the doctrine of the resurrection. We conclude with a personal statement to the effect that Jesus really did rise from the dead and that this should be understood not just as historical fact but an article of faith.

## Drawing Near to God in the Old Testament

We continue this chapter with the dedication of Solomon's temple, which was a tremendous moment in the history of the Jewish people. In the Old Testament, there is an underlying uncertainty about God's presence and God's attitude. Sometimes, God is close, and all is well. But his presence can be withdrawn, because of sin or disobedience, and then everything is wrong. The Jewish nation desperately needed to feel the nearness of God, but yet, this experience was frightening. Anyone who presumed to come too close was in grave danger of being overwhelmed by the infinite greatness and glory of God. And the presence of God presented demands of obedience and of morality, which were far from being comfortable. The story of the Old Testament is one of a constantly reoccurring cycle, of the people coming close to God, accepting his demands as the price of not overwhelming them, and assuring them of his continuing presence and support. And then, gradually rebelling against his discipline, as selfishness, pride, and self-sufficiency take over. When this happened, it was the job of the prophets, people of spiritual insight, to bring the people back to God and restore a right relationship with God. It is a universal pattern that we can recognize even in our own lives.

The presence of God then was desirable, even necessary, but uncomfortable, quite possibly dangerous, and for a long time, rather unpredictable. The building of the temple marked an important stage in the religious development of Israel. It pointed to a more permanent and predictable relationship with God, but still, there was the commitment to loyalty and obedience, and there was the basic assumption that to approach God required humility and penitence. Forgiveness was the prime gift that people needed from God. Certainly, it was what needed to come first. No one could possibly have the nerve to approach God proudly and presumptuously.

Moses meets God in the holy and burning bush and is sent back to the land of Egypt to lead Israel out of slavery. He is hesitant about this. To begin with, there is the desire to know "what God" is speaking—this results in the disclosure of the divine name and its mysterious explanation, "I AM WHO I AM."[1] Then, Moses tries further delaying tactics—first, maintaining that the Israelites wouldn't believe him, then suggesting that he would be incompetent at the job. And finally, when God has "dealt" with both of these excuses, he simply asks God to send somebody else. To get so many people to follow him, Moses must have been quite a charismatic leader.

Moses already had experience of exile. He knew what he was leading the Hebrews into. Moses knew that the motif of the Passover night would always mark his people; they would eat bitter herbs and unleavened bread. One of the things that can be seen in the life of Moses is the sense of struggle. True faith can only take place when people are prepared

1. Exod 3:14.

to strive with God. It is only when Jacob struggles with God by the fords of the Jabbok that he becomes Israel.[2] So, what God did Moses meet? He met the God of his fathers, the God of the promise, the Liberator God, who heard the cries of his people and was acting to set them free. Moses encountered the God who was so much alive that his name meant life, his name meant the continuing power of creative existence. And Moses standing in the crevice of a rock is promised that he will see the back of God—even if not his face. That is as far as God is prepared to go; there is a boundary, an inequality between humanity and divinities that even Moses ultimately cannot cross. But Moses' request for God's presence to be with Israel is at least partially answered in his own person, for as he comes down the mountain, his face shines like the rays of the sun reflecting the glory of God. He has so lost himself in his concern for his people that he has become, in his person, one of the means by which God's presence will journey with Israel from Sinai.

The Old Testament speaks of an elusive God. It is the back of God that Moses glimpses for a moment—not his face. The Old Testament God is the same God as the one who meets two disciples on the road to Emmaus[3]—but disappears as soon as he is recognized—or who tells Mary in the garden not to cling to him.[4] He cannot remain with us unless we are willing to let him go. If we did not have an elusive God, we could not have a longing for the vision of God, nor could we experience faith and even life itself as a journey. A journey in which God is always one step ahead of us, a journey that sometimes can lead us to places we have never been before, and at other times, lead us back towards familiar scenes to know them more deeply than we did the first time. We stand, then, on the Emmaus road, like those two disciples despairing and failing to understand the message of the Scriptures. It is only when, finally, through the Old Testament that we have begun to grasp why the Cross has happened and that the Cross is then transformed into the resurrection.

• • •

We stay with the Old Testament and consider the ministry of the prophet Jeremiah, who is often thought of as a prophet of doom and disaster. On account of his feelings of suffering, disillusionment, and despair, he is

2. Gen 32:22.
3. Luke 24:13–35.
4. John 20:17.

sometimes referred to as dismal Jeremiah or Jeremiah, the prophet in the mire. However there is also much in the book of the prophet Jeremiah about salvation. There is no life in the Old Testament that more closely resembles the life of Jesus than that of Jeremiah. Like Jesus, he wanted an inwardly felt religion. For this reason, both Jesus and Jeremiah found themselves in dispute with the religious leaders of their day. Jeremiah accused these leaders of turning the temple into a den of robbers. This accusation is identical with the one Jesus brings some centuries later against the sanctimonious traders in his Father's house. Jeremiah went to the temple and stood on the steps to deliver God's message. He told the people that their worship of false gods wouldn't help them when their enemies sent powerful armies to march against them. Jeremiah told them that they were wrong to listen to false messengers, who told them that everything was going to be easy and peaceful. Jeremiah had been sent to warn them, but the people laughed at him.

Jeremiah tried to show the people something that would help them to understand. So he went to the workshop where the potter turned clay on a wheel to make plates and jugs. God is like a potter, explained Jeremiah, and we are like the clay. He went out to the valley where the people had disobeyed God. They had even killed their own children and burnt them as an offering to statutes that could neither hear their prayers nor help them. Jeremiah hurled a heavy clay jar to the ground, and it broke into pieces. Jerusalem and all its people will be like this broken pot, explained Jeremiah. God will let our enemies break us completely. Jeremiah didn't like the message he was commanded by God to give. This message was that because of the people sins, God would allow the Babylonian superpower to conquer and invade their country. And worse still, to destroy their temple. Jeremiah's message was to tell the people of Jerusalem that resistance would be useless. They would be beaten in battle and carried off into captivity. Then, and only then, after a period of time in exile in Babylon would they begin to see sense again, stop worshiping idols, and obeys God's law.

Jeremiah was not very popular. The Babylonians had surrounded the city and were laying siege to it. It was difficult enough in any case to keep up morale. All anyone needed now was a miserable prophet telling them God actually wanted them to be defeated. Sometimes, God spoke to Jeremiah by showing him pictures. On one occasion, God showed him two baskets of figs. One basket was full of good, ripe figs, while the other held shriveled and bad figs. God wanted Jeremiah to understand that if the people gave themselves up to the king of Babylon, they would be like the good, ripe figs, and if they did not, they would be like the bad figs. We wonder if there are any similarities here with the siege of Baghdad by American and British forces in 2003? The Church of England, with many, had opposed war with Iraq in favor of a diplomatic solution, and Anglican bishops called upon Saddam Hussein to relinquish power as the best hope of saving lives. If the situation in the Gulf can be likened to that of Jeremiah's Jerusalem, we must be clear in our own minds that the people of Iraq were not being punished for any lack faith.

Eventually, the Babylonians enter Jerusalem as Jeremiah had predicted. They ravaged the city and sacked the temple. They carried all the so-called important people into captivity, with only the poor and weak left behind. Jeremiah stayed in Jerusalem until a group of freedom fighters assassinated the governor the Babylonians had put in charge. Terrified of the Babylonians, some of the people decided to escape to Egypt, taking Jeremiah with them. Jeremiah believed that the future lay with the return of the exiles to their own land after a suitable period of penitence in Babylon. That is, they could use their time in exile to repent of their sins and turn afresh to God. The new covenant of which Jeremiah spoke was to be brought about six hundred years later by Jesus Christ. Like Jesus, Jeremiah drew attention to the hypocrisy of external religion without an internal consecration of the heart. Like Jesus, Jeremiah wept over Jerusalem. But there is a point at which the parallel breaks down. In Jeremiah, there is no saving power as there is with Christ. Since no claim of divinity can be made for Jeremiah, any comparison with Christ has to be inadequate. At the Last Supper, Jesus explained to his disciples that a new covenant between God and his people was now being made through himself. From now on, the law would be written on people's hearts and rooted in love.

## Drawing Near to God in the New Testament

We can take it for granted that both James and Paul counted on the emptiness of the tomb, whether they knew the Jerusalem tradition or not. For Pannenberg, the expression "resurrection from the dead" has a metaphorical character.[5] This expression stands not for something we can experience in our everyday life, like a mountain or a tree. It is rather

5. Pannenberg, *Jesus*, 89.

a metaphor, a way of speaking in an image. Just as we arise from sleep in the morning, in a similar way, those who are dead shall also rise. This metaphoric sense of the expression could already be found in the Old Testament when the notion of resurrection was first mentioned and where the terms "rise" and "awake" are used in parallel.[6] The frequently used interpretation of death as sleep has similar implications.[7] However, for Pannenberg, the resurrection of the dead was not understood by primitive Christianity as a revival of a dead body.[8] Pannenberg's description of the resurrection of Jesus as a historical event is as follows: if we approach history from the conviction that the dead do not rise, then we have already decided that Jesus also did not rise. If, on the other hand, we take seriously the apocalyptic expectation with regard to the hope of the resurrection, then we can accept provisionally that Jesus did rise from the dead, that is until such a time as contrary evidence is made available. Thus, for Pannenberg, the appearances of the resurrected Lord must be examined in the light of the eschatological expectations for a resurrection from the dead and, in this sense, can be understood as a historical event.[9] Clearly, there was a tradition in which the expectation of resurrection, from the dead, be it for all people or only for the righteous ones, was alive and kicking. This is the Jewish apocalypticism that gained more and more ground after the time of the Babylonian exile and had penetrated deeply into the thinking of Jewish theology.

Pannenberg's answer to those who say that the resurrection would be an event that violates the laws of nature is as follows: firstly, only a part of the laws of nature are ever known; secondly, in a world that, as a whole, represents a singular irreversible process, an individual event is never completely determined by natural laws, since everything that happens is contingent, and the validity of the laws of nature is itself contingent.[10] In other words, general laws do not make possible an absolute certain prediction about the possibility or impossibility of single events, except in the case where all possible conditions can be taken into account.[11] Thus, for Pannenberg, there is no justification for affirming Jesus' resurrection as an event that really happened if it is not to be affirmed as a historical

6. Isa 26:19.

7. Dan 12:2; 1 Thess 4:13, 15; 1 Cor 11:36, 15:6.

8. Pannenberg, *Jesus*, 75.

9. Pannenberg, *Jesus*, 98.

10. Pannenberg, *Jesus*, 98.

11. Pannenberg, *Jesus*, 98.

event.[12] Thus, whether or not Jesus rose again from the dead is not made certain by faith, but only by history.[13] This approach is claiming that faith cannot ascertain anything certain about the events of the past that would perhaps be inaccessible to historians.[14] Pannenberg goes further to say that the judgments about whether an event has happened or not is a matter for the historian and cannot be prejudiced by the knowledge of natural science.[15] However, in this sense, Pannenberg does understand the resurrection of Jesus as a historical event, that is, an event that really happened two thousand years ago. Thus, Pannenberg concludes that the best explanation for such events as the disciples' experience of the appearances of Jesus and the discovery of the empty tomb are indeed to be found in the concept of the resurrection.[16]

• • •

According to Rudolf Bultman, the resurrection is not an event of past history with a self-evident meaning but, along with the cross, forms a single, indivisible cosmic event.[17] However, the cross is not an isolated event as though it were the end of Jesus, which needed resurrection subsequently to reverse it. When he suffered death, Jesus was already the Son of God, and his death by itself was the victory over the power of death. St. John brings this out most clearly by describing the passion of Jesus as the hour in which he is glorified, and by the double meaning he gives to the phrase "lifted up," applying it both to the cross and to Christ's exaltation into glory.[18] Bultman is well aware that the resurrection of Jesus is often viewed in the New Testament as an authenticating miracle. For example, we are told that God substantiated the claims of Christ by raising him from the dead. Then again, the resurrection narrates both the legend of the empty tomb and the appearances that insist on the physical reality of the risen body of the Lord. For Bultman, these are mostly later embellishments of the primitive tradition. James and Paul would know nothing about them. For Bultman, a historical fact that involves a resurrection from the

12. Pannenberg, *Jesus*, 99.
13. Pannenberg, *Jesus*, 99.
14. Pannenberg, *Jesus*, 109.
15. Pannenberg, *Jesus*, 98.
16. Pannenberg, *Jesus*, 109.
17. Bultman, *Synoptic Tradition*, 36.
18. Bultman, *Synoptic Tradition*, 37.

dead is utterly inconceivable.[19] In other words, the resurrection of Jesus cannot be understood as a miraculous proof by which the skeptic might be compelled to believe in Christ. The difficulty is not simply the incredibility of a mythical event, like the resurrection of a dead person. For that is what the resurrection means as is shown by the fact that the risen Lord is apprehended by the physical senses. Nor is it merely the impossibility of establishing the objective historicity of the resurrection, no matter how the witnesses are cited, as though once it was established, it might be believed beyond all question, and faith might have its unimpeachable guarantee. The real difficulty is that the resurrection is itself an article of faith, and you can't establish one article of faith by invoking another. You cannot prove the redemptive efficiency of the cross by invoking the resurrection. For Bultman, the resurrection is an article of faith because it is more than the resurrection of a dead body, rather, it is an eschatological event. In other words, it has something to do with the future. For apart from its credibility, the bare miracle tells us nothing about the destruction of death. Moreover, such a miracle is not otherwise unknown to mythology.[20]

For Bultman, the resurrection is not a mythological event added in order to prove the saving efficacy of the cross but, rather, an article of faith just as much as the meaning of the cross itself. Indeed, faith in the resurrection is the same thing as faith in the saving efficacy of the cross of Christ. Hence, you cannot first believe in Christ and then, in the strength of that faith, believe in the Cross. Thus, to believe in Christ means to believe in the cross as the cross of Christ. Without that efficacy, it is the tragic end of a great man.[21]

So, how do we come to believe in the cross as the cross of Christ and as the eschatological event par excellence? How do we come to believe in the saving efficiency of the cross?[22] For Bultman, there is only one answer. This is the way the gospel is proclaimed. It is always proclaimed together with the resurrection. Christ meets us in what has been preached, and in the word of preaching, he is the crucified and risen Lord. Thus, the faith of Easter is faith in the word of preaching.[23] According to Bultman, it would be wrong at this point to raise again the problem of how this

19. Bultman, *Synoptic Tradition*, 37.

20. Bultman, *Synoptic Tradition*, 38.

21. Bultman, *Synoptic Tradition*, 39.

22. Bultman, *Synoptic Tradition*, 39.

23. Bultman, *Synoptic Tradition*, 39.

preaching arose historically, as though that could vindicate its truth. That would be to tie our faith in the word of God to the results of historical research. The word of preaching confronts us as the word of God, so it is not for us to question its credentials. It is we who are questioned, we who are asked whether we will believe the word or reject it. But in answering this question, in accepting the word of preaching as the word of God, and the death and resurrection of Christ as the eschatological event, we are given an opportunity of understanding ourselves.[24] Faith and unbelief are never arbitrary questions as they offer us the alternative between accepting or rejecting that which alone can illuminate our understanding of ourselves as people who are crucified and risen with Christ. According to Bultman, the historical event of the rise of the Easter faith means for us what it meant for the first disciples, the self-attestation of the risen Lord, the act of God, in which the redemptive event of the cross is completed.[25] Thus, we cannot buttress our own faith in the resurrection by that of the first disciples. For the first disciples, faith in the resurrection is itself part and parcel of the eschatological event, which is the article of faith. In other words, the apostolic preaching that originated in the event of Easter Day is itself a part of the eschatological event of redemption. Through the word of preaching, the cross and the resurrection are made present. Thus the eschatological future is now here in the word of preaching.[26]

• • •

In the New Testament, God was present in the midst of his people in the person of his Son, Jesus Christ. For those who recognized him, for who he was, coming into his presence presented moral demands. "Follow me."[27] "Go sell all that you have."[28] "Go and sin no more."[29] It brought also a kind of fear prompted by a sense of unworthiness. "Depart from me for I am a sinful man."[30] Jesus, hidden under form of flesh, but in truth, the presence of the living God. Here he was, and those who were drawn to Jesus could go to him. Some did not recognize him, some shied away

24. Bultman, *Synoptic Tradition*, 39.
25. Bultman, *Synoptic Tradition*, 40.
26. Bultman, *Synoptic Tradition*, 40.
27. Matt 16:24; Mark 8:34; Luke 9:23.
28. Matt 19:21.
29. John 8:11.
30. Luke 5:8–10.

from the challenge he presented, but he was there to be found by those who wanted to. Through the Holy Spirit, we are never out of God's presence, for this is a constant reality. Whether it be Solomon's Temple or any other parish church, no building can contain God. But God has made a covenant with his church—he has promised. This is the house of God, a special place. Here, we can come and meet him. "This is my body, this is my blood."[31] "Whosoever sins you forgive they are forgiven."[32] Through the Holy Spirit, Jesus promises to act decisively through the priests of his church. Are we prepared to take these promises at their face value, to confront Christ face to face? Or do we timidly keep on the edge of things, afraid or unwilling to commit ourselves? We can never play down the importance of the church. It is the place where we find forgiveness and peace of mind in the presence of God. Having found this, we can go forward in confidence to do his will.

• • •

The next section of this commentary deals with baptism, confession, and the cross. But first, let's think about Lent, when we see Jesus at his most human, wanting food, wanting reassurance, but also full of clever ingenuity. At the end of the story, Jesus is aware of who he is and what he needs to do. He has been through his time of trial and has come out ready for his mission. Like many religious leaders before and since, he spent time literally in a desert. In the middle of sterile nothingness, he found all that he required. Lent is about taking time out in a meaningful way to enrich our spiritual life and to reacquaint ourselves with the essentials of our faith. God loves a cheerful giver, so do not begrudge time and offering during Lent. Make a good Lenten observance. Make it your Lent rule to attend the stations of the cross and the Lent course at a church where they do that sort of thing. In the desert of this world, may you find true riches and holy nourishment, so that you may grow in grace. Let us all pray for each other that these blessings may be ours at this time.

In the film *The Last Temptation of Christ*, our Lord is tempted to come down from the cross, take his life into his own hands, and marry Mary Magdalene.[33] In this film, we are asked to consider what would have happened if Jesus had indeed taken this course of action. You can imagine

31. Matt 26:26–28; Mark 14:22–24; Luke 22:19–20.

32. John 20:23.

33. Scorcese, *Last Temptation of Christ.*

the situation. Jesus gets down from the cross, is married, and raises a family. If this had happened, could New Testament writers have still preached Christ crucified and risen? If he did, it wouldn't be based upon a real historical figure but rather an idea. And ideas by themselves do not last. In our Gospels, we are told about three temptations that urged Jesus to use the power he had as God's Son to win praise for himself instead of carrying out God's work.[34] Let us look at these temptations. The first temptation is that Jesus is tempted to turn stones into bread. Clearly, physical exhaustion lays people open to the temptation of losing sight of all other claims in the effort to supply their needs. So, the suggestion came to Jesus that if he was the Son of God, then he could turn stones into bread. The temptation was to prove that he was the Son of God by doing what only God could do. But the Son of God was also a human being. His acceptance of human experience could only be real if he lived as we live, dependent on the heavenly Father. Jesus' answer to this temptation is to identify himself with his humanity. "It is written, one does not live by bread alone."[35] There are spiritual values that must come first. The heavenly Father will care for his children as he cared for his people in the wilderness. In the second temptation, our Lord thought of himself as standing on a mountain top with the whole inhabited world spread out before him. The temptation here was that he could, if he chose to, lord it over this world as do the earthly rulers, whose kingdoms are based upon intrigue and bloodshed. Jesus is tempted to win power for himself at the cost of disloyalty to the will of the one who sent him—God the Father, the Almighty. Jesus' answer to this temptation is to say, "It is written, worship the Lord your God and serve only him."[36] In the third temptation, our Lord felt himself carried like the prophet Ezekiel to a pinnacle of the temple. It was a high and sacred place, suggesting both danger and protection. Looking down from the dizzying height, there came to our Lord a suggestion to test the reality of his sonship by one supreme act of faith—to risk even life itself by throwing himself down so that God might lift him up to safety. To this temptation, Jesus' answer was, "Do not put the Lord your God to the test."[37]

34. Matt 4:1–11; Mark 1:12–13; Luke 4:1–13; see also, for implicit reference to the temptations, John 6:26, 31 (turning stones to bread); John 2:18 and 6:15 (rejection of the temptation of worldly power and fame); 1 John 2:16 (rejection of the lust of the flesh).

35. Luke 4:4.

36. Luke 4:8.

37. Luke 4:12.

In the film *The Last temptation of Christ*, we are asked to contemplate what would have happened if Jesus had got off the cross and lived to an old age in his earthly body. Just as Jerusalem is about to be destroyed, Judas rushes in and accuses Jesus of being a traitor. In the film, as in the Gospel, Jesus is no traitor. He dies on the cross and rises to a new and everlasting life. He was tempted as we are, but he was without sin. For sin is the response of the human mind and will to temptation when we forget our allegiance to God. Happiness does not depend upon money, although it is very important to our well-being. No, it depends upon our relationships with those we care about. For no happiness can be perfect until it is shared. Kind words and kind looks are all acts of charity. Kind smiles and warm handshakes. Cheerfulness is also an act of charity. Do you not find yourself refreshed by the presence of a cheerful person? So, in charity, we try to give that pleasure to others. If you feel that you are not a very charitable person, don't lose heart. Do as well as you can today and perhaps tomorrow you may be able to do better. For every day is a fresh beginning. Charity is not just about our relationships with fellow Christians. It is to be extended to the whole of humanity. A Christian should show charity towards all people on account of the fact they are all made in the image of God. As Christians, we must witness in our lives a belief in the sacredness of the human personality. When we look at Jesus, we can see a model of true charity. For he lived in such a way with his disciples that he released them to become their true selves. So, how should we enter the season of Lent? We must break with our bad routines in order to place ourselves in a position where God's grace can take better effect. Not by fasting, or even by prayer, can we guarantee success and a fresh start and nearness to God. If our Lenten exercises are done to make us feel good or noble, we are unlikely to find God drawing nearer to us and helping us with his closer presence. Everything is dependent upon God's love, not our efforts. The Lenten discipline must be seen as part of God's plan. If Lent is to mean anything for us, we must accept the good news of God in Christ Jesus. The good news is this—Jesus loves us and will forgive us our sins if we are truly sorry.

• • •

Cleanse your hands, you sinners, and purify
your hearts, you double minded.

—James 4:8b

Clearly, the preceding text is not just about Lent but also baptism into a new life here on earth. So, we must ask what is this new life into which we have all been baptized? What does it involve? James is talking about how God empowers the humble so they can do his will. James speaks directly to notorious sinners, calling for them to engage in the moral reform of their lives.[38] To be a Christian means participation in the life, death, and resurrection of Jesus Christ. To know Christ is to share the cross he bore and to share the life he lives. This involves washing away of sin and a new birth in which the power of sin is broken. When we are immersed in the liberating death of Christ, our sins are buried with the old self. Thus, the old self is crucified with Christ, and the new self is raised here and now to a new life in the power of his resurrection. We have all been immersed in the liberating love of Christ Jesus. But how confident can we be that God will not only raise us here and now to a new life in the power of the resurrection of Jesus Christ, but that ultimately, we will be one with him in the world to come? We can be very confident because our faith is based upon the powerful promise of God. But does this mean that because the power of sin has been broken, our salvation is a forgone conclusion? The answer to this question has to be "no." For the Christian life involves a confession of sin and a conversion of heart. Repentance consists of three aspects: contrition, confession, and amendment. Contrition is the dislike of sin because this comes from a genuine love of God. A sinner who has repented sees sin as an affront to God and as a disrespect to the love they see in the passion and death of Jesus Christ. Sin damages our relationship with God and our fellowship with other Christians, so contrition can lead us to a state of reconciliation and peace. In other and technical words, we separate ourselves from God and from each other by the sins that we commit, but God forgives us. God's side of the relationship never changes and never ceases to love us. Our membership of the body of Christ then is renewed by confession. Confession is a means of returning to God and to the family fold. Whether we confess our sins during public worship as part of the general confession at Holy Communion and evensong, or whether we go privately to a priest, the main thing is that we take seriously our failure to love God as he would want us to. This means that we must regularly examine our conscience. If our confession is sincere and is truly from the heart, then it must involve a total surrender to the love of God. Without this, the words "I am sorry for" are meaningless.

38. Barclay, *Letters of James and Peter*, 123.

Confession, then, is a truthful acknowledgment of our sins. It is self-accusation and the acknowledgement to God of our wrongdoing. As sinners, we receive God's pardon on the understanding that we must have a firm resolve not to commit the sin again. In life, and in death, and beyond death, we are in the presence of the risen Lord. We who are immersed in the life, death, and resurrection of Jesus Christ must look forward to the final kingdom that is yet to come. We must do this without losing sight of the kingdom that is already here. We have hope in the life with God in the future, beyond death, in the resurrection of the dead, because it is based upon the certainty of life with God in the present.

• • •

Staying with baptism and confession, we have, in so many ways, betrayed these crucial sacraments. We have not been faithful to the promises that we made or were made on our behalf. We have done wrong and we must admit it. We put much store in what we think of God or what we decide about God. Surely, the important thing is what God thinks of us and our duty towards him.[39] What, then, is our duty to God and how does this relate to other duties that we may have?[40] To be true to the teachings of Jesus, we must not forget the duties of fasting and almsgiving. Fasting is literally abstinence from food and drink, but it really includes all forms of self-denial, which helps us in resisting temptation. If we are able to deny ourselves in lawful things, we shall be better able to deny ourselves in things that are unlawful. Almsgiving is the giving of money, goods, or time to the special service of God. The practice of giving alms is a recognition of the sovereignty of God. By making a return of some of our goods to him, we acknowledge that all we have is his. Almsgiving is a great safeguard against the love of money. So, what do we mean by charity? A disposition to think kindly of others? Practical kindness? No, it is more than this. We could sum up Christian charity in one word that is at the heart of our faith. That word is *love*. With love, we can forgive and be forgiven. Love is all about giving not merely money for worthy causes but the giving of ourselves, our emotions, our intellect, and our time to others. So, how can we be charitable, you may well ask? Well, wisdom is knowing what to do next. Skill is knowing how to do it. And virtue is

39. James, 4:3.

40. James, 4:5.

actually doing it. We need to look at our relationships with others and be satisfied with nothing but our best.

So, what does baptism mean? So, what is this new life into which we have all been baptized? What does it involve? It means that through Christ Jesus, we are not only united with each other but we are in communion with God. For we have all entered into an agreement—a new covenant between ourselves and our Creator. To know Christ is to share the cross he bore and to share the life he lives. This involves washing away of sin and a new birth in which the power of sin is broken. When we are immersed in the liberating death of Christ, our sins are buried with the old self. Thus, the old self is crucified with Christ, and the new self is raised here and now to a new life in the power of his resurrection. To be a Christian means participation in the life, death, and resurrection of Jesus Christ. We have all been immersed in the liberating love of Christ Jesus. But how confident can we be that God will not only raise us here and now to a new life in the power of his resurrection but that ultimately, we will be one with him in the world to come? We can be very confident because our faith is based upon the powerful promise of God. We must live for the sake of Christ and of his church, which has one great hope. It looks forward to the final kingdom that is yet to come without losing sight of the kingdom that is already here. We have hope in the life with God in the future, beyond death, in the resurrection of the dead because it is based upon the certainty of life with God in the present. In life, and in death, and beyond death, we are in the presence of the risen Lord.

So what did Jesus mean when he said, "I am the living bread that comes down from heaven."[41] Clearly, he meant something radically different from the conventional understanding of the words "bread" and "life." The bread we are talking about is the spiritual food that is able to sustain life, not only in this world but also in the world to come. The life we are talking about is life with God, beyond death in the resurrection of the dead. In our Gospel reading, Jesus promised that he would raise us up on the last day. When Christ appears again, there will be a general resurrection of the dead, which will be followed by the end of the world. As for the nature of the resurrection body, it will not have the same characteristics as the body we have now. But the identity of the individual will be preserved in spite of the change. We shall acquire a new instrument for our personality, which will be nevertheless a proper successor to the

41. John 6.51.

present body and will actually be linked in definite continuity with it. The new body will be immortal, the final victory of life over death. In heaven, we will live with God forever. So, what can we say of this place called heaven? Heaven is the blessed condition of unending happiness in the presence of God. It is a company of just people made perfect. We shall be different from each other, but we shall have been purified. We will find ourselves in a world where there are no things but only persons. In heaven, we shall meet all those we have known and loved. We shall know each other as we really are, with all the sins and weaknesses gone. In heaven, there will be no tears, neither sorrow nor crying. There will be no more pain, for these things will have passed away.

So what did Jesus mean when he said, "I am the living bread that came down from heaven."[42] The bread of life is the teaching and self-offering of Jesus. For the bread of life is the food of eternity because it comes from God who is in heaven. The living bread offers us a new relationship with God in which our hunger is satisfied. And if we want to receive this bread that is the gift of real life from Jesus Christ, then we must believe in him. For we live and die in the faith of Christ so that in the world to come, we may live with him forever. In our eucharistic meal, we witness to the joy of the resurrection. As Christians, we come together to remember him in the way he gave us. In this sacrament, we are nourished and strengthen to confess by word and action the Lord Jesus Christ, who gave his life for the salvation of the world. The Eucharist is the real presence of the crucified and risen Christ. By the power of the Holy Spirit, bread and wine become the sacramental signs of Christ's body and blood. So, this is how we fix our values on the eternal values of heaven. God, who made the heavens and the earth, is still a loving God who knows all his children. God sees all, forgives all, and heals all in the fullness of eternal life. God sent his Son Jesus to live in our flesh and to suffer all the troubles and the pains of human life, so that we might become as he is, perfect and loving, bringing good to all. As authors of this commentary, we could not say the things we have said, and will go on to say, without that faith. For through it, we can find the strength to face all that life brings. Through faith, we can trust and live freely in this life and the next. So, we meet here, in this book with our readers and mindful of the Lord's table, standing in the coolness of his empty tomb, trembling

42. John 6:51.

with awe at the greatness of the hope that has dawned on the world. So, in this service of Holy Communion, be comforted and have strength.

• • •

Anyone, then, who knows the right thing to
do and fails to do it, commits sin.

—James 4:17

In the uncertainty as to the future, there is no excuse for inaction but, rather, a sign to accept our dependence on God's love.[43] There is a great deal of questioning going on at the present time in every possible direction, and so there should be. Mother Linda and Father David have questions of our own. The courts and Parliament face an increasing pressure to modify their structures to reflect more realistically the present-day situation. Education, too, is under the microscope with the whole set up of higher education and the universities under review. The health service, the prison service, and the police—no matter where you look, this questioning is at work. It is not least evident in the church. We are a conservative people. By and large, we don't like change, that is, as long as things are ticking along in a reasonably satisfactory fashion. It is only when things break down, when a crisis point is reached, that there is any real likelihood of change. Western society has changed so rapidly and so much that make do and mend will not suffice. So, we must ask what are the important things, what are the desirable things—how can society best hope to bring them about. One might expect the Christian faith to provide the basis for some answers. There can be no one Christian social or political theory. But as it regards human freedom, human dignity, and the infinite value of every individual in the sight of God, Christians ought to have no doubts where their duty lies.

During the Trinity period, we think about hope and its relationship to faith. We learn that it is about aspirations—about looking forward to the future. Ultimately, for us as Christians, it is about going to heaven. But quite a lot happens before then. So, hope is about all aspects of life, home, work, and church. It is an expectation of what God has on offer for us in this life and in the next. Hope can be seen as that bit of heaven come down to earth. We get to glimpse at a small part of the divine hope. Clearly, hope for the Christian is contained in the person of Christ. Thus,

43. Barclay, *Letters of James and Peter*, 131.

hope in the future is to be found in our knowledge of God as revealed to us in his only begotten Son. This, in turn, leads us to ask some important questions. What are we, as Christians, as the church, here for? And these questions must be asked and answered, however imperfectly, before we can judge the best way of achieving our ends. If all this seems very general, let us try to apply it to one area in particular. At this time of the year, services in most churches are less well attended. Clearly, I am talking about the Church of England. When this happens, there are various possible lines of approach. One might think, in terms of the church, putting on services in response to demand, and the inference would be that if a particular service no longer met a need at a particular time of the year, it should be withdrawn—just like a retailer might remove an unpopular or slow selling line from the shelves of a supermarket. This would be a very cynical approach to our subject. One might, again, think in terms of the church putting on services in competition with other attractions, like Sunday shopping. If the response is not good, or falls off, the service needs to be brightened up—made more attractive—more popular hymns, fewer prayers, shorter and more interesting readings, brighter and more controversial sermons. Or perhaps, the time of the services or their length could be altered. Again, practical terms like these must often be considered, but an approach along these lines would be very inadequate. What we need to do, surely, is to get down to some basic thinking—to try to see our services not as isolated religious occasions or observances, but as fitting into the pattern of our whole life as Christians. What part does public worship play in the Christian life? What might it fulfill, and more to the point, what function ought it to fulfill?

The idea of squeezing God into a gap of an hour or so each week of our lives doesn't really make much sense in terms of a committed Christian life. The central truth of the Christian faith is the triumph of Jesus Christ over sin through his death on the cross and his resurrection to a new life. In this hope, we look forward to our own resurrection, when God will transform our bodies into copies of Jesus' glorious body. He will change us so that our scared and twisted lives will be filled with new hope and love. Our hope in the resurrection is that God is preparing us even now to share the fullness of eternal life. Thus, it is God's plan that we should enter the blessed condition of unending happiness in his presence. For it is God's will that all that depart this life will be with him in heaven at the last, which brings us to a consideration of what we mean by a resurrection.

• • •

This brings us to the New Testament's discovery of Jesus' empty tomb in light of what we learned from Pannenberg and Bultman. This tradition is the Easter account common to all the Christian Gospels and appears in its most original form in Mark.[44] Clearly of great importance is the question of the connection between the findings of the empty tomb and the appearances of the resurrected Jesus. It is widely accepted that the basic appearances took place in Galilee, while the empty tomb was found in Jerusalem. Now, we have to see how these two things are connected. Whether the discovery of the empty tomb was the reason the disciples of Jesus went to Galilee in the hope of meeting the resurrected Lord there, or whether the largely male group of disciples returned to Galilee because their journey to Jerusalem had come to such a catastrophic end. According to the earliest reports, these disciples were not present at the crucifixion or burial of Jesus and were not interested at first in the empty tomb. Meanwhile, the women disciples, as we find everywhere in the tradition, discover that Jesus' tomb was empty. It would be difficult to explain these events if all the disciples were still at Jerusalem, the place God's final decision regarding the imminent end of the world. So, why did these disciples go to Galilee and come back to Jerusalem in order to form the center of the Christian community there? It is likely that the appearances and the discovery of Jesus' empty tomb had happened independently of each other and became connected only in latter stages of the tradition. The independence from each other of the two traditions forms weighty reason for the fact that the Easter events were not the imagination of disturbed people but the starting point in the unique but real event that occurred prior to all human experience of it. Thus, the two traditions, by their mutuality, complementing each other, let the assertion of the reality of Jesus' resurrection appear as historically true.[45] We, the authors of this commentary, are taking it for granted that James countered on the emptiness of Jesus' tomb, whether he knew the Jerusalem tradition or not. Without having a reliable testimony for the resurrection, the readers of James would not have survived as a faith community.

We know what Peter and John believed—that their Lord and Master had indeed risen from the dead, but what was it that led them

44. Mark 16:6.

45. Pannenberg, *Jesus*, 89.

to believe?[46] This question is important in a world where many people find it difficult to believe in anything. No one else had ever risen from the dead in this way. It is true that our Lord raised Lazarus, the brother of Martha and Mary, but that was a quickening of the old body for a further period of earthly life. That Jesus rose from the dead was something entirely different. It was a resurrection to the fuller life in which the soul is no longer confined within the limitations placed upon it by the body. Hearing the news that the tomb was open and that their Lord no longer lay there, Peter and John at once hurried to the tomb. John, being younger than Peter, arrives first and looks into the tomb but does not enter. Yes, the body has gone! What could have happened to it? Surely, no one can have stolen it. Who could have wanted to do such a thing? Peter arrives and goes into the tomb, and he sees something that would have led him to summon John to his side. When John sees what Peter has noticed, he believes, too. What was it that gave the clue as to what had actually happened? The strips of linen are lying there as John would have noticed, but so is the burial cloth that had been about Jesus' head. The burial cloth is lying there a little apart from the strips of linen, but both are undisturbed. This is it that first lead them to realize the truth of what had happened. St. John goes to a lot of trouble in distinguishing the strips of linen that would have been wrapped around our Lord's body from the burial cloth, which would have been about his head. The important thing is that his head was wrapped separately from the linen that enfolded his body. Now, if our Lord's tomb had been broken into, it is unlikely that the robbers would have been so careful as to lay the burial cloth rolled up in a place by itself—so as to give the impression that Christ had risen? We must remember that the tomb had been guarded and intruders would not have wasted time doing that. In fact, they would probably have hurried away taking grave clothes and all. Moreover, even if the body had been unbound, what would have happened to all the spices with which it had been embalmed? We are told that they weighed over one hundred pounds. They would have been scattered all over the floor, and that would never have given the impression of a resurrection. Rather, it would have made it clear that the tomb had been robbed. Peter and John certainly did not see anything like that. So, how should we understand what St. John tells us? There were the strips of linen lying in the same position as when they had been placed around our Lord's body. And there was the burial

46. John 20:8.

cloth, lying as it had been entwined around our Lord's head. These are the facts that point to Jesus' resurrection from the dead.

Our Lord's body had withdrawn from the grave clothes, leaving them undisturbed. Jesus said that he would rise from the dead and he did so. He has promised that we, too, shall rise and, trusting in his word, we believe that we shall. And that is why we are bold to come to be partakers of his risen life here and now when we receive him to ourselves at the Holy Eucharist under the humbler form of the bread and wine. Staying with John, let's consider what happens in the evening on the first day of the week after the crucifixion. Note how careful St. John is to tell us about the time at which our risen Lord appeared to his disciples. It was, we are told, "*at evening, being the first day of the week.*"[47] That never-to-be forgotten day, when what the world and the disciples themselves judged to be the disaster actually ended in triumph. When what seemed to be complete collapse of a lost cause was found to be but the beginning of a campaign that was to embrace the whole world. Things were moving a fair pace, much had already happened that day, and at any moment, the authorities might burst in and arrest the followers of Jesus. For the whole of Jerusalem was wild with excitement. Early that morning, Mary Magdalene had gone to the sepulcher only to find the stone rolled away and the tomb empty. As we have already explained, Peter and John had at once set out for the spot and found it as she had said. As soon as the news reached the authorities, they announced that the body of Jesus had been stolen, even though soldiers had been placed on guard. So, they would have us believe the very thing against which they had taken such elaborate precautions. If the body of Jesus had been stolen, would they have done nothing about it? They knew full well that it had not been stolen, and so as the disciples were gathering together, it was with doors shut and fastened. It must have been with very mixed feelings that the disciples were gathered there; two disciples had come all the way from the neighboring village of Emmaus, even at this late hour, to bring the great news that they had seen their risen master. Jesus had gone into their home with them, and he was known by them in the breaking of the bread. Such news was too good to be true. And there were many, even among the disciples themselves, who could not bring themselves to believe it. But while they were listening and questioning each other "came Jesus and

47. John 20:19.

stood in their midst."[48] Imagine yourself to be one of their number. For a brief second, there is a hush as we wonder if we are seeing things, but no sooner has the thought entered our minds when we realized that the others have also seen what we see. So, what do we make of all this? We know that everyone in the room recognized him as their Lord, whom they had seen crucified, whereas the only people who have had doubts about it are those who were not there. What we must do is to decide for ourselves whether we are going to believe those who were there, or whether we prefer to believe those who were not. I know whom I would rather believe. Peter and John and Andrew jumped to their feet, and so do all the others. And in the excitement of the moment, our Lord greeting "Peace be unto you" is lost amidst the welcome. And we see his feet and his hands and his side bearing the wounds, but he is about to speak again and we listen.[49] We realize now, quite clearly, that our Lord's mission is to be carried out by us, his disciples. He is now giving us his commission to carry on the work that he has begun.

• • •

So, what was it like for the first disciples in the days and weeks following what they thought was the disaster of Jesus death upon the cross? They had been in great distress, not knowing what to do or where to go. It must have felt as if their world had come to an end. Then came Easter Day, as we now call it, and the wild, crazy, joyous story of the women that they had seen Jesus. They were meeting together, for comfort and consolation, turning together against the icy wind of doubt and fear, like a flock of sheep gathers and turns against the winter snowstorms. They must have talked over so many events and sayings, new understandings were beginning to emerge. But they would only be thought of as mad if they went ahead on what had already happened. Jesus still had to be public knowledge to be credible. After all, a handful of half-demented Galileans with a trumped-up story of someone risen from the dead would not convince anyone of anything. So, what was it that changed the disciples from being a rag bag of frightened people in mourning into what we now call the early church? How did Jesus infuse them with his own vitality? Jesus appears to his disciples at the sea of Tiberius.[50] At first, they did not recognize him and return to their boats.

48. John 20:19–21.

49. John 20:21.

50. John 21:1–14.

But when they realized who he was, there was no more doubt; this was not the first occasion on which Jesus had appeared after his resurrection from the dead. Jesus had revealed himself alive to his disciples, and they knew that the cross was not the end. The women had seen the Lord. The disciples with and without Thomas present had seen him also. The disciples had to come to terms with the physical reality of Jesus' death and resurrection. They had to come to terms with the difficulty of believing that anyone could live after death in a visible and understandable way. That is what the story of Thomas, called the doubter, is all about, for we are all doubters at times, and we understand exactly what he must have felt like. When you are in doubt about your faith, unsure if it is real for you, remember Thomas and be comforted.[51]

So, how did Jesus come back to life? This question naturally comes to mind. But it is futile to speculate as to how when we are faced with the miraculous works of God. To do so implies we have the capacity to understand the ways of God. Rather, let us ask ourselves why, for there is always a very good reason for everything that God does, and with his help we are usually able to find it. It was seen with our beloved Lord; he was there all the time at the Sea of Tiberias, but it was only when he desired to make his presence specifically known that he made himself visible to human eyes. We must remember always that Jesus is God, even when leading an earthly life, and now he is no longer subject to the limitations of time and space, unless for some special reason he desires to be so. There is a further point that must be considered in connection with the appearance of the risen Lord to his disciples. Jesus makes himself known to us in the breaking of the bread, when the Christian family meets to celebrate the Eucharist. Again, it is futile to ask how this can be. The resurrection has taken place, and Jesus is once more able to enjoy the freedom that was his before he became incarnate. Thus, in this absolute freedom that belongs to God alone, he gives himself focus under forms that we can perceive. If Jesus' resurrection did not happen, then Jesus is not the Son of God and what he taught would made no sense to the original readers of the Letter of James. But it did happen and Jesus is the Son of God. In the Gospels, this central truth unfolds in the Easter story. Jesus is not dead but alive and reveals himself to his disciples, who, at first, do not recognize the risen Christ because they had difficulty believing what they saw.

51. John 20:24–25.

We know from reading the Letter of James that his readers, despite many problems, remained firm in their faith. The resurrection of Jesus was the hope upon which their faith was founded. They had hope in this life and in the life to come. We, too, must share this hope—that Jesus will remember us in his kingdom and that, when we die, he will fill us with new life now and forever. Faith in the resurrection is really the same thing as faith in the meaning of the cross. The cross was a symbol of shame and failure, yet Christ made it the sign of love and hope. It was the suffering and death of Good Friday that made Easter Sunday possible. Without the cross, there would be no empty tomb to bear witness to the resurrection. It was a resurrection to the fuller life in which the soul is no longer confined within the limitations placed upon it by the body. We don't know how it happened, but we know that it did happen. Therefore, we are not afraid of any criticism that may be leveled against our belief, nor are we afraid of any new light that scholars and scientists may throw upon the subject. The more it is examined, the more clearly its truth will stand out. Something happened that changed the lives of Jesus' disciples, who had been so afraid at the time of the crucifixion. Something happened that changed the lives of millions of people in every age and nation, which it is still doing today. Christ, though he died, was still the life; death never had him in its power, nor can it hold us, his disciples. To be a Christian is to believe that when we die, we also are raised from the dead and transformed into a new and everlasting life. Resurrection means a new life in a new body and to live with God forever. In this hope, we look forward to our own resurrection, when God will transform our bodies into copies of Jesus' glorious body. Our hope, then, in the resurrection is that God is preparing us even now to share the fullness of eternal life.

• • •

Baptism, Eucharist, and resurrection are crucial to our Christian faith. So what did this say to the first readers of the Letter of James and still has to say to Christians everywhere, not least to us. Do we thank God and never stop thanking him for our faith, and for all the many graces we have received through Jesus Christ? It's easy to take it all for granted; sometimes, we even feel we ought to be given a medal for still practicing our faith when so many don't. How could we get it so wrong and be so arrogant?[52] But really, it is a matter for constant thanksgiving and submit-

52. Jas 4:3.

ting ourselves to God in Christ Jesus.[53] There are so many things that we don't have to worry about.[54] Credit crunch—don't tie up your treasure.[55] Mortgage, debts—consider the lilies of the fields.[56] Family disputes—put your hand to the plough and don't look back.[57] Insecurity—God could count the hairs on your head.[58] God knows you so intimately and still loves you. Many people are apparently too clever to believe. They look for worldly wisdom and the faith of Christ crucified, which won't fit into that sort of context. It was and remains a scandal, a stumbling block, inspired by the devoted irrationality of a love that will not let us go. Many others are too cynical to be impressed. Their sense of their own neediness makes them close down, not offer thanks to God that, despite all, God still loves us and desires dialogue and kinship with us. But by the grace of God, we believe, and it really is something to thank God for as we are liberated to be free creatures in the sunshine of his love and in the strength of his call.

The New Testament reminds us that we belong to one church. St. James addresses his letter to the twelve tribes in the dispersion.[59] We need to be thanking God always for the faith of all Christians and, so, reminding ourselves of our place in the great family of God, the two-plus billion of us who know that we are called and the countless millions whose faith is known to God alone. There is no place for narrow parochialism, imagining that God favors his people in one place more than those elsewhere. We have been called by God, we have accepted his call, and we are now waiting for our Lord Jesus Christ to be revealed. Supported by the sacraments, by the gifts of the Holy Spirit, we are to remain faithful until our Lord comes to claim his kingdom. In these days, where darkness—Gaza genocide and famine, financial crisis in the West, global terror—is counterpoised with hope—ceasefire, sense of life being more than material—more than ever, we are called as Christians to witness to this hope and to the life of faith. These few short years we have on earth should be about pledges, future promises that spring from our acts of love and justice. We foreshadow the final coming of the kingdom and its righteousness. James's converts, like Paul's, thought this would be soon—certainly in their lifetime. We cannot

53. Jas 4:7.
54. 1 Pet 5:6–7; Phil 4:6–7; John 14:27; 2 Tim 1:7; Ps 55:22; Matt 6:34; Prov 3:5–6.
55. Matt 6:19.
56. Matt 6:28.
57. Luke 9:62.
58. Luke 12:7.
59. Jas 1:1.

be sure that it won't be at any time. But we have to accept the possibility of a much longer timescale, and this, in many ways, imposes a strain different from that on the early Christians. It isn't so easy to remain in a state of constant readiness over a very long space of time. But our Lord will expect to find us ready, whenever he comes. And so we have to plan our life, accordingly, submitting to certain rules, cultivation of good habits, constantly on guard against temptations and carelessness. We do need to learn to live from moment to moment and not get sucked in to the glamor that the concrete possessions of now are all that there is. It is absolutely essential to show forth in our lives what our lips say on Sundays. We have to make the fullest possible use of all the gifts of the Spirit, so that God will keep us steady and without blame until the last day.

We have a duty—not a tiresome duty, but one full of grateful joy—to keep firm our own faith, to care for our own souls and also, by every means, to present the faith to others. We can't guarantee that people will take notice—but this mustn't be an excuse for not trying. And this doesn't mean trying to wrap up the faith in clever terms, but simply presenting our crucified Lord—letting him win those who are able to respond to his love. So, staying with the theme of joining organizations like churches, why do we do this? Usually, because we want to—we decide. And we want to, or feel obligation to, because the group stands for something we feel is very important—the saving of a park from a motorway, the preservation of church music, or whatever. We join organizations because they offer us something we want—fellowship, recreation, a purpose in life, and so on. What about the church? In the summer months when there are no great festivals, when holidays are in the air, and if we are not actually away, the weather is so much better suited to going off into the country than to going to church. The long procession of Sundays after Trinity is the testing time. This is when we get down to the really basic implications of our faith. Why do I go to church? Why do I call myself a Christian? If we haven't worked out satisfactory answers to questions like these, our religious observances will inevitably be at the whim of circumstances.

So, what is the proof of our Christian faith? The proof of our faith is that we declare that we are broken by sin, that we have no power to help that, and we have been rendered almost helpless. And yet, we still have some choice in the matter. For our choice is whether or not to accept the salvation offered to us in Christ Jesus. We can say, "No!" We can say, "Not yet!" We can say, "Mostly!" We can say all sorts of things, but we have to answer the question that God put to us when he became

Emmanuel, God with us. Our faith is that we believe not only that God made us but that God lived in our flesh and still lives with us. We do not have a distant God or a far-flung goal to struggle and yearn towards. We have an immanent God, a God who, as it were, rolls up his sleeves and pitches in with us. One of the reasons that we so love the great festivals of Christmas and Easter is that, at those times, we don't have to do anything except weep in joy and awe at the love of God visiting us in Christ Jesus. At the stable, at the crib side, in the holy hush of the straw-filled shed, to be small in the presence of God's smallness, that is serenity. And Easter morning, at the empty tomb in the dazed presence of the terrified women, trembling on the beginning of understanding. So, the proof of our faith is to show the world that we love each other as God first loved us. Love is not a tranquil state of serenity, although it can be sometimes. Love is dynamic and interactive and demanding. The gospel makes each and every one of us an alien in every worldly culture. It stops us from blending seamlessly into the crowd. We stand out because we stand for something. And that carries with it the pain of separation and also carries the compassionate urgency of mission, the imperative to reach out and proclaim the gospel. Our faith, then, is the foundation that commits us to a way of life, supported by prayer and worship, by sacraments, and by the community life of the family of the church. And the whole scheme assumes a Christian family—Christian parents and home, in which infant Christians will grow up to responsible maturity; and the wider family unit of the Christian congregation, supporting and able to organize for action—to be those productive branches. The risks of God's plan are enormous. The risk that many newborn Christians will be abandoned, spiritually neglected, and never reach maturity. The risk that adults, as well as children, will reject their family ties and responsibilities—turning their backs on spiritual support, without which, the Christian way of life is impossible to maintain. The risk that people will stop coming to church and that Christ's work will be hampered and slowed down by human failure expressed in infrequent attendance. But God has made us free—to love or not to love, to respond to or reject his unchanging love. This is a risk he is prepared to take. May we never lose sight of God's plan and his hopes for us in this world.

## Endnote: Biblical Intelligence and Form Criticism

If we are to understand the Bible intelligently, we must recognize the mythical language in which it is set and proclaims its message. As authors of this commentary on the Letter of James, we are only too conscious of the distance that separates our contemporary world and its conceptual apparatus from that of the first century. A group of theologians including Bultman, known as form critics, advocate a process of demythologization of Scripture. This is a way of comprehending the Bible text through a realization of its intention. For Paul Ricoeur, this is a vital part of biblical interpretation.[60] He relates the question of demythologization to what he calls the hermeneutic cycle: to understand it is necessary to believe, to believe it is necessary to understand. This is not a naïve reading of the text.[61] So, faith in what the text is concerned with must be deciphered in the text that speaks of it and in the confession of faith of the primitive church, which is expressed in the text. This is what is known as a hermeneutic understanding of the nature of Scripture, which puts the question of its inspiration and authority into a theological perspective. The Bible is a human record of God's revelation of Scripture, and if it is to be understood as inspired, then inspiration will have to be seen within the life and faith of the community that gave birth to these Scriptures.

According to Ricoeur, demythologization is operative on two principal levels. Firstly, it is modern people who demythologize the cosmological form in primitive preaching.[62] Myths are expressed in terms of the understanding that people have of themselves in relation to the foundation and the limits of existence. Demythologization is to interpret myths by relating their objective representations to the self-understanding that is shown and concerned in it. At a second level, demythologization requires restoration of the original intention.[63] Ricoeur comments that this hierarchy of levels is the key to reading Bultman correctly. In other words, Bultman does not just find the myths, discover their meaning in relation to human existence, and dispose of them. Rather, Bultman looks for their deeper meaning and intention. In contradiction to Pannenberg, it is possible to affirm Jesus' resurrection as something that really happened in the life and faith of the community in which it originated without calling

60. Ricoeur, *Essays on Biblical Interpretation*, 58.

61. Ricoeur, *Essays on Biblical Interpretation*, 58.

62. Ricoeur, *Essays on Biblical Interpretation*, 60.

63. Ricoeur, *Essays on Biblical Interpretation*, 61.

it an historical event. Following Bultman, we can say that the cross and the resurrection are articles of faith forming one single cosmic and eschatological event. Jewish funeral practices would call into question Pannenberg's understanding of metaphoric perceptions of what was meant by the term "resurrection" on the part of primitive Christianity.[64] For this reason alone, we cannot totally rule out the possibility that between his crucifixion and ascension, Jesus was perceived and preached about as a revived corpse. This would be a very effective way of communicating the redemptive significance of the cross to people who were expecting a physical resurrection.

So, what should we preach at funerals in the Anglican church? We start by acknowledging that to lose someone is painful and continues to be painful. We are each one of us, precious and unique, both to God and to each other. The church has always recognized the pain of bereavement and sought to bring reassurance and solid comfort in its prayers and in its worship. The church has one great hope. It looks forward to the final kingdom that is yet to come. We have hope in the life with God, beyond death, in the resurrection of the dead. In other words, we have faith that our dearly departed have a future and that in heaven, we will meet all those we have known and loved. It is on the basis of this understanding, that the church mourns her departed and commands them in faith and in trust to God. So, we meet in the name of Jesus Christ to honor the dead and to comfort one another in our grief. In our pain and in the company of others, we say goodbye to those we love but see no longer. We give thanks for their uniqueness and identity, although we are sad that they have been taken from us now. The sorrow that we feel must be put alongside the joy of all they meant to us. Perplexity is seen in the light of faith. When Jesus walked this earth in our flesh, he did so to show us once and for all that we might become as he is. That demonstration holds a rich promise to all. For just as Jesus came into his throne through his death and resurrection, uniting forever the human within the divine of his being, so we, in our turn at our death, become more fully and more clearly the image of God that we were made to be. Death is the final process that makes each one of us more fully human. In death, there is a delight for the one who dies in that they get themselves back; they discover with wonder just how marvelously they have been made. Christ conquered death and entered into glory. Confident of his victory, we entrust our loved ones to God's merciful keeping as they draw near him.

64. Rahmani, "Ancient Jerusalem's Funerary Customs."

# *Chapter 5*

# Endurance in the Faith

## Introduction

ARE YOU SITTING COMFORTABLY? Once upon a time, in a sunlit clearing deep in a dark and dangerous forest lived three bears: Daddy Bear, Mummy Bear, and Baby Bear. Daddy Bear was a genial sort of beast who loved to sing and dream. Mummy Bear was short and quick, a busy bear whose rapid fingers and agile brain were never still. She managed her family with anxious care. Sometimes her tiny frame would quiver with vexation at the easygoing Daddy Bear and his perpetual optimism.

Baby Bear loved his parents dearly and, in his turn, knew how to manage them. He understood how to float like a butterfly alongside happy Daddy. He also knew how to sting like a bee beside busy Mummy. The bears' home was lovely, full of laughter and sunshine inside, even on a gloomy day. Flowers and creepers adorned the walls and birds sang in every room. The house was strong and safe and beautiful.

One day, the bears decided to venture on a honey hunt through the forest. Daddy Bear hummed, Mummy Bear buzzed, and Baby Bear bubbled as he tried to do both at once. Finally, all was ready and they set off. Daddy Bear thought that he was valiantly leading the way, but Mummy Bear, as usual, nipped his heals to guide him in his path. Baby Bear kept them both firmly in sight. So, the happy trio vanished into the silence of the forest. Quiet fell over the clearing. Some hours later, when the afternoon had just laid down for its nap, a little girl slipped into the clearing. She had traveled a long way and felt very small in her distance from home. She saw the bears' house, snug and solid before her, and her eyes widened with joy. This house is gorgeous she thought. They must be wonderful, whoever lives here, said Goldilocks to herself. She was irresistibly drawn to the front door.

As she neared it, she saw that the door stood ajar. She knocked at the door, and it opened wide to let her in; what could she do but enter? "I'm here," she called. "Is anyone home?"

Fresh fruit and nuts gleamed their invitation on the table and she ate hungrily, but daintily, having first washed her hands. A clay pitcher of water pearled with coolness in a corner; she quaffed the clean water gratefully. "It's strange how much I feel at home," she felt; meanwhile, weariness was tying up her feet so that she could hardly move. Exploring, she found a bedroom with rosy colored curtains and a little bed just exactly her size. "I wonder if they'd mind," she murmured, as she sank into the pillows. She slept, and as she slept, she smiled. The sun moved on and left a space for a greedy evening that gobbled up the day.

The bears returned, sticky and tired, from their expedition. Mummy Bear was furious when she spotted signs of their visitor, that she did with vigilant speed. Daddy Bear smiled, maybe it's the bear fairy coming to visit us, I'm sure everything will be fine. Mummy Bear gave him a hard stare and there was no need for words. But Baby Bear saw her look; he knew when his mother was offended. "Let's search the house," he suggested, so they did. They found her. Little Goldilocks was still asleep, dreaming of a beautiful city, full of golden houses and welcoming people. Mummy Bear and Baby Bear howled with fury at the desecration of the spare room. Baby Bear was especially angry; maybe he was jealous at this interloper so close to his own size.

Before Daddy Bear had time to realize what they were up to, they fell on Goldilocks and ripped her limb from limb. Bears are wild and dangerous creatures and so are human beings. Goldilocks died, still half in dreams; she died without a sound. So, Daddy Bear made a lovely song up in memory of the smile on her face. Do we identify with Daddy Bear, content to make up a lovely song in memory of the smile on our Lord's face just before they crucified him? We do not intend to demean our Lord's passion, but the story of Goldilocks and the three bears could also be used as a way of explaining Linda's ministry in the Church of England. This was included as a case study in *Faith in Church Newspapers.*[1]

1. Isiorho, *Faith in Church Newspapers*, 17–24.

At the time of publishing this commentary, we are into the run-up to Christmas. Advent is the four-week countdown, and it is the same every year. According to the radio and television, everyone is full of Christmas merriment and good cheer. We doubt if this includes the jobless, homeless, and poor. The minds of those who look forward to Christmas are planning the details of the feast, making puddings, and reserving the turkey; thinking of the old reassuring, comforting picture of the baby Jesus, inoffensive, snoozing on a quiet and meek Mary; no threats, no danger, and, we venture to suggest, no resemblance to the gospel of Christ. No wonder we need Advent to stir us up before Christmas. For Advent does not just refer to the first coming of our Lord. It is also about the awesome mystery of his second coming, and with the second coming comes judgment.

We all know what it is like to sit in front of the fire on Christmas Day surrounded by the debris of wrapping paper, turkey, empty bottles, and to think to ourselves, "Well, it's over for another year." And sadly, many people forget the reason for this time of celebration. Christmas marks the birth of Jesus Christ, and in words from a well-known carol, we pray that he may be "born in us today." Christmas should herald a new beginning and give hope for the future. There are people for whom the message of peace gives courage and meaning to life, where once there was only despair. The shepherds who came to the stable went back to the fields, "glorifying and praising God for what they had seen."[2] Ordinary life resumes, but Jesus makes it different.

So, how many hundreds, probably thousands, of pounds have been spent by all of us on presents and provisions for Christmas this year? And why? There's more going on here than rampant consumerism and kids' "pester power," as the advertisers term it. Objects convey messages. They can be concrete expression of respect, regard, and affection. What's that got to do with Christmas? God gives presents, too. That's what the crib reminds us of. The greatest and most expensive present in the history of the world. Salvation in the form of a baby. Why a baby? So that God is small enough for us to reach out to without fear, to hold our arms out to with most innocent of loves—the love that a baby inspires in most human hearts. So, enjoy the richness of our human celebration. Be glad of all the trouble that you go to make this season special. And remember that

2. Luke 2:20.

behind our earthly festivities lie the incalculable opulence, splendor, and strength of God's love for each one of us.

## Waiting for the Lord

Be patient, therefore, beloved, until the coming of the Lord.

—James 5:7

No doubt we have all, at some time or other, had a visit from the Jehovah's witnesses. It's Friday night, you've just had a glass of sherry, and you are feeling a little sleepy. There are two people standing on the doorstep, a man and a woman. They introduce themselves as Jehovah's witnesses. Still half a sleep, you ask them if there has been an accident. The JWs pride themselves on being able to build a Kingdom Hall in less than forty-eight hours. The local JW leader in the town where my mother lives could not understand why anyone could object to an all-night building site. Half an hour before they started the hammering, drilling, and the singing of campfire songs, a team of missionaries had been around to every house on the estate to let people know that the world was coming to an end and to sell them a copy of the JW magazine *The Watch Tower*. This paper has been known to carry predictions as to when this event will happen. Despite what the Jehovah's Witnesses may say, nobody knows when Jesus will come again. That he will return, however, is certain because he has said so. In this, we can be confident because it rests on the powerful promise of God.

So, what is this second coming all about? The purpose of the second coming of Jesus Christ is stated in the creed. He shall come to judge the quick and the dead. So, what about judgment? What does it involve? Jesus, who is both God and man, shall judge us. He will judge us fairly because he knows our failures, our temptations, and struggles. Thus, we face our judgment through God's merciful and forgiving love revealed to us in Christ Jesus, who himself has gone through suffering. Hell was never intended for humankind, and we can only arrive there through a willful, deliberate, and continued rejection of God's goodness. Thus, it is not part of God's plan that we should go to hell and face everlasting torment. But rather, that we should enter the blessed condition of unending happiness in his presence.

So, what is the Christian gospel about? For Jesus' disciples, a golden age was about to dawn. But Jesus warns them that discord and confusion—that even the most established things will be shaken.[3] In times of peace and comfort, people are often content with things as they are. It is only when the established order is shaken that they recognize their need of Christ. So, our Lord warned his disciples to expect change and uncertainty in human affairs. The day of judgment will be the day of justice, when all life's inequalities will be put right. So, does that mean we leave it all to God and let the world go its own course? The answer has to be "No!" The readers of the Letter of James are to discern the signs of the times and not to be taken unawares when days of confusion and distress of nations come. We have not only to realize the instability of earthly things: we must learn to recognize that the crumbling of empires is a sign of the coming of the true kingdom.

How do we discern the signs of the times? As Christians, we can only do this with the help of the Bible, supported by church tradition, and reason. The Jehovah's Witnesses believe that God will come again to exterminate all those who do not believe the way that they do. They believe in a revengeful God who will wage a holy war against his own creation. They preach pits of fire, sulfur, and brimstone. The Gospels portray Jesus as a dangerous liberal who came into the world not to condemn but to save sinners. God does not send thunderbolts out of the sky to make us obey him. The choice is entirely our own. If we come to God, we come not out of fear but in love. From the time Jesus first came into the world, we have had this choice before us. God's patience, mercy, and understanding we cannot measure. We only know that he is still waiting for us.

How should we understand the return of Christ? Our Lord has not been slow concerning his promise to return. We would suggest that Jesus has come again in many more ways and in many more times than at first seem clear. Christ comes again and again into this world. He comes invisibly into the hearts of his followers. In the previous chapter, we considered Jesus' coming again in the glory of his resurrection. Jesus' disciples were quick to see, in the events of Easter, a fulfilment of his promise to return. But his coming again on Easter Day was not for the setting up of an earthly throne or for vengeance upon those who had crucified him. Jesus' coming again at Easter was to reveal the glory of God's righteousness.

Having considered Jesus' coming again in the glory of his resurrection, let us now think of Jesus coming again in the glory of his kingdom. If Christ reigned supreme in every human heart, if everyone hailed him

3. Matt 24:29; Rev 6:12–13.

as Lord and God, what a changed place the world would be. For Christ comes in the glory of his kingdom, when in temptation, we stand firm in our allegiance to his gospel. We thank God for the rewarding peace and calm of the quiet-conscience loyalty to Christ the king. So, how should we understand the second coming of our Lord Jesus Christ? And what about the child of the Bethlehem nativity? The baby that was born in squalor to redeem the dirt. The Almighty one, by whom and for whom all things were made, lay helpless in the arms of his young mother. We must follow our God-given instinct to reach with yearning love to the Christ child, who makes himself small enough for us to grasp. And with all the painful tears of joy, we shall enter the birth of the new age, where we shall grow with our Lord and become as he is. For Jesus has become as we were. As Christians, we have nothing to fear from the second coming of Christ. God did not appoint us to suffer wrath but to receive salvation. Christianity offers forgiveness to sinners, not condemnation. Jesus associated with sinners, and it was for them that he came into the world.[4] God has given us the perfect relationship to himself through our Lord Jesus Christ. It is what Christ has done, and what he still does, that makes our salvation possible. It is because Christ rose again from the dead that we can live with him in this life and the world to come.

• • •

The Letter of James calls upon us to put our faith into action. So, how do we do this? What are the means of channeling our love and respect for God and our service of him and our neighbors? The apparatus of organized religion—church buildings, church services, prayer and sacraments, clergy, PCCs, and churchwardens. These should be the means of building up and maintaining that real faith and commitment. The church is also the means of channeling to us the love and power and presence of God. Religion is often seen as a last resort in times of trouble. When the bottom falls out of our world, and we can do absolutely nothing about it—in desperation, we turn to God—perhaps, somehow or another, he can help. When our faith in ourselves is completely shattered, then we find the humanity to turn to God. How often, when the crisis is past, do we turn back to self-confidence and forget about God. It happened time and time again in the Old Testament and throughout the history of Christianity, too. True religion means

4. Luke 5:32; 1 Tim 1:15.

giving God the central place all the time, not merely using him to fill the gaps when all else fails.

We often sing the hymn "Will Your Anchor Hold in the Storms of Life," a song with familiar images in our thinking and talking about the Christian faith—images that point to the sureness, the security, the reliability of our faith. Another image is that of foundations: 'The Church's One Foundation," "Christ Is Made the Sure Foundation." The trouble is that, so often, we take the foundations of a building for granted. This part of any building is usually hidden away from sight underground. It's only when the cracks start to appear in the superstructure and bits start to fall off that we are forced to dig down and see what is happening. It's an enormous job making good the foundations of a building—enormously complex and expensive, and rarely can a proper job be done. It is usually a question of how effectively the foundations can be shored up and patched. We can't afford to let this happen to the spiritual foundations of our faith. Once the cracks appear, we are in a dangerous position, and when the building collapses in a storm, it is a long and difficult job to rebuild.

The Christian faith is for the whole of life, in every conceivable circumstance—not just an insurance against misfortune. It is a great pity that this later impression has often been given, and many people think of God only in times of trouble. When things are going well, it is all somehow irrelevant. But the Christian faith is relevant at all times, in prosperity as well as adversity. And we must take care not to forget this. In the introduction to the marriage service, Christian marriage is spoken of as "signifying unto us the mystical union that is betwixt Christ and his church." If the relationship between Christ and the church can illustrate the relationship of marriage, we can perhaps turn the illustration around and be helped in thinking about our relationship with Christ. For better for worse, for richer or poorer, in sickness and health, but not till death us do part. Rather, till death unites us perfectly in the life that is to come. We live in an age in which faith is not easy. The foundations are constantly being shaken by the traffic of materialism. But we do well to remember that Christ is the same yesterday, today, and forever. The rock cannot be shifted. Those whose faith is really founded upon the rock of Christ are the true pillars of the church. We need to nourish and maintain our spiritual foundations. We can only do this by living a Christ-centered life. And there are no short cuts, no easy ways out—we can't put this job out to contractors—we've got to do it ourselves. A Christ-centered life is one that involves regular prayer, reading the Holy Scriptures, penitence, and feeding on the body and blood of Christ in the holy sacrament of the altar. There is no substitute for these practical means of grace for those who really wish to make Christ the center of their lives—the rock on which their faith is grounded.

• • •

So, we ask again, how do we find the Christian hope in situations of despair? And if hope is about aspirations, how do we relate this to our faith? It is about looking forward to the future, yes. But it is a Christian vision of the future that is required. It is about where we want to go. And ultimately, it is about going to heaven. But quite a lot happens before then. Hope can also be seen as that bit of heaven come down to earth. Thus, we get to glimpse a small part of the divine hope. Clearly, hope is contained for the Christian in the person of Jesus Christ. Thus, hope for the future is to be found in our knowledge of God as revealed to us in his only begotten Son. We have to trust God, who has the overall plan. So, the Christian hope is to live with confidence in the newness and fullness of life, and to wait the coming of Christ Jesus. The Christian hope is waiting the completion of God's purpose for the world.

• • •

## The Covenant with God

The first covenant that God made with the human race was with Noah; the last was the great covenant through Christ Jesus. The word "covenant" is intrinsically dynamic. It means we're coming together. It is a word that has movement and change and mutuality as ideals attached to it. The word is used to show an agreement between God and humanity and suggests a common process that obliges both parties to certain actions. We sin when we seek our good apart from God or look to his gifts instead of to him. But God has reconciled us to himself through his Son, our Savior Jesus Christ. This is the good news of God in Christ Jesus, to which a response must be made. Jesus is certainly the chosen one of God and the way in front of him was the way of the cross. If we are to follow Christ, we must deny self and bear that cross also. That cross must be lifted high with an ever-new willingness by the higher and better self, which is one with Christ Jesus. The daily temptation to leave it and to leave Christ has to be denied. The call to grasp it tighter and press on more firmly has to be obeyed. Jesus had a clear and unique sense of destiny that was fulfilled in Jerusalem when God put all things into his hands. He would suffer and be put to death. He died to gain for us pardon and eternal life. But if Christ pleads his death before God in heaven, does this mean that in order to save us, God required a blood sacrifice? Surely, the answer has to be *no*. If the world had accepted his message, his death would have been unnecessary. Christ died for our sins in the same way that soldiers die for their country. God did not say that in consideration of Jesus' death, he would overlook our sins and allow us to escape that everlasting torment that our sins merit. No, Jesus saves us not so much from the consequences of sin as from sin itself—but this requires repentance on our part. Our sins are forgiven in the church through baptism and confession, and both of these require prayer. It is by prayer that the bond between our souls and God can be strengthened. In fact, prayer is essential. Without it, our vision of God would soon fade away. It is not only essential for us to pray, but it is natural to us. Our souls were made by God and for God in order that we might have communion with him. So, when we pray, we are doing that for which we were made.

As Christians, we come together on the first day of the week—the day Jesus rose from the dead—to remember him in the way that he gave us. The Eucharist prayer helps us to do this. In this sacrament, we are nourished and strengthened to confess by word and action the Lord Jesus Christ. In the Holy Eucharist, we find the real presence of the crucified and risen Christ. By the power of the Holy Spirit, bread and wine become the sacramental signs of Christ's body and blood. Amen.

• • •

In the early days of the Christian church, from the day of Pentecost on, the early Christians preached the gospel with an urgency that was compelling. It is possible from the Letter of James to build up a picture of the message they proclaimed—a message that impelled those who heard it to action. So, what was the content of their preaching? The prophecies are fulfilled and the new age inaugurated by the coming of Christ, who was born of the seed of David; who died for us according to the Scriptures, to deliver us from the present sinful age; who was buried, rose on the third day, according to the Scriptures; is exalted to the right hand of God the Father, and will come again as judge and savior of all. So, from reading the Letter of James, we have an opportunity to rediscover the Christian gospel for our own time—the relevance of the good news for our age, and then boldly preach the gospel to all people, as the author of James did in the power of the Holy Spirit. But we must, first of all, rediscover this for ourselves.

• • •

One of the challenges of the Letter of James is to hold fast to what we believe in the face of skepticism and hostility and, above all, in this present age, apathy. How can we meet those challenges when they come? In chapter 3, we discussed the virgin birth and acknowledged that for some people, this claim was impossible and was their last defense against faith. It reminds us of the scene at the end of C. S. Lewis's Narnia series in *The Last Battle*.[5] Aslan is a lion who moves between two worlds, the world that we inhabit and the world of Narnia, a world of fabulous creatures. Aslan is clearly Christ, the great Lion of Judah. The end of the world has come, and Aslan has arrived after his sacrifice on the stone table, his death to usher those who will come into the New Narnia. The entrance to this is through a tiny stable where it is very dark and where people stumble in some confusion until they find the other door and go through, and on, and up into the new world. Sacrifice, death, return, stable will all ring bells for Christians and, yes, that is what C. S. Lewis is referring to. Scores of people and creatures stream through the stable and find the way into the new world, but there are some beings that are stuck. These are apelike creatures, which suggest to me that C. S. Lewis thought that such people are not fully human, just closely related. They could not see the other door and wondered grumpily why everyone else was tramping around in the dark. Why was there so much fuss about this stable? Some of the humans who had gone through asked Aslan what was going on. They were distressed that these unfortunate creatures were still enchained in the old world and apparently unable to see the new that was freely available to them. We have always found this so helpful a picture. You can, out of your own determination, turn your back on God and on what God offers to us all in Christ Jesus through the incarnation. That is what the virgin birth and the stable are all about. They are about God saying that the first Advent came about in ways that challenge us to believe. And remember that we were created to explore and take risks even when

5. Lewis, *Last Battle*.

we get it wrong, as Adam and Eve did in the first great adventure of the apple. So, when people ask you about Christmas and the virgin birth, tell them that it is a matter of faith. Tell them that since they are asking about it, then they are already knocking at the door of the stable themselves, otherwise it wouldn't bother them. Tell them to go on worrying about it because what they might not realize is that any such concern is not an internal and private dialogue proper only to themselves; it is a genuine process of prayer under the influence of the Holy Spirit. It is the struggle of their faith to be born in the Christmases and our lives as we look to the final coming and the promise of his glory. Even so, come, Lord Jesus, come. Amen.

## Warning to Rich Oppressors

Come now, you rich people, weep and wail for
the miseries that are coming to you.

—James 5:1

This text is about greed and the accumulation of wealth at the expense of those less fortunate. James wants his readers to prioritize the kingdom of God, not earthly riches that can only bring judgment.[6] The warnings by James are offered to rich people because they are responsible for the plight of the poor. In the Old Testament, the prophets of the eighth century condemn the rich for their oppression of the poor. They speak out against the bribes and corruption. They take up the traditional cause of the widow and the orphan, who were, from the earliest times, the classic example of those who needed the protection of the guardians of justice.[7] Instead of administering this justice, the rulers had become the despoilers of the helpless. The ruling class increased their own houses and land by taking advantage of the distress of small farmers, who were subject to sickness, crop failures, inflation, and excessive taxation. Now, the peasants were offered loans, and if they were unable to pay them back at a later date, their land would be taken away and their children would be sold into slavery.

6. Barclay, *Letters of James and Peter*, 131.

7. Isa 1:17, 23; 10:2; Jer 7:5–7; Ps 10:14, 68:4–5, 82:3, 94:6, 146:9; Prov 23:10; Lam 5:3; Zech 7:9–10; Exod 22:22–24; Job 24:3, 29:12–13; Deut 10:18, 14:28–29; Mal 3:5; Ezek 22:7; Esth 2:7.

Let us not imagine that these prophets are dangerous left-wingers who would favor a Communist dictatorship. So, why are we accused of party politics when we speak out against the captains of industry, the directors of utility firms, who have given themselves massive pay rises, and the millionaire farmers and entrepreneurs who don't want to pay any taxes. Standing clearly in the tradition of eighth-century prophets along with the Letter of James, we believe there is a prophetic warning here for the business community of the UK, that they will be judged by this gospel.

> Listen! The wages of the laborers who moved your fields, which you kept back by fraud, cry out, and the cries of the harvesters have reached the ears of the Lord of hosts. (Jas 5:4)

The rich are only rich because they have exploited the poor, and their wealth is a sign of injustice.[8] The laborers here have been denied their pay.[9] James is speaking out against external forces that were working against the gospel. He is preaching at a time before the church became an institution and an instrument of the state. The church family is the household of Christian faith, and in James's time, the local church in a particular place was very likely a household and likely oppressed by these oppressors. It would be a bigger unit than our average nuclear family, including several generations. We read in the New Testament of whole households being baptized that transcend the boundaries of blood relations, of geography, of life and death. So there were no church buildings or churchwardens, and the faithful would meet at home for their worship. James warns not only against external oppressors but that the church should not be cozy to them and become complicit in their sinful behavior. James 5:4 calls to mind the parable of the unforgiving servant in Matthew's Gospel. This is about forgiving others as we are forgiven.[10] In this parable, we are reminded of the Lord's Prayer: "*Forgive us our trespasses, as we forgive them that trespass against us.*" So, we pray that God will so forgive us as we forgive others. Is this request conditioned by our forgiveness of others? Does this mean that God will not forgive us unless we forgive them that trespass against us? Are we not fit to receive mercy from God until we have shown it to others? But the lesson of the

8. Barclay, *Letters of James and Peter*, 137.

9. Deut 24:14–15; Lev 19:13; Prov 3:28; Jer 22:13; Mal 3:5; Sirach 34:26–27; Wis 2:13–20; Luke 10:7; 1 Tim 5:18.

10. Matt 18:34–35.

parable is not "forgive in order to be forgiven," but "forgive because you have already been forgiven."

The condemnation of the unmerciful servant is that after receiving mercy, he went to look for a fellow servant that was in debt to him, and having found him, offered him no mercy whatsoever. This relates to the oppressors James is talking about in his letter. The aim of this parable is to enlighten us, so that we see who we are and what Jesus has done for us. The threat of damnation is to alert us to our true state, as those who have been forgiven. We are in debt to God for work undone, for time and talents wasted. We cannot make good any part of what is owing. If we are hard to others like the oppressors in the Letter of James, while we cringe before God, our penitence is proved to be only the selfishness of cowards. Clearly, the qualities of love and forgiveness cannot be separated. As Christians, we are committed by our Lord's command to care for all people—whether they are Christians of whatever sort or not. Whether we consider them nice or not—whether they show any appreciation for our efforts or not. There are people, as we all know, to whom it is very difficult to show love. They could be difficult to approach. There are people who seem to resent any attempt at being friendly or helpful. Jesus said we were not just to love those who love us but everyone, including the difficult, the spiteful, those who hate us and abuse us. It should be one of the characteristics of a Christian that they are prepared to offer love even though they know that there is a strong probability that they will be rebuffed—even though they have been rebuffed by that very person, not once but many times before. Doesn't Jesus set a high standard?

If we think in terms of achieving this standard from the Letter of James and his understanding of the Christian gospel immediately, or even quite quickly, we shall be disillusioned. But the fact that it seems impossible is all the more reason that we should start somewhere, however inadequately—at least try to aim in the right direction. When Jesus commanded us to love all people, our enemies included, he must have meant love in another sense than we generally think of it. We must understand that these loving feelings are not always a reliable guide. We can't control our feelings to order. Nor will it be the kind of love that meets with any positive response, necessarily, in the person to whom it is directed—indeed, as we have already considered the response may even be the opposite. If we love our enemies, they are not necessarily going to stop being our enemies. But we pray that through the love we try to show, they may come to love, not us so much as Jesus, whom we serve.

## Trust in Earthly Wealth

Your gold and silver have rusted, and their rust will be evidenced against you, and it will eat your flesh like fire. You have laid up treasure for the last days.

—James 5:3

So, what is this text about? Judgment, self-examination, or salvation? And what about mercy? This is the difficult one as we read the Letter of James. If sinners are to be saved, then sins must be forgiven. But this can only happen through the love and mercy of God. So, how, then, does God do this? The forgiveness of sins is to be obtained in the Holy Catholic Church, and this happens in three ways. In baptism, in prayer, and in penance. All sin is washed away in baptism. By prayer, we refer to the petition in the Lord's Prayer, "*Forgive us our trespasses.*" And by penance, we refer to sacramental confession with a view to gaining absolution. I am sure James would counsel Christian converts as well as those who had been thought to have lapsed in the faith. They would have had something like an Alpha and an Emmaus course. So, let us then first look again at baptism. The first Christians truly believed that their sins had been washed away and that they were beginning a new life in Christ. What has all this got to do with the children who are baptized in our local church? And how can a baby have a living faith? From early times, children of Christian families were baptized. It was recognized that we who are born of earthly parents need to be born again, for holy baptism is an act of God upon the soul, which confers his special blessing and protection. But baptism by itself without commitment cannot give a child a Christian upbringing. Those who are too young to profess the Christian faith are baptized on the understanding that their parents will bring them up in the faith of the church. For this reason, parents and godparents are asked to affirm their allegiance to Christ and their rejection of all that is sinful.

So, what about prayer? If the bound between the soul and God is weakened by sin, it is strengthened by prayer. From reading the Holy Scriptures, we learn that prayer is a duty and a necessity and involves much more than merely asking for certain things. Our prayers must be offered in faith and through the merits of our Lord and Savior Jesus Christ. The Lord's Prayer, as its name implies, was composed by Jesus Christ. It is the prayer that we should most frequently use. And what can we say about penance? A penitent is a sinner sorry for their sin. Doing penance is putting right what has gone wrong between ourselves and God. It involves positive steps to change our lives by repenting of our sins and turning afresh to the Lord. The first Christians confessed their sins to one another to renew their membership of Christ's body. Today, we can make our penitence known to the church by approaching the priest as its local head, and they are given authority to welcome penitents back into the fold. The Church of England invites sinners, who cannot otherwise make their peace with God, to make their confession before a priest. It is a blessed privilege open to all who heartily desire it. We can receive the most direct assurance of pardon that Jesus Christ empowers the church to pronounce. In this, we must remember that, strictly speaking, to absolve is not to forgive because God alone forgives.

## Suffering Through the Lens of James

> Indeed we call blessed those who showed endurance. You have heard of the endurance of Job, and you have seen the purpose of the Lord, how compassionate and merciful the Lord is.
>
> —James 5:11

The message of James is clear—don't give up. It is endurance that made possible the witness of the prophets. Jesus had encouraged endurance as a necessary means of salvation.[11] James talks about Job's anguish as he considered the possibility that God had forsaken him, even though he never lost his faith.[12] So, as we approach the conclusion to this chapter, we want to first look at some of the Old Testament ideas about endurance, which are to be found in the book of Job. The basic storyline is simple. A man who has everything is afflicted with great ill fortune until all that he has is taken away from him, and he is left in great misery and distress. All his children are killed in freak accidents; his flocks and other such wealth is destroyed; his skin breaks out in a loathsome rash of sores. But in all this, Job did not utter one sinful word. After a long period of silence, he finally opened his mouth to regret the day upon which he was born. Job is someone who presumes to know the mind of God. Behind the storyline is the working out of several questions to do with problems of suffering.

11. Matt 24:13.

12. Barclay, *Letters of James and Peter*, 144.

Why do people suffer? Is it because they deserve it? And where does suffering come from anyway?

At the sight of Job's suffering, his three friends begin to weep and wail. One of Job's friends tells him that he has brought this trouble upon himself and that he should not resent it when God rebukes him. Job replies that he has never opposed what God commands and that, in times like these, he needs loyal friends. He asks his friends not to condemn him. Another friend tells Job to put his heart right before God and to put away all wrong from his home. Only then could Job face the world again, firm and courageous in his faith. Job responds by declaring himself innocent and asks why God is treating him like an enemy. But his friends ask if any man can be really pure and right with God. Job declares that the comfort his friends give him is only torment, for Job wanted someone to plead with God for him, as a man pleads for his friends. Job wants to know why his friends are tormenting him, since they regard his trouble as proof of his guilt. As far as they are concerned, Job is only hurting himself with his anger. They tell him to make peace with God and stop treating him like an enemy. But Job does not give up his claim to be right, since his conscience is clear. Eventually, Job's three friends give up trying to answer him. At this, a bystander tells Job that no one has the right to tell God what to do or accuse him of wrong.

In the book of Job, there is an all-knowing narrator who introduces the main characters and gives the readers information that the participants in the story do not have. As a literary device, it involves the readers in the drama in such a way as to be highly sympathetic with Job. This style of writing is also found in the Gospel of Mark, when the reader is let in on the secret that Jesus is the Messiah, who brings the good news of God. Thus, the reader begins to wonder about the disciples who seem unaware as to whom Jesus is. Job blames God for his suffering and wishes he were never born. However, it is not the suffering that concerns him but the misery of not knowing the true meaning of life. For the meaning or purpose of life is hidden from him, and the one who hides it is God. The protest that Job addressed to God is this: Why should the way of the wicked prosper? Why do those who are treacherous thrive? The questions raised about the cause and ultimate meaning of suffering leads Job to ask not simply *Why* but *Why me*? Job is a good man, so why has misfortune come upon him? When God finally begins to answer Job at the end of the book, he answers in the most irritating of ways, by posing further questions. Job admits that he had talked about things he did not understand. He is ashamed of all he has said and now repents in dust and ashes. After this, God blessed the last part of Job's life even more than he had blessed the first. It is through Jesus that we can understand the spiritual drama of Job. For it is the testimony of our Lord that shows this state of affairs in which the wicked prosper can only last while this present world runs its course.

• • •

Are any among you suffering? They should pray.

—James 5:13

We conclude this chapter by staying with the concept of suffering and faith. One of the constant struggles for us in the Christian faith is to deal with the question of suffering. We are sure you have heard it said before, "Why does a good God allow bad things to happen?" It is something that we have all asked, and many of us will have been asked often by people in harrowing circumstances. Why does God give me so much hardship when others, who never give him a moment's thought, seem to sail through life without a care? I've always tried to be a good Christian but is it really worthwhile persevering, trying to say my prayers, making my Communion regularly, when so many people have obviously decided it's all a waste of time? Why does God allow such suffering in the world? All of us, some time or another, find ourselves thinking like this—and many fail the test and give up. Clearly, our faith is tested. But isn't this testing something we should be prepared for? Doesn't it make a tremendous difference to the way we react to such temptations to despair if we think of them as a way in which God strengthens our faith? It all sounds great and noble, doesn't it? Jacob's faith, Abraham before him, journeying in faith, Jesus talking about putting aside anxieties—the stories have all been written and they have a comforting, tidy air of completion. We don't know about you, but we sometimes get rather frustrated with these stories of heroism in the faith. How are we supposed to live up to the ideals of complete faith? It's as if we are being asked to gamble in some crazy, religious kind of roulette. What we do have to remember is that these stories do come to us in retrospect. The perspective of history always makes things seem to hang together. I bet Abraham and his family felt just as uncertain as you or I might in similar circumstances. We know that Jacob, for all his conning and other faults, spent a lot of time being very miserable and uncertain. And Jesus didn't have an easy deal. For most of us, our leaps of faith are not to these Olympic standards. Falling in love and getting married, that is a huge leap of faith. And faith and love are close partners, after all. Having a child, now that's a dangerous journey. Making a new friend is perilous because friendship makes us vulnerable. Changing our natural inclinations so that we can do acts of charity and generosity—that, too, is living the life of faith. When you check on a neighbor, visit the hospital, do the thousand and one acts of kindness that I know Christian people do, these are all demonstrations of faith and monuments along life's pathway to the call of God's love working in us.

So, what, then, is this thing called faith? Faith is one of those words that is always cropping up and whose meaning is usually taken for granted. What do we mean when we talk of the Christian faith? Basically, faith is believing—believing in God as revealed in his Son, Jesus Christ. The creed is a summary of the Christian faith. In a very practical way, God must be so real to us that we are prepared to put our trust in him. God sees the whole picture—we see only a limited part. God had a plan for Israel, his chosen people, and right at the beginning of it, he had a key part lined up for Abraham. Obviously, Abraham would not be able to grasp the ultimate importance of his part—the question was whether he was faithful enough to trust God and get on with it without asking too many questions. So often, people think of faith in terms of feelings and emotions. It's worth giving some thought to the fact that it may have more in common with standards of discipline. This isn't to say that unless we automatically respond to God's call without a second's hesitation, we have no faith—or if we have misgivings about what God asks of us, we have no faith. Abraham's faith was tested and so is ours, and we have to learn to trust him. Life and faith are not always full of excitement, rushing around moving mountains, but more often being quietly faithful. Being quietly faithful in our prayers and in our worship, in our communion, in trying to love our neighbor, and trusting in God so that it really makes a difference to our whole outlook on life.

So, what is our Christian hope? What is the point of living a life of faith? How can we be sure that God is good and just and fair? This question has vexed people since the dawn of time. Life is what is given to us. In one lifetime, we can have truly little control over anything except our own hearts and those we must struggle with. Life is uncertain, and we have to learn to survive in the light of that fact. The Christian hope is that our persistence will be rewarded at the end of time. We hope that God will hear and will ultimately rescue us. This is no insurance policy that removes the worst of life's stressful and painful difficulties. The hope is that God, who had the first word, will also have the last say; that God is faithful; that God is loving and just; and that all will be well. God sees all, forgives all, and heals all in the fullness of eternal life. God sent his Son Jesus to live in our flesh and to suffer all the troubles and pains of human life so that we might become as he is, perfect and loving, bringing good to all. We could not write this book without that faith and the prophetic guidance that has been freely given. And that, for us, is part of our traditional understanding of Christian evangelism and discipleship. Through it, I will find the strength to face all that life brings. Through faith, we can trust and live freely in this life and the next. So, how does this relate to *the Letter of James and the disestablishment of the Church of England*? How do we proclaim the faith of the church? This is the subject matter of this commentary.

David recently had a three-way conversation with two men whose wives had died within the last year. As their conversation progressed, it became clear that trusting in our Christian faith was not the issue but rather what they had to go through to realize that faith. David also thought, at the time, that he was ministering to their need to talk about their experiences, but Linda had been ill, and we wonder now if they were ministering to us, just in case David should be where they were. Fortunately, Linda is on the mend, but no one knows what is around the corner. In our experience, a so-called crisis of faith is usually about suffering and how we are going to engage with the anguish we face. There are not many easy answers, if any at all. We live this life in faith and in trust to God in the divine and everlasting arms. The suffering is upsetting because it is real, not a fantasy. So, do we want to live in a real world or one that does not really exist?

So where does suffering come from? Are we, because of our sinful ways, responsible? Do we deserve to suffer and is it our fault? Does God punish us for our sins? These are real questions that need to be addressed by the Christian faith. The starting point, if not the answer, can be found in New Testament Scripture. There is no divine retribution for the sins that we commit in this life, even though many people like the idea of a punishing God. Clearly, some dreadful things happen because of sin, but that is not the same thing as punishment from God. Jesus does not connect sin exclusively with calamity. In Luke's Gospel, we hear about the Tower of Siloam that fell on eighteen people, and Jesus says that they are not worse sinners than anyone else who lived in Jerusalem at that time.[13] I am sure there were cowboy builders then as there are now.

• • •

In the modern world, suffering is no longer a fashionable concept. The old adage *suffer in silence* is laughed at today. We are astounded, when someone is not fit or not thin, if we have some other cause of unhappiness. It seems that we are under some unwritten and unspecified obligation to be healthy, radiantly so; happy, ecstatically so; and both continually. When Linda was explaining to some agnostic friends of hers a few years ago about the relationship between her and Jesus and a sense of vocation, they remarked, "But it doesn't seem to make you happy." They were genuinely shocked when she retorted, "What's happiness got to do with it?" So, what does the word suffering mean? It comes from a word that has the idea of bearing and carrying. The one who suffers is under a heavy load of some kind. We have to, therefore, suffer as Christians because part of our calling is to bear one another's burdens. Suffering, then, is central to the Christian life. I think we are called into suffering in two ways: firstly, through the works that God has prepared for us to do; secondly, through living as a loving intercessor in and for the world.

What James says about suffering ought to be compulsory reading for all those who say that Jesus makes everything better, as if he were reduced to the triviality of rosy spectacles on a grey day.[14] For Jesus does not make everything better in that individualized and tritely personal sort of way. Many of us can vouch for the fact that at the personal level, Jesus and his sweet, irresistible call makes things worse with more conflict, more uncertainty, and demanding what always feels like just that bit more than we can give. Yes, of course, underneath are the everlasting arms, but they are everlastingly requesting, beseeching, commanding us in all kinds of arduous labors. God has promised not to try us beyond our strength, but he sure does define our absolute limits. There was a campaign a few years ago to pray the news, to make it part of our Christian life to prayerfully give attention to the news each day. That was a call to take on the burden of suffering. The ears of those turned towards God who weep for the pains of others are powerful protests against the unrighteousness of the world. Tears are prayer and are part of suffering. Perhaps you are not

13. Luke 13:4.

14. See Jas 1:2–4; also, Rom 5:1–5.

a natural weeper, but you can remember before God what is laid on your heart. It doesn't have to be a complicated prayer couched in technical language. We need to practice prayerful alertness. Remember that we are the body of Christ here on earth. Remember that God chooses to come to us in human size, which means that God depends on us being human to achieve the divine plan. Prayer must be accompanied by action, but only through prayer do we discern what action is needed. Then, perhaps the Letter of James will remind us of that God, who made all things and loves all his children. To pray is to suffer—to pray is to be called into the life of Christ. To pray is to live a positive but costly life—the only life that can makes changes for the better.

• • •

Are any among you sick? They should call for the elders of the church and have them pray over them, anointing them with oil in the name of the Lord.

—James 5:14

James was concerned with health in its widest aspect. God created people whole. James understands that Jesus showed God's concern to restore that wholeness or health, which we had lost. Wholeness is more than just physical well-being. Wholeness, as God meant us to be, is the health of body, mind, and spirit. All of us *should* accept the possibility of illness, or accidents involving broken limbs, or rheumatic disability, and mental health issues in older age. We are sympathetic to those who suffer. We demand a high standard of medical care and constantly press for improved treatment, and research into illnesses and complaints, as yet unconquered by medical science. In whatever way we can, we cooperate with God in relieving physical suffering and promoting health, whether as doctors or nurses, helpers, visitors, or intercessors. This is our Christian duty. But, as Christians, we know that the material, physical side of life is only one aspect. It is important, but not the most important. For one thing, the physical world is only a temporary one—we believe in life eternally. It is all too possible to have physical health and all the material requirements and yet be sick.

Mental health is at least as important as physical health. Yet, here, attitudes are quite different. People are embarrassed and frightened. They will talk openly and at length about operations and rheumatics. When it comes to mental illness, there are hushed whispers. Mental illness is just as crippling and just as distressing to the other members of a family. Depressive illnesses are perhaps the fastest growing of all disabling illnesses at the present time. People who are mentally ill are ordinary people who are ill. And what about the spirit? The most neglected aspect of health, and yet, in the end, the real key. What is the use of physical and mental health if we don't know what to do with them? Spiritual health is concerned with the answers to questions like, who am I? What should I be doing with the life and gifts God has given me? What is life really about? What is life eternal? It is concerned with attitudes and a sense of purpose. It depends on our realizing that we can't be spiritually healthy on our own; we depend on God—on his grace, his love, his inspiration, his forgiveness, and his strength. The way God made us, we can't be whole people; we can't, in the highest sense, find happiness unless we are healthy in spirit. We ought to think in terms of spiritual sickness, and the right treatments for the sins that cause it. We can gain an insight into the importance of spiritual health that leads to life eternally in all its fullness. Having gained this insight, it is up to us to accept the healing power of God through the sacraments of the church.

## Endnote

The Christian Church *certainly* had very humble beginnings among the readers of the Letter of James. We are told that there was no rush of learned and influential people to join the faith. The early church then was anything but fashionable. The author of James had to ask and try to answer the question, why, since the gospel was such good news, so vitally important, did it fail to make much impression on the so-called wise, the mighty, and the noble? Well, the message just didn't get through to them. The Pauline tradition tells us that to many Jews, the cross was a stumbling block, and to the Greeks, the intellectuals, it was foolishness—they just couldn't see the truth and relevance of the gospel. And this must have been puzzling and frustrating to the readers of the Letter of James, who would have been bursting with the importance of the message they had heard and understood and accepted. We, the authors of this commentary, have heard over the years from Anglican pulpits that Jesus chose twelve ordinary men to be his apostles, which leads us to ask just how ordinary were they? Peter was a fisherman *working for* a family firm with hired men, and Paul made tents in his spare time. John was a scholar; Luke, a physician; and Matthew, some kind of an accountant. So, should we think of these apostles as a group of simple fishermen or, perhaps, as a cross section of the skilled and professional people of their day? Well, let's look at this in more detail. In Palestine, the first Christians were tax collectors and outcasts of society. In Asia Minor, Greece, and Rome, many were slaves. There were a few from the higher ranks of society—Joseph of Arimathea, if he was a real historical character, must have been at least on the fringe of the apostolic band and seems to have been a man of some influence, in that he was able to approach Pilate and ask for Jesus' body after his crucifixion. We have mentioned that St. Luke was a physician, not that this implies the professional status of a present-day medical doctor, but it implies education and learning. A woman called Chloe figures in the Epistles, and she seems to have been a person of some financial substance.

We must be careful to remember that James's thoughts were directed to the particular situation that faced the church at the time he was writing and the people he was addressing. It would be quite unjustifiable to conclude that the church was only for the poor, although the marginalized clearly have a significant place in the program of change that was being considered. At that particular time and place, the educated and wealthy had clearly not been led to accept the Christian faith. And perhaps, this was not something to be despondent about but something to accept as part of God's will. After all, many times before, God had worked wonders through the most unlikely people in the most adverse circumstances. The message of James is that Christianity, therefore, must be for all people, rich and poor alike; but that does not mean that the rich are allowed to exploit and create a class of the poor.

So, how willing are we to put ourselves at God's disposal and to trust him? Do we want to let everyone know—to invite them to use the many opportunities to express, in worship, fellowship, and study, their love for God and to take their place in his church? Are we willing to challenge injustice? One important means of proclaiming the gospel is simply talking to people about our faith and the righteousness we seek in Christ's name. We talk anyway about the weather and the price of things—why not make sure our neighbors and acquaintances know where we are coming from. This has to be a mission imperative. It is a matter for great thanksgiving, which ought to spill over as we seek to keep firm our own faith and to extend this privilege to others.

# Conclusion

## *Disestablishment as the Contextual Theology of Liberation*

WE WRITE FROM LOVE and loyalty for the Church of England, but some will find our views shocking; some may even refuse to accept that this is the reality for a failing institution. This is a carefully written book that deserves careful reading. It will be eye opening for many, reassuring some that they are not as alone as they sometimes feel. From the start, we should say as authors that, because we are Anglicans, we find ourselves critical of the Church of England. This is because we are very familiar with its foibles and idiosyncrasies, and this will sometimes involve using polemic to challenge its senior leadership. It follows from this that we reserve the right to speak truth to power during a very challenging time and to call out incompetent and corrupt leadership. However, our critique is motivated by a genuine love of the Church of England. We care deeply about this organization and want to see it liberated from state control.

So, what does disestablishment of the Church of England mean? A disestablished church would cut its formal links with the king, Parliament, and government. But this does not mean that people would no longer be able to say they were C of E unless they came to church each week and were on our electoral role, even if they know what that meant. In other words, the church would not abandon its responsibility to the people who live in England. It follows from this that the church is of necessity in the world, and the Letter of Janes teaches us that we are Christ's church militant here on earth. We can't escape from the tensions of this, from the responsibilities that it entails. In the deepest sense, the church cannot be godly and worldly at the same time. We cannot serve God and mammon. So we need watchfulness concerning the purpose of the church. It is here to devoutly serve God in all good works, doing all to the glory of his name—God, at the very center of everything, a sure trust in his protective and supporting power, and a clear view of the fruits of godliness—all this must be our aim. If our godliness, our primary concern for God and for the will of God and things of God, does not show itself in our lives, then it isn't worth very much. The message of James is clear: if we don't take use of the protection and strength of God to get on with his work, then we have no right to ask for its privileges.

The church is the household of faith. All Christians who have been baptized are members of this household. The family can be identified at different levels: at the local level, the national, and the worldwide. There has been a great deal of attention devoted to household reorganization in the Church of England. We now have an Archbishop's Council as well as General Synod. All this change may seem somewhat confusing. But most of it is necessary, and much of it is overdue. There can be no justification for maintaining a chaotic household, possibly in debt for lack of proper management, neglectful of the family house, wasteful of the family resources, with parts of the family out of touch with others. If, for a long time, it has not been possible to tackle these things for very good reasons. If, for a long time, no one has been convinced of the need to do anything—this is no good reason for shirking the tremendous task that faces us now when circumstances are changed. So, change is often necessary. But it is possible to imagine a household where the fabric of the building is in top condition, well maintained and modern, with every useful aid and gadget to enable the household to function smoothly; with efficient management of money and resources; and a faultless routine for meals and recreation, and yet, something essential is lacking. Something that can't be measured or produced to order. Something that can only be described in terms of warmth and purpose in life. There is nothing specifically godly about conservatism—keeping things the way they are because that's how they always have been. Nor is there any guarantee that a refurbished, reorganized, reunited church will necessarily be any more about the will of God. This essential factor depends on the will of individual Christians—to be godly, the church needs the total commitment and dedication to God.

In our introduction, we have discussed Anglicanism as the local expression of the Christian church, focusing upon universality embodied in the historical formularies of the Church of England. We now draw some conclusions as we explore the colonial legacy of that tradition as it is experienced within a contemporary context. To do this, we must examine the diverse cultural, political, and social influences emanating from the relationship between church and state in the light of increasing calls for the disestablishment of the Church of England.[1]

This book also opened, albeit towards the end of the introduction, with a consideration of the sociology of transcendent reality. This was done to demonstrate that contextual theology was serious about the sociology of religion and about making its own contribution to that subject within the mainstream of religious activity. The combination of theism and English ethnicity is found in a deep Anglicanism, in which the Church of England as an institution looks back to its past. However, the church also promotes a belief in a transcendence that is essentially eschatological and, as such, is concerned with the future. The challenge of a split temporal dimension is important for the church. The *kairos* of the cross rests upon the *chronos* of the world. The commentary on James explores the possibility that Christians who follow the teachings of this letter are likely to experience alienation from the Church of England and to perceive its liturgy and ethos as the exclusive concern of the privileged and their life experiences. The mode of involvement of the less privileged in the Church of England is likely to be shaped by their experience of individualized exclusion and marginalization, and this can be found in institutionalized practices that work against them. It is the values and norms that form part of Englishness, and not the Christian gospel, that governs the treatment of those who did not go to public schools and join and promote a network of privilege. It is inclusion and exclusion in the Church of England that governs the mode of involvement of Christians within that institution.

From the start of this commentary, there has been an implicit hypothesis, and the authors now seek to make it explicit, which is as follows:

*The hierarchy of the Church of England promotes favoritism of the rich and wealthy because it is just as much concerned with promoting a post-colonial English culture as it is the faith of the universal church.*

1. Buchanan, *Cut the Connection.*

As far as we, the authors, are concerned, this hypothesis was upheld by our theological commentary. Chapter 1 set the tone by defining the Christian faith as doing the word of God. James's readers are encouraged to take on this faith by the way they live their lives. So, there is a dichotomy between accepting the word and actually doing it. There is a call to prayer to maintain an authentic faith; and in this, there is no room for artificial piety or hypocrisy, which we, the authors of the commentary, identify with the establishment. In chapter 2, Jesus is the author and finisher of the Christian faith, the completion of expectations from the Old Testament, and the beginning of a new era. With the guidance of the Letter of James, we can realize the relevance of the good news for our age. Again, a claim to faith must be put into action, and without this action, there is no genuine faith. As it says in our hypothesis, the hierarchy of the Church of England promotes favoritism of the rich and wealthy because it is just as much concerned with promoting a post-colonial English culture as it is the faith of the universal church. We launched chapter 3 by praying for the humility of our scholarship. Many of the senior pastors don't have to worry about this because there is a lack of scholarship amongst the hierarchy, and this has made its own contribution to the Church of England crisis. It is about identity and praxis and is reflected in its choice of leadership. The church does not know how to manage its appointment system because control is with the state. English ethnicity is bound up with the Church of England, and if the church is in crisis, then so is Englishness. The quest for an English identity that leaves behind the colonial past and the British identity of empire would involve a process of change that many privileged Anglicans will find difficult. It involves an explicit realization of the Christian faith that is advocated by the Letter of James. So, should this tell us that disestablishment is well overdue? Chapter 3 ended with the theology of the cross, and chapter 4 was about Jesus' resurrection from the dead. The implicit implications for disestablishment of the Church of England to be found within this theology will be left to readers to consider following our further conclusions. So, how should we understand the return of Christ? Chapter 5 is about waiting for the second coming and acknowledges that our Lord has returned to this world in many more ways than we could possibly imagine. So, we are asked to be patient and to discern the signs of the times with the help of the Bible, supported by church Tradition, and reason, which is the Anglican way of doing things. This leads to *warnings to rich oppressors* concerning greed and the accumulation of wealth at the expense of those less fortunate. There is nothing wrong with wealth if it is used for the common good. In a set of parishes on the Northamptonshire/Leictershire border, there were at least six millionaires, and we know that two of them were engaged in projects that help those in situations of poverty. In David's last parochial situation, two very kind and generous people funded a private ambulance to get Linda to our retirement location. In that same benefice, there were many discrete acts of charity in support of the parsonage house and its household. We mention all this because, as authors, we are indeed advocates of a socialist society, but this does not prevent us from acknowledging the good in all people under God. In chapter 5, we made it clear that Christianity was for all, rich and poor alike. So, the Letter of James calls upon us to put our faith into action. However, the actions of the Church of England hierarchy are found to be wanting, and the system they support calls for the disestablishment of the same.

There is a concern with maintaining a church structure, and the characteristics of that structure is a point of contention between competing groups. The political agenda is not necessarily theistic but cultural, often involving issues of ethnicity and class. We can identify a group of people in the church institution who are reactionary and opposed to any form of change. These church civil servants and their supporters operate from the center and can be in conflict with General Synod, the church's parliament. They can also be identified as a certain class of people with a history and occupying a definite position within the English class system. They are the retired brigadiers who had always been around in the church and know how to move in church circles. Another group of people are identified as innovative and aspiring, and some of them are younger. There is also something in here about the tension between rural and urban.[2] A modern feature of Englishness can be found in the actions of wealthy people, who move out of towns to live in the countryside, some of whom are very influential in the Church of England. This leads us back to the novels of our introduction that were used to explore different types of Englishness and how clergy were portrayed in works of fiction—Henry Fielding, Jane Austin, George Eliot. We are looking there at a shift through squirearchy, to gentry to petty bourgeoisie, and this is one of the tensions in Susan Howatch's series. *Nouveau riche* clergy finding their way on to the bench of bishops and various boards around the church all have implications for our hypothesis about Englishness,

2. See Isiorho, *Faith in Church Newspapers*, 2.

although this group is no longer in the ascendancy because their distinctive contribution has not moved the church on. This is the Englishness of the Church of England to say the polite thing, in this case, that which might be considered politically correct but not really mean it. This leads us to ask the question, how serious is the church institution about any of its policies?

In this context, we explore the mode of involvement of those who, like us, value the church but not its establishment. This has been the focus for this book. The political agenda to which this mode of involvement relates is seen in the response from the church hierarchy, which claims there is not a problem because the institution upholds the lot of the poor and underprivileged. Our research would suggest that the Church of England's conceptualization of a classless society, where we are all equal under God, is actually a technique allowing the institution to avoid the very issues upon which such a concept should be constructed. Institutional exclusion from the decision-making processes in the Church of England clearly owes its origin to values located within English ethnicity, but these values are then expressed in the actions of policymakers who operate within a system that denies their culpability. By adopting the stance of challenge to institutional exclusion, the church locates exclusion as a problem within the collective and, as such, does not see it as an error of the institutional functionary who are archdeacons and bishops. Thus, they abdicate personal and individual responsibility. There is no serious note of personal contrition on the part of senior officeholders for policies that are intentionally or unintentionally discriminatory. There is no real attempt to confront the processes that characterize their own mode of involvement. It could be argued that it is only when senior managers are able to confront their exclusion of the underprivileged, both individually and personally, that they will be able to detect and challenge it as it operates at an institutional level. It appears that the church hierarchy prefers to blame the institution but never their own personal part in it. Thus, their own position is protected. If mistakes are made by the institution, then it is the institution that is criticized by its own mangers, who, then are seen as courageous because they have acknowledged the problem. The political agenda here is about finding a convenient concept that will act as an alibi and, in doing so, make the Church of England look as if it were following the New Testament. The Church of England operates historically in response to social need. It waits for society to set the agenda on social concerns before it is seen to address them. The Church of

England commissioned a number of reports to maintain an authoritative voice within the discourse of society and out of fear that it had become ghettoized to its own concerns. Church reports are concerned with looking back, even though they are meant to be about looking forward. This also helps to explain why the Church of England is locked within a social dynamic that has more in common with an English novel than with a genuine interest in a belief in God. Thus, the Church of England does not see these reports as acts of mission but rather as acts of authority and of preservation of authority. *Faith in the City*[3] and *Seeds of Hope*[4] are really about maintaining the church's status within the political establishment.[5]

That the Church of England felt that it should make a special effort to say anything about urban priority areas is interesting in itself. It should be within the normal vocabulary and discourse of the church to address the issue of justice without having to commission a series of reports. A biblical perspective tells us about defending the poor and needy and not gleaning your field to the edge. This answers the issues of social justice, since it is the Black communities in our society that are most likely to live in the urban areas of deprivation. Furthermore, the emphasis on equality to be found in the Letter of James should not leave Christians in any doubt about their responsibility to resist injustice.

## Prayers That Lead to Change

The good Samaritan is a well-known parable in which Jesus used figures in first-century society who have expectations upon them.[6] Today, we would draw upon bishops, members of Parliament, and rich farmers who think they should be exempt from paying taxes. As David has said in another publication, the Samaritan carried his equivalent of a first aid kit and was ready not to look away.[7] So, when we meet a stranger, we are also a stranger to them, but the relationship is not an equal one. We encounter strangers who belong to social groups, some of which are less dominant and powerful than others. For example, if we belong to the

3. Archbishop of Canterbury's Commission on Urban Priority Areas, *Faith in the City*.

4. Church of England Committee on Black Anglican Concerns, *Seeds of Hope*.

5. Isiorho, *Black Clergy Discontent*, 215–17.

6. Luke 10:25–37.

7. Isiorho, *Faith in Unions*, 112.

majority group and encounter a stranger who belongs to a minority ethnic, religious, or sexual group, then we may have the power to make them conform to our norms.

So, how do we and how should we receive Christ in the stranger? What do you think? Clearly, there is not a level playing field between us and those we encounter as strangers. This homily does not examine how virtuous an outsider is. Instead of this approach, we want to look at the relationship between prayer and action. In the good Samaritan parable, Jesus tells a story that defines neighbor not in terms of race, religion, or proximity but in terms of vulnerability. Those of you who have been on safeguarding training will appreciate this important concept. In this context, it means whoever is in need is your neighbor. Jesus does not ask who was the Samaritan's neighbors. Rather, he asks who *acted* like a neighbor. The answer, of course, is obvious to the lawyer and to us: it is the Samaritan, the one who went out of his way to help another. But this changes things. Suddenly, the neighbor is not simply the one in need but rather the one who provides for *our* need, the one who takes care of us. Which raises an interesting—and often uncomfortable—question: Who has been our neighbor by caring for us as of late? This is uncomfortable because we spend so much of our time, energy, and money to need as little as possible from those around us. Is it a fear of being a burden or a concern about "owing" others? Are we afraid of being vulnerable because, if we show our need, that need may not be met? Whatever the reason, however, so many of us are absolutely mortified by the idea of showing our deepest needs to others. We have a hard time receiving a compliment, let alone serious aid or help. Yet, if we are reading this parable right, it seems that according to Jesus, being a neighbor involves not only giving help but also being willing to receive it—even and especially to and from those we do not normally see as "like us." The only way we can see ourselves as the Samaritan—the one called to give help and healing to those in need—is first to recognize how often we have been the traveler left for dead.

When Jesus tells the parable of the good Samaritan, he is giving a clear steer to his followers. This is a teaching the readers of the Letter of James would have no difficulty in comprehending and acting upon. After delivering the parable, Jesus goes to see Mary and Martha.[8] We all know the story: Mary wants to listen to what Jesus has to say, but Martha is

8. Luke 10:38–39.

concerned with getting a meal ready and demands that Mary should help her in this task. As far as Jesus is concerned, Mary has chosen the appropriate course of action and questions are now raised about prayer and action.[9] It is one thing to affirm that Mary has chosen the better part. It is quite another to affirm that it will not be taken away from her. So, Jesus does not send Mary back to the kitchen to help Martha and confirm the traditional roles of women. However, this story is not just about gender roles. After all, Mary was not the only person in the room who could help with preparing supper. Luke assumes that the most important response we can give is to receive Jesus' word. This means prayer comes before action. And this prayerful action can call us to relinquish roles and patterns of behavior that we once thought as "tried and tested."

• • •

The next section of this commentary is about liberation theology. So, where does the theology of Gutierrez and the Letter of James fit into this? Well, our commentary deals with questions concerning salvation, justice, and the knowledge of God. This is an opportunity to give greater clarity to what we understand about those concepts through the lens of an eminent biblical theologian. So, the next section of this conclusion will focus upon the work of Gustavo Gutierrez and the use of the Bible in the construction of a Latin American theology of salvation.[10] We will review this theology from a sociological perspective in order to place it into the context of a model for change, which has been influential in the Anglican church.[11]

In order to understand how Gutierrez uses the Bible to construct liberation theology, we will review his 1983 work *The Power of the Poor in History*.[12] He begins by explaining God's revelation in proclamation in history. He starts from the faith assumption that the Bible is the word of God. However, he admits that it is difficult to approach the Bible from any other approach but interdisciplinary. He readily concedes that some

9. Luke 10:42.

10. See Duffield, "Changing Liberation Theology," 61–62.

11. See Green, "Liberation Theology and Urban Theology," 39–40. He notes six principles of salvation/liberation that the comfortable classes found offensive, which includes the following: full salvation must include liberation; all theology is contextual; the life of faith demands a dynamic of action and reflection; theology must always be concerned about power; theology must hold fast to God's concern for the poor and marginalized; theological work is a witnessing spirituality. See also Green, *Let's Do Theology*.

12. Gutierrez, *Power of the Poor*.

will read the Bible and adapt the message to their own time, while others will desire to reinterpret it from their own experience. This last approach, he believes, goes to the roots of the Bible message. He suggests we start with Christ, as the fulfillment of the promise of God the Father, so as to understand the unity between the Old and New Testaments. This, he explains, will make our reading christological yet, at the same time, a reading in faith not constructed by specialists but by a community knowing itself to be the Bible's intercession. He stresses that Christ is the Lord of history and of the community's own life. He further maintains that the reading of the Bible will be historical, God revealing himself in the history of the people, and this leads us to rethink his word in the context of our own history.

Gutierrez suggests that our reading of the Bible will be a militant one, for the questions about the word of God will arise out of Christian practice. He believes we should reclaim the militant reading and that we need to read from the perspective of the persecuted in the cause of right. He describes how God reveals himself in history and he gives an example in Deuteronomy.[13] Gutierrez maintains that the reference to Jacob expresses the historical origin and modest beginnings. In the liberation from oppression in Egypt, the God of biblical faith is revealed. He explains that this is an open-ended history—open to the future. There are, he stresses, to be many liberations from oppression, for example, in Latin America. Faith, he points out, is to be found in the light of the present, not in remembrance of the past. Gutierrez sets out what he thinks are the essential elements of a liberation theology for the establishment of justice and right. For him, the God of the Bible governs history and also orientates it in the appropriate direction of the establishment of justice and right. He is the God who takes sides with the poor to liberate them. This liberation, he points out, is not a demonstration of God's power—but to bring about justice. Gutierrez attempts to explain the semantics by telling us that to know God is to do justice. He goes on to explain the context in which the word *knowledge* is used—to know is not entirely intellectual; to know means to love. Sin becomes the absence of love; therefore, to know God as liberator is to liberate, is to do justice.

For Gutierrez, our relationship with God is expressed in our relationship to the poor. For Gutierrez, to mock the poor is to insult their

13. Deut 26:5–9.

creator.[14] What Gutierrez calls the touchstone of injustice is to sin—not to love, not to know. He illustrates this by saying that if someone pretends they believe, the truth of this will be discovered in their practice with regard to the poor. Thus, knowledge of God is found in actual practice. Justice in the Bible, he maintains, is what unites one's relationship with the poor to one's relationship with God. This is necessary for justice to mean holiness. He goes on to make the statement that Jesus Christ is God become poor. Gutierrez raises the question of Christianity being linked to one culture, i.e., White and western, and feels that this is a subversion of history. It could be said that Latin American history is, in fact, a memory of Christ who is present in all, especially in the despised, minorities and exploited classes. He advocates non-support of the prevailing domination. A new spirituality is to be found, and a new proclamation of the gospel made. He visualizes a church of the people marked by a response of the poor to the call of Christ and foresees a time when there will be, as he calls it, social appropriation of the gospel, when the poor dispossess those who consider it their private property.

In his earlier work, *A Theology of Liberation* (1973), Gutierrez examines the relationship between salvation and liberation of people in history.[15] He looks for the meaning of the struggle against an unjust society. He attempts to explain what is meant by salvation and acknowledges the difficulties in doing so but emphasizes that the salvation of the whole person reflects that it is taken for granted that the concept is easily understood. He says that investigation reveals two main threads that have closely linked stages. The first is interested in the numbers of persons being saved, the possibility of being saved, and the part played by the church in this, i.e., the universality of salvation and the church as the mediator. The second thread is concerned with the possibility that there is more to salvation than simply asserting the possibilities from outside the church. A search has begun for the means to widen the possibility of human salvation. People are saved if they open themselves to God and to others, even if they are not aware they are doing so. Salvation is the communion of people with God and the communion of people among themselves. Thus, it embraces all human reality. Gutierrez sees sin, then, as a break with God—a historical reality. A breach of communion of people with each other is an obstacle to life reaching a fullness called salvation.

14. Prov 17:5.

15. Gutierrez, *Theology of Liberation*.

Gutierrez appears to be concluded that there are not two histories—one profane, the other sacred, closely linked—but rather one human destiny assured by Christ, the Lord of history. The Bible, he maintains, establishes a close link between creation and salvation, and that link is based on the historical and liberating experience of the Exodus. Creation, he believes, is presented in the Bible not as a stage before salvation but as part of the salvation process. He illustrates his point by reference to the political liberation from Egypt, which he feels is both a historical fact and a fertile biblical theme. The creative act is linked with Israel freed from slavery. The liberation of Israel is a political action, and he cites it as second Isaiah.[16] Gutierrez notes that the words and images refer to two events, creation and liberation from Egypt. Creation and liberation, he says, are but one salvific act. The liberation of Israel is a political act—it is breaking away from misery and is the beginning of construction of a just society. He is using the Bible here to show that a liberating theology for Latin America would liberate and create at the same time.

Gutierrez talks in terms of recreation and complete fulfilment. He sees the long march of Israel towards the promised land as a historical process in which Israel and, indeed, Latin America, can establish a society without oppression and alienation. The religious is expressed in political terms, and the political in religion. For Gutierrez, human beings are a work of creation and, as such, are expected to continue that creation through their labors. There is a need, then, for people to participate in the building of society. It is the place of human beings to work to change the world to a liberated one by confronting and struggling against division and oppression. He feels the true agents of the quest for unity are those who are oppressed, whether it be economically, politically, or culturally. By building a just society, we are part of salvation.

Gutierrez concludes that salvation includes all people. The struggle for a just society is part of salvation. He goes on to describe change in terms of development, a change from the less human to the more human condition. Poor human conditions affect first those who are too poor to have essentials of living. Also, this includes those who are oppressed by the social situation that has come into being through the abuse of ownership and power, exploiting the workers or by unfair business practices. More human conditions, he says, imply the transition from need to the possession of necessities. Nowhere today is this more evident than in the

16. Isa 51:9–10.

Latin American countries. He sees the work of human beings in transforming and developing nature as the conclusion of creation but only if it is development that considers the concerns of social injustice and oppression and works towards change in this area. For Gutierrez, the social injustice and oppression of the so-called third world pose a great challenge to the faith of Christians in these countries. There is, in his view, an optimistic vision in Latin America that attempts to reconcile faith and the world and to encourage commitment to change. Liberation does not justify the status quo. He feels that a start must be made with a rejection of the existing situation that is unjust. This, he says, allows us to go to the root of the problem and to create a new social order based on justice. The rejection, he says, does not produce an escapist attitude but rather a will to revolution.

For Gutierrez, political liberation has economic roots. There is an effort to struggle and the struggle, he maintains, is the human activity whose goal is to be enlightened by faith. He stresses that an unjust situation does not happen by chance, destiny is not a determinant. There is human responsibility behind it. In the liberation approach, sin is not viewed from an individual reality that does not challenge the order in which we live. Sin is seen as social and historical. Sin is evident in oppressive situations in the exploitation of others. Sin, for Gutierrez, is alienation, and he explains how it demands a radical liberation, which implies a political liberation; and it is only by taking part in the historical process of liberation that it is possible to reveal the alienation present in every political alienation.

• • •

We move now from theology to class analysis; Gutierrez has had to explain and defend his concept of liberation theology against criticism. He has been accused of making an explicit appeal to Marxism. The next section of this chapter will seek to detect if there is any Marxist influence in Gutierrez's writings. In order to do this, we will need to isolate those parts of the two systems of thought that are commensurable and, as such, share a similar observation language. Clearly, both Marx and Gutierrez share an interest in class analysis, but can this be said of other concepts? What does Gutierrez mean by the term *alienation* and is there an eschatology, a sense of future, in Marx's thought? We will seek to find out if Gutierrez has used Marx or Marxism as a tool of analysis.

For Marx, the conflict or struggle between classes produces consciousness and is the means whereby change comes.[17] This conflict, then, is both inevitable and necessary. For Gutierrez, far from being desirable, class conflict is a painful historical fact that Christians must come to terms with if they are to play a part in resolving it. For Gutierrez, this involves evaluation, not just of the social conflict itself but of the factors that produced a world divided into privileged and dispossessed. In accepting Marx's categories of ownership and non-ownership of the means of production, Gutierrez adds a global dimension to the analysis by declaring that we must also do away with the factors that produce a world divided into superior and inferior racial groupings. The deep and underlying causes of poverty and injustice in Latin America, according to Gutierrez, are to be found in the centers of power that lie outside Latin America. Thus, low educational standards, a limited economy, and an unsatisfactory legal system are the direct result of dependence upon a system of world capitalism, whose center of ownership and control is in the West. This system of neocolonialism must be rejected.

For Gutierrez, the social economic class conflict between labor and capital is not to be transformed into a narrow militant class struggle conducted exclusively by ideological and political means. Rather, the challenge of the gospel is how to combine real and effective opposition to the system of oppression without hatred towards our fellow human beings. Clearly, there is an effort to struggle, and the struggle Gutierrez maintains is the human activity whose goal is to be enlightened by faith. For Gutierrez, the key to understanding the full significance of God's action in history is the concept of eschatology. Within this perspective, Gutierrez locates faith not in a remembrance of the past but as a concern with the present in as far as it provides an opening to the future. It is the attraction of what is to come, i.e., a new action of God that is the driving force of history. This bias towards the future lends meaning to, and is expressed in, the present while simultaneously being nourished by it. So, meaning is given to the here and now as a pre-condition and foretaste of what is to come. The present and the future are part of a continuous process, as are creation and salvation—thus, the revelation of the final meaning of history gives value to the present. Gutierrez rejects either-or position of spiritual versus temporal redemption. The spiritual does not eliminate the earthly realities but, rather, it is through these temporal,

17. Marx, *Capital.*

earthly historical events that we can open up to the future of complete fulfillment. Eschatology, for Gutierrez, is the theology of hope that takes shape in the unjust present and leads us forward to the just future; hope in a new humanity. Hope mobilizes the liberating function in history. In recent years, the term *utopia* has recovered its original meaning in order to express the aspirations of many who want to establish new social relations among human beings. The term is not synonymous with illusion, lack of realism, or irrationality but rather a dynamic element in the historical becoming of humanity. Through its relationship to historical reality, we discover the two aspects of denunciation and annunciation so crucial to the liberation process. Utopia means a denunciation of the existing order and an annunciation of what is to come, i.e., the new society.

To engage in denunciation of injustice is a prophetic process that involves a radical critique of the present order. We must denounce the system that takes no account of the dignity of human beings and their most elementary needs. People have a basic right to freedom and autonomy. To be part of the process of liberation is to champion these rights. We must take a clear position regarding both the present stage of social injustice and the revolutionary process that is attempting to abolish that injustice and build a more human order. For Gutierrez, this denunciation takes place by confronting a given situation with the reality that is announced. To announce the gospel is to proclaim that the love of God is present in the historical becoming of humankind and that there is no human act that cannot, in the last instance, be defined in relation to Christ. The annunciation of the gospel is made real and meaningful only by living and proclaiming it within a commitment to liberation—that is through a concrete and effective solidarity with the poor.

In order to detect any Marxist influence in Gutierrez's writings, we must now ask ourselves the following questions that relate to the possibility that there is also an eschatology in Marx. So, to what extent can we speak of a Marxist eschatology? Is Christian faith utopian and, if so, in what sense? How can we distinguish between optimism, pessimism, and hope? In one sense, Marx's thought is eschatological in that it speaks of the birth of humanity from the revolutionary overthrow of capitalism. In this new post-revolutionary society, human alienation will be overcome, and, in this respect, Marx's eschatological reasoning can be seen to be derived only partially from Hegel. However, the idea that humankind needs to be reconciled with itself and with the world is fundamentally transformed in the hands of Marx. Alienation was the suppression of creative human power by actual social conditions of capitalism, whereas, for Hegel, this was exclusively a phenomenon of the mind.[18] What makes Marx's thought truly eschatological is the fact that the revolutionary overthrow of the capitalist system by the industrial proletariat, once achieved, will be irreversible. Marx viewed utopias as myths designed to help humanity escape from reality so bringing satisfaction to impulses and desires frustrated by social reality. Thus general psychological interpretation of utopias runs parallel with Marx's criticism of religions offering an opium to the people. Christianity's harmonious, eschatological picture of life in a heavenly realm was not only an illusory, utopian goal but one that allowed people to endure their alienation from one another, from themselves, and from society. Since they could bear their situation better because of the illusory belief, they were less likely to seek to change oppressive conditions in the present. Religion is thus presented by Marx as a genuine protest against social conditions, but one that is negatively utopian in the sense that it encourages an endurance of situations rather than seeking to change them. At certain stages in the historical development, claims Marx, utopianism, i.e., religion, reflects the only available form of constructive protest against existing poverty, suffering, and injustice. However, once the goal of the social movement becomes attainable in reality, there is no longer any place for utopianism. Thus, religion is seen as an obstacle and a reactionary distraction from the working-class movement.

Despite Marx's critique of religion, we must now ask whether his own system of analysis contains certain utopian elements in the illusionary sense in which he used the word. Marx avoided predictive descriptions of the future society, but he believed that, after the revolution, all would be well. Is this not also utopian? Thus, an understanding of utopianism in Marxist eschatology provides us with a critique of Marx based upon his serious neglect of morality issues. Marx was optimistic in his conviction that the transformation of structures and circumstances in themselves would be enough to effect a radical change in consciousness. Revolutionaries are not free from the possibilities of corruption, as Marx believed of the proletariat. Believing that the proletariat is free from such corruption on the grounds of its historical mission is a harmful illusion, since it ignores the chance that the very group that may seek to establish justice may also become perpetrators of injustice once they

18. Hegel, *Phenomenology of Spirit*.

have power themselves. Having established that there is such a thing as a Marxist eschatology, we must seek to find out to what extent Gutierrez has used Marxism as a tool of analysis. According to Gutierrez, Marx had constructed a scientific understanding of historical reality based upon his empirical studies of exploitation of one class by another. For Gutierrez, these class categories provide new insights into historical initiatives and, thus, allow for the elaboration of a science of history that would make humankind more aware of the socioeconomic determinants of its ideological creation.

For Gutierrez, Marx's scientific analysis is based upon a dialectical conception of history that, as a result of its analysis of the present, is necessarily advancing towards the future as a classless society based upon new relationships of production. If we follow the French Marxist Althusser, as Gutierrez appears to do, it is possible to make a distinction between the young Marx who talked about alienation and humanism and the mature Marx who had outgrown these pre-scientific and romantic terms. It would seem that Gutierrez wants to add the Christian gospel to a neutral and perhaps agnostic Marx, who became user-friendly as a tool of scientific analysis. It must be remembered that Marx did not study religion in any detail after 1845. Gutierrez's adoption of Althusser presupposes a useful distinction that can be made between scientific analysis on the one hand and ideological and political struggle on the other. Marx's ideas on class and party would seem to rule this out. In elaborating the incisive formula of the Communist Manifesto, Marx and Engels affirm and develop the idea that the working class truly exists as a class only when it has given birth to a political party.[19] That is to say, the mass of individuals brought together by their identical or similar relationship to the productive process becomes a class only when it emerges as a single force, moving towards a final objective and conscious of the historical path leading to that aim. For Marx, the Communist Party is part of the working class, namely, the most advanced, most class-conscious and, hence, the most revolutionary part. By a process of natural selection, the party is formed of the most class-conscious, most devoted and far-sighted workers. This party has no interests other than the interests of the working class. Thus, for Marx, the Communist Party is the organizational and political lever that the most advanced section of the working class uses to direct the proletarian and semi-proletarian masses along the right road.

19. Marx and Engels, *Manifesto of the Communist Party*.

Gutierrez's support of Althusser's scientific Marxism and, by implication, rejection of the so-called young Marx, seems somewhat strange. For sure, Gutierrez and Marx share a conception of human nature that does not exclude Marx's early writings. Marx's use of the term *alienation* is derived from his concept of class and its relationship to the division of labor. This concept of class, and its relationship to the division of labor, cannot be conveniently assigned exclusively to a young or mature stage in Marx's thought.

Gutierrez constructs a Latin American theology of liberation based upon the Christian gospel. Contrary to popular thought, he seems actually to reject this idea of equating Marxism with Christianity. In fact, he warns against any hasty synthesizing that makes for converging patterns, especially the concept that revolution becomes redemption. For Gutierrez, the task of the church is to politicize by evangelizing, and he recognizes that, in the Latin American context, this means subversion. He also believes that there is only one vocation to salvation that embraces all people, and, consequently, their actions in history, whether Christian or non-Christian, gain religious significance. Gutierrez sees his task as a theologian of liberation to uncover the complicities of power. The challenge for Gutierrez is how not to exclude our enemies from our love. Far from making an explicit appeal to Marx, he is more interested in the work of Althusser, which, he believes, opens up new possibilities for liberation.

## Endnote: *The Book of Common Prayer*

We consider again how *The Book of Common Prayer*, although now an unfamiliar form of service to many Church of England attenders, remains the normative form of service today. In the 1950s, it was the regular diet. It has a particular ethos that conveys a particular theology and ecclesiology. In the *The Book of Common Prayer* liturgy, the priest uses courtly and courteous language when addressing God, thus vesting power in God. The priest also uses request to the people, e.g., "Let us pray." This suggests the common condition of priest and people. Thus, the priest addresses God as petitioner-surrogate. By contrast, in the modern service, which is the most frequent worship experience for the Church of England today, the priest uses the same verbal forms to address God and the people. The focus of power is on the human person, and the priest conducts the service as a power-agent. White culture of post-modernity is highly fragmented and intensely individualized, which represents a sharp contrast to the culture of worshipers from multicultural community. Clearly, the liturgical preference of these communities is more likely to be shaped by social experience than it is by personal choice. These differences are associated with attitudes to morality, politics, and social policy and are reflected in liturgy. Thus, the more the mode of involvement of a church is centered upon the needs of the upwardly mobile, the less included marginalized people are likely to be.

The liturgy is a means of interaction between the institution and the individual. The tension behind the liturgy is the inevitable hostility towards any change, both within the institution and the recipients whose lines in the dialogue are dictated by and gradually internalized by frequency of repetition. Changes in the liturgy expose the divisions within the church that, because of the Christian drive to orthodoxy and unity, excites guilt. Changes of liturgy, institutionally, are not about contextualizing the church into the present so much as about retention of power for the writing hierarchy. This powerful group also has to appear to maintain tradition as an essential part of identity and authority. Anglicanism has always had a missionary imperative, but the abstract notion of mission becomes very different when the birds come home to roost. In writing *The Book of Common Prayer*, Thomas Cranmer responded to the need of the baptized, compiling the liturgy into one tome to be a tool for mission overseas. This imperative, in its inclusivity, is at odds with the dynamics of a secular culture that maintains a moat mentality, which is how the shocked post-war England could be described.

It can be argued that the English have attempted to tame the Church of England and *The Book of Common Prayer* as conveyors of quintessential Englishness. Remember the old joke: there is a fog in the channel, and the continent is cut off. England was the new omphalos that connoted donor and export. Post-nineteenth century Englishness had to distance itself from that because otherwise it could not have continued with the glorification of empire. "Church of England" became a loaded code term for self-justification and hypocrisy of the most blatant and, therefore, most precarious kind. For the British, to confront and deal with racism and the racializing process is to erode the national concepts of superiority that centuries of aggressive colonialism have embedded deep within the national psyche. Alongside this is the Church of England as the church of the state and nation, so a lot is at stake when bishops and leaders are challenged about trying to be more than nice to marginalized and poor people.

The Church of England, in its present state, is attempting to span a gap of the most uncomfortable dimensions. On the one hand, it is the established church, an organ of the state, whose interests and identity are generally perceived to be coterminous with those of conservative middle England. On the other hand, in part due to a renaissance of vigorous hermeneutics inspired by liberation and feminist theologies, the church is beginning to rediscover its prophetic voice. Like a latter-day minor prophet, the Church of England talks about rivers of justice but, burdened by the downside of its Englishness, namely, its reserve, does it theologizing with gloves on. It talks about action, a most seductive oxymoronic state.

The Church of England has always regarded itself as the local English expression of the Catholic and Apostolic Church. In Tudor times, "English" connoted respite from decades of civil war, aggressive opposition to Roman Catholic states, such as Spain, and a particularly English relish of the growing English language and cultures. In post-colonial times, the Church of England must find itself in a non-oppositional identity. It must now focus on the insular level and drop the notion of global significance that it once carried. It can no longer even claim to be *primus inter pares*. Perhaps, the main call to the Church of England should be to rediscover what it means to be English on the edge of the third millennium. In this time of huge political changes, a period of uncertain and shifting frontiers, maybe now it is possible to discover what Englishness means and to distinguish this from Britishness. So far, we have identified approaches and expressions of liturgy, particularly those that unite passion, prayer, and ritual into a genuine sacramental dignity. We have looked at the love affair with language that is an enduring English trait, and we have considered the notion of fair play. These in themselves are not essentially racialized and are potentially profoundly inclusive. During the nineteenth century, the English looked at slavery and knew it was wrong. They normalized the concept of basic human freedom. Why should not an English church seek its own identity founded on justice and mercy, and thereby normalize and institutionalize its opposition to establishment. Freeing itself of British colonial inheritance, Englishness could reimage itself if it wanted to.

## Endnote: Franz Fanon and Post-Colonialism

So, what, then, of Anglicanism and its colonial legacy? We now draw conclusions about the missionary policies of the Church of England in the context of the British Empire. Our focus is an understanding of the possible relationship between Christian evangelization and the institutions of colonial imperialism. We are using the term *colonialism* to describe the exploitation and domination of the non-white world by European states and their church structures. Using Fanon's typology of colonialism, neocolonialism, and decolonization, we will seek to relate periods of colonial development to periods of missionary expansion and decline.[20] The heyday of nineteenth-century colonialism was also the heyday of church mission in India and on the continent of Africa. Missionary policy during the first half of the nineteenth century had to take account of the independent status of former colonies and the new colonial system of economic controls, which replaced force of arms. The Church of England's missionary policy was also influenced by two world wars and the process of decolonization.

So, what is the link between Anglican missionary policy and colonial imperialism? Christian mission during the second half of the nineteenth century went hand in hand with European colonial expansion. So closely linked were these two phenomena that Jean Comby, in her book on Christian mission activity, has a chapter called "The Missions of Colonial Imperialism."[21] In discussing this collusion, she explains that colonialism opened up the missionary field and allowed the missionaries to establish schools and hospitals. Comby accepts that the missionary work needed colonialism. What she does not adequately consider is the extent to which colonialism needed the missionaries and the extent to which their involvement aided further colonial conquest. If missionary activity can make colonial expansion respectable, then, at a certain point of development, it is possible that the relationship between Christian evangelism and colonial imperialism could be reversed. However, the collusion debate is soon dropped by this author in favor of an empirical account of mission activity throughout the world.

According to Stephen Fryer, British rule in India owes its foundation to the East India Company and the activities of an adventurer named

20. Fanon, *Wretched of the Earth.*

21. Comby, *How to Understand the History.*

Robert Clive.[22] The Battle of Plessey in 1757 saw the overthrow of the ruler of Bengal and, from then on, the extraction of India's wealth by the British was no longer a matter of sharp business practice but direct and explicit plunder. Previously, they had sent silver to pay for Indian goods; now, they could take what they wanted with force of arms. Prior to British rule, India was a prosperous country whose economy combined agriculture with manufactured goods, which were marketed throughout Asia and Europe. These products included cotton, silk, and woolens. Traditional skills included working with stone, gold, silver, ivory, glass, tannery, perfumery, and paper making. For Stephen Neil, British rule in India meant the introduction of civilized government and the encouragement of trade.[23] Fryer took a different view, explaining that the exploitation of India required some serious reorganization.[24] British rule meant the deindustrialization of India, turning it into an agricultural colony of British capitalism. The British abolished the Indian tradition of linking taxation to the harvest. They introduced instead a revenue system that required Indian farmers to pay fixed sums to the government regardless of crop yards. When harvests were bad, they were forced to borrow money from money lenders, who charged high rates of interest. The result was starvation for many. British rule ended the Indian textile, metalwork, glass, and paper industries. India now exported to Britain raw cotton, wool, jute, oil, seeds, dyes, and hides, but imported British textiles, which had virtually free entry. Indian silk and cotton were blocked by prohibitive tariffs. British rule meant that India no longer traded with the rest of the world.

British rule meant a favorable climate for missionary activities. Church mission schools received grant aid from the British government. Initially, the missionaries went all out for conversion, using the language and imagery of Western civilization. When it became clear that the Western version of the Christian gospel would conflict with Indian society, they had to rethink their strategy. The new approach was to see evangelism as a long-term educative process capable of penetrating other faith perspectives. The gospel would now be presented in a way relevant to the situation of those to be converted. However, Protestant missionaries resisted attempts to foster indigenous leadership. The appointment

22. Fryer, *Black People.*

23. Neil, *History of Christian Mission.*

24. Fryer, *Black People.*

in 1912 of Bishop Vedanayakam Samuel was met with hostility by those who wanted to maintain a foreign mission.

According to Stephen Neil, missionary activities in southern Africa were dependent upon the favor of tribal chiefs.[25] In West Africa, the strategy that amounted to European domination of the mission field was seriously revised with the consecration of Samuel Adjai Crowther as the first non-European bishop. Neil comments upon the enthusiasm associated with this appointment and informs us that this enterprise was fully justified, and that Africans should be allowed to take the lead. However, this writer goes on to say that enthusiasm is no substitute for common sense, claiming that the bishop was too old for this work and that he received insufficient help from the Church of England. Furthermore, the bishop did not speak an East Nigerian language and had to rely upon interpreters. Following the death of Bishop Crowther, the Church Missionary Society did an about-turn and reconstituted the mission as a joint African European project under a white bishop. In patronizing tones, Neil tells us that this was the right course of action in view of the irregularities in the way the former diocese had been run.

Colonialism as a category of dominance and privilege was challenged many years ago by Franz Fanon, whose seminal text *A Dying Colonialism* identifies three distinct phases of colonialism.[26] Firstly, there is an extractive phase in that the colonies are viewed as a source of raw materials, and this leads to the accumulation of capital. Secondly there is a consumer phase when the colonies become markets for European manufactured goods. And thirdly, there is an ultra-colonialism phase where American capital dominates all markets. This phase coincides with liberation movements and national independence struggles that threaten colonial interests. In the first phases of colonialism, Fanon identifies the peasantry: traditional authorities and a trading group who act as a commercial intermediary in the extraction of raw materials. In the second phase, Fanon identifies a number of discrete classes, including a petty bourgeoisie, a proletariat, and a lumpen proletariat. The neocolonial period is characterized by the continuing differentiation of classes. Fanon writes from the perspective of the oppressed, offering a scientific exploration of the relationship between racism and class rule, focusing upon the identity politics of both oppressed and oppressor. His psychology

25. Neil, *History of Christian Mission.*

26. Fanon, *Dying Colonialism.*

of colonial domination is about the distortion of human relationships and how these are to be challenged through the politics of decolonization. His challenge is to oppressive and redundant social systems. Racism, for Fanon, serves distinct economic and political functions, while at the same time, it is the product of a complex and diffuse historical process, which is not necessarily related to class position. For Fanon, the two important classes are the colonizer and the colonized: the ruler and the ruled. In *A Dying Colonialism*, he uses the term *Algerian* to cover the entire subjected population. Clearly, Fanon is aware of social strata. In the colonial context, class divisions tend to be fixed and the means of production less developed than in European states. The ruling class is distinguished by its racial difference from the indigenous population rather than by its ownership of the means of production. It is the relationship between the indigenous classes to the national culture that brings about political consciousness. For Fanon, it is the peasantry, not the industrial proletariat, who are the revolutionary class. They are the victims of land alienation and market exploitation. They are the inheritors of a pre-colonial traditionalism. They are also inheritors of a tradition of revolt, and their demand is for land. This class cannot be bribed and has no stake in the material interests of colonialism, as have the petty bourgeois and the proletariat. In both *The Wretched of the Earth* and *A Dying Colonialism*, Fanon talks about the importance of an education program for this revolutionary class.

## And Finally: Disestablishment and Colonialism

As the established church, the Church of England has a peculiarly resonant influence in wider English society. We need to reclaim the apostolic and catholic fundamentals of our tradition in order to achieve two goals: the reinvigoration of the church and the integrity of the church's mission in England as a major force for justice as well as for salvation. It is important, therefore, to look at what it means to be a member of the Church of England, bearing in mind the emergence of the hectic welter of the modern period with an archbishop's resignation over safeguarding failures. So, what of the future? At the time of writing this commentary, the Church of England was still without an archbishop of Canterbury. Clearly, the government of the day with the power to make Crown appointments would want a safe pair of hands and not someone with the intellectual and scholarly determination to oppose their policies in the House of Lords.[27]

This commentary on the Letter of James has been concerned with establishing the link between the Church of England, its disestablishment, and liberation theology as its true mission. In this, it has been useful to follow Gutierrez since he has sought to blend two traditions sometimes seen as opposing. He has used Marxism as a conscious tool to temper and hone the way that the church does mission. Putting the two horses of theology and sociology in one yoke leads to a more thoroughly ploughed field. The Church of England exhibits the traditional English suspicion of intellectual methods. This study of Gutierrez suggests that we cannot afford to eschew the vigorous methods of self-inquisition that the theologians of South America have presented to Rome and to Christendom. Gutierrez locates oppression within systems that alienate the workers and marginalize them into voiceless poverty. This process looks very different from the West; however, his praxis can help us to find our focus. The oppression here is probably, for our purposes at least, cultural rather than economic. The Church of England can be described as a repository of contemporary oppression because it has been the meeting point of other oppressions, such as the slave trade. The conquest of non-European lands by the colonial powers was welcomed by the Church of England, who saw it as an opportunity to evangelize. The colonial expansion of the nineteenth century left behind a legacy that contributed to the alienation of colonized people and their descendants. The interface between church and state is exemplified in Anglican support for Colonialism with an archbishop of Canterbury presiding over a failing and archaic structure.

27. See Isiorho, *Faith in Church Newspapers*, 109.

# Bibliography

Anglican Communion. *The Lambeth Conference, 1948: The Encyclical Letter from the Bishops, with Resolutions and Reports*. London: SPCK, 1948.

Archbishop of Canterbury's Commission on Urban Priority Areas. *Faith in the City: A Call for Action by Church and Nation (The Report of the Archbishop of Canterbury's Commission on Urban Priority Areas)*. London: Church House, 1985.

Augustine. *The City of God*. Translated by Henry Bettenson. New York: Penguin Classics, 2003.

Austen, Jane. *Northanger Abbey*. London: Signet Classics, 1965.

———. *Pride and Prejudice*. London: Penguin Classics, 2003.

Austin, George. *Affairs of State: Leadership, Religion, and Society*. London: Hodder & Stoughton,1995.

Barclay, William. *The Letters of James and Peter*. Edinburgh: Saint Andrew, 1976, 2003.

Bell, George. *Christianity and World Order*. Harmondsworth, UK: Penguin, 1940.

———. *The Church and Humanity (1939–1946)*. London: Longmans, Green, 1946.

———. "The Church's Function in War-Time." *Fortnightly Review*, Sept. 1939. The Bell Society. https://richardwsymonds.wordpress.com/tag/the-churchs-function-in-war-time-fortnightly-review-sept-1940/.

———. *Randall Davidson—Archbishop of Canterbury*. 3rd ed. London: Oxford University Press, 1952.

Berger, Peter. *A Rumor of Angels: Modern Society and the Rediscovery of the Supernatural*. London: Penguin, 1969.

———. *The Social Reality of Religion*. London: Faber & Faber, 1968.

Bonney, Norman. "The Monarchy, the State and Religion: Modernising the Relationship." *Political Quarterly* 81.2 (2010) 199–200.

*The Book of Common Prayer, and Administration of the Sacraments and other Rites and Ceremonies of the Church of England According to the Use of Church of England*. Oxford: Oxford University Press, 1662.

Bowker, John. *Church Times*. Mar. 14, 1997.

———. *The Sense of God*. Oxford: Clarendon, 1973.

Buchanan, Colin. *Cut the Connection: Disestablishment and the Church of England.* London: Darton, Longman and Todd, 1994.

Bultman, Rudolf. *The History of the Synoptic Tradition.* New York: Harper & Row, 1968.

Carr, Wesley. *Say One for Me: The Church of England in the Next Decade.* London: SPCK, 1992.

Cesarani, David, and Tony Kushner, eds. *The Internment of Aliens in Twentieth Century Britain.* New York: Routledge, 1993.

Chadwick, Owen. *Church and State: Report of the Archbishops' Commission.* London: Church Information Office, 1970.

Chandler, Andrew. *The Church and Humanity: The Life and Work of George Bell. 1883–1958.* London: Routledge, 2012.

———. "The Church of England and the Obliteration Bombing of Germany in the Second World War." *English Historical Review* 108 (Oct. 1993) 930–31.

———. *George Bell, Bishop of Chichester: Church, State, and Resistance in the Age of Dictatorship.* Cambridge: Eerdmans, 2016.

Chapman, Mark, et al., eds. *The Established Church: Past, Present, and Future.* London: T&T Clark, 2011.

Church of England. *Common Worship Services and Prayers for the Church of England.* London: Church House, 2024.

Church of England Committee on Black Anglican Concerns. *Seeds of Hope: Report of a Survey on Combating Racism in the Diocese of the Church of England.* London: General Synod, 1991. Comby, Jean. *How to Understand the History of Christian Mission.* London: SCM, 1996.

Comby, Jean. *How to Understand the History of Christian Mission.* London: SCM, 1996.

Douglas, J. D., ed. *The New Greek-English Interlinear New Testament: A New Interlinear Translation of the Greek New Testament.* Translated by Robert K. Brown and Philip W. Comfort. United Bible Societies' 4th ed. Carol Stream, IL: Tyndale, 1993.

Duffield, Ian. "Changing Liberation Theology." In *For Church and Nation,* edited by Chris Roland and John Vincent, 57–66. Sheffield: Urban Theology Unit, 2013.

Eade, John. "Changing Landscapes in an Inner City Area: Mosques, Conservation, and Culture in Tower Hamlets." Conference paper, Religion, Minorities and Social Change, Bristol University, Sept. 1991.

Eliot, George. *Adam Bede.* Oxford: Oxford University Press, 1871.

———. *Middlemarch.* Harmondsworth: Penguin, 1994.

Fanon, Frantz. *A Dying Colonialism.* Translated by Constance Farrington. New York: Grove, 1959.

———. *The Wretched of the Earth.* Translated by Constance Farrington. New York: Grove, 2002.

Fielding, Henry. *Joseph Andrews and Shamela.* London: Penguin, 1999.

Fryer, Peter. *Black People in the British Empire.* London: Pluto, 1989.

Gillman, Peter, and Leni Gillman. *Papers of Francois Lafitte.* London: Quartet, 1980.

Graham, Elaine. "The Establishment, Multiculturalism, and Social Cohesion." In *The Established Church: Past, Present, and Future,* edited by Mark Chapman et al., 124–40. London: T&T Clark, 2011.

Green, Laurie. *Let's Do Theology.* 2nd ed. London: Continuum/Mowbray, 2009.

———. "Liberation Theology and Urban Theology." In *British Liberation Theology: For Church and Nation,* edited by Chris Roland and John Vincent, 34–53. Sheffield: Urban Theology Unit, 2013.

Gutierrez, Gustavo. *The Power of the Poor in History*. London: SCM, 1983.
———. *A Theology of Liberation*. London: SCM, 1973.
Habermas, Jurgen. "Religion in the Public Sphere." *European Journal of Philosophy* 14 (2006) 1–25.
Habgood, John. *Church and Nation in a Secular Age*. London: Darton, Longman, Todd, 1983.
———. "Church and Society." In *Celebrating the Anglican Way*, edited by Ian Bunting, 33–41. London: Hodder & Stoughton, 1996.
Hastings, Adrian. *A History of English Christianity*. London: SCM, 2001.
Hegel, Georg Wilhelm Friedrich. *Phenomenology of Spirit*. Translated by A. V. Miller. Oxford: Oxford University Press, 1976.
Hempton, David. *The Religion of the People: Methodism and Popular Religion c. 1750–1900*. New York: Routledge, 1996.
Husband, Charles. "The Political Context of Muslim Communities: Participation in British Society." Seminar paper, Les Populations Musulmanes en Europe, Nov. 7–9, 1991.
Isiorho, David. "Black Clergy Discontent: Selective Interviews on Racialised Exclusion." *Journal of Contemporary Religion* 18.2 (2003) 213–26.
———. *Faith in Church Newspapers: A Contextual Theology of Identifiable Black Actors and Race Related Issues Found in the Church Times and the Church of England Newspaper*. Eugene, OR: Wipf & Stock, 2024.
———. *Faith in Unions: Racism and Religious Exclusion in the Faith Workers Branch of Unite the Union 2017–2020*. Eugene, OR: Wipf & Stock, 2022.
———. "For the Big Society." In *For Church and Nation*, edited by Chris Roland and John Vincent. Sheffield: Urban Theology Unit, 2013.
———. *Mission, Anguish, and Defiance: A Personal Experience of Black Clergy Deployment in the Church of England*. Eugene, OR: Wipf & Stock, 2019.
Jasper, Ronald C. D. *George Bell: Bishop of Chichester*. Oxford: Oxford University Press, 1967.
John Rylands Research Institute and Library. "The Role of Women Within Methodism." https://www.library.manchester.ac.uk/rylands/special-collections/subject-areas/methodist-archives-and-research-collections/using-the-collections/researching-women-in-methodism/the-role-of-women-in-methodism/.
Julian of Norwich. *Revelations of Divine Love*. Translated by Grace Warrack. London: Methuen, 1901.
Keenan, William. "Post-Secular Sociology: Effusions of Religion in Late Modern Settings." *European Journal of Social Theory* 5 (2002) 279–90.
Lafitte, Francois. *Internment of Aliens*. Harmondsworth, UK: Penguin, 1940.
Lewis, C. S. *The Last Battle*. Chronicles of Narnia. London: HarperCollins, 2009.
Lloyd, Jennifer M. *Women and the Shaping of British Methodism: Persistent Preachers, 1807–1907*. Manchester: Manchester University Press, 2013.
Lockhart, John. *Cosmo Gordon Lang*. London: Hodder & Stoughton, 1949.
Rahmani, L. Y. "Ancient Jerusalem's Funerary Customs and Tombs." *Biblical Archaeologist* 44.3 (1981) 171-77.
MacKinnon, Donald. *The Stripping of the Altars*. London: Colin Fontana, 1969.
Marx, Karl. *Capital: Critique of Political Economy*. Vol. 1. Translated by Ben Fowkes. London: Penguin Classics, 1984.

Marx, Karl, and Friedrich Engels *Manifesto of the Communist Party*. Peking: Foreign Language Press, 1975.

McDowall, David. *Britain in Close-Up*. London: Pearson/Longman, 1993.

Morris, Rob, ed. *Church and State in 21st Century Britain: The Future of Church Establishment*. New York: Palgrave Macmillan, 2009.

Neil, Stephen. *Anglicanism*. Harmondsworth, UK: Penguin, 1958.

———. *A History of Christian Mission*. Harmondsworth, UK: Penguin, 1964.

Pannenberg, Wolfhart. *Jesus—God and Man*. London: SCM, 1968.

Percy, Martyn. "Opportunity Knocks: Church, Nationhood, and Establishment." In *The Established Church: Past, Present, and Future*, edited by Mark Chapman et al., 26–38. London: T&T Clark, 2011.

Purcell, William. *Fisher of Lambeth: A Portrait from Life*. London: Hodder & Stoughton, 1969.

Ricoeur, Paul. *Essays on Biblical Interpretation*. Philadelphia: Fortress, 1980.

Sanders, Andrew. *The Short Oxford History of English Literature*. Oxford: Clarendon, 1994.

Santer, Mark. "The Freedom of the Gospel." In *The Church and the State*, edited by Donald Reeves, ch. 8. London: Hodder, 1984.

Scorcese, Martin, dir. *The Last Temptation of Christ*. Universal City, CA: Universal Pictures, 1988.

Silva, Trinidad. "Naming the Wise: The 'Sophos', the 'Philosophos', and the 'Sophistes' in Plato." PhD diss., University College London, 2017.

Slack, Kenneth. *George Bell*. London: SCM, 1971.

Steiner, Rudolf. *Isis Mary Sophia*. Great Barrington, MA: Steiner, 2003.

Sykes, Stephen. *Unashamed Anglicanism*. London: Darton, Longman, and Todd, 1995.

Therbourn, Goran. *European Modernity and Beyond*. London: Sage, 1995.

Thompson, Edward. *The Making of the English Working Class*. Harmondsworth, UK: Penguin, 1970.

Williams, Alwyn. *The Anglican Tradition in the Life of England*. London: SCM, 1947.

Williams, Rowan. "A Church of the Nation, or a Church for the Nation." In *The Church and Humanity: The Life and Work of George Bell, 1883–1958*, edited by Andrew Chandler, 209–19. Abingdon, UK: Ashgate, 2012.

Wise, John. *The History of John Wise, a Poor Boy*. London: Religious Tract Society, 1830.

Woolf, Virginia. "George Eliot." In *The Common Reader*. New York: Harcourt, Brace, and World, 1925.

Wright, Patrick. *On Living in an Old Country*. London: Verso, 1985.

www.ingramcontent.com/pod-product-compliance
Lightning Source LLC
LaVergne TN
LVHW050629100826
845148LV00011B/1792